WORLD CLASS CONTRACTING
5th Edition

Gregory A. Garrett

NAVIGANT

Wolters Kluwer
Law & Business

Editorial Director: Aaron M. Broaddus
Cover and Interior Design: Craig L. Arritola

Copyright Notice

Notice of Trademarks

Product No.: 0-4506-500

ISBN: 978-0-8080-2568-9

CONTENTS

PREFACE

Today, what every company wants in both the public and private business sectors is a fast, effective, and seamless integration between itself, each customer, and its supply partners using the power of the Internet. Building successful business partnerships via outsourcing is a must for survival!

Buyers worldwide are becoming more informed and demanding as they require sellers to assume greater business risks to win the buyer's valued business; mergers, acquisitions, and longstanding partnerships of former competitors are increasing; and the integration of products, services, and solutions is growing at an exponential rate in business transactions. Thus, contracts are becoming more complicated to plan, negotiate, create, and administer.

Make no mistake – outsourcing is here to stay! Globally, companies and government organizations have increased their contracting for goods and services with the specific intent of focusing more on their core business and allowing suppliers or sellers to do the "other work." Competition is growing, speed to market is critical, and costs must be reduced, but only those with a solid understanding of contract management will achieve ultimate success.

There is power in contract management – today and tomorrow. All business professionals, especially executives, must realize the power of the expectations that have been created by their organizations' contract management actions. The business deals an organization made several years ago and how it manages the resulting contracts and projects dramatically affect its success and reputation today. Likewise, the contracts an organization negotiates today and performs tomorrow will significantly affect its profitability and reputation in the marketplace of the future. Professional contract management is vital to ensure that both buyers and sellers perform as expected and get what they have mutually agreed to in their contracts.

DEDICATION

To my wife Carolyn, sons Christopher and Scott, and daughter Jennifer for their love and support.

To my parents for their love and confidence in my success.

ACKNOWLEDGMENTS

Creation of this fifth edition of World-Class Contracting is at the request of numerous colleges and universities worldwide who have selected this book for their undergraduate and graduate business programs.

I would especially like to thank the following individuals for their support in making this 5th edition possible.

Dr. William C. Pursch

Dr. Rene G. Rendon

Special Acknowledgments (for the first edition): To the members of my former team at ESI International, a global training and consulting firm, for their numerous contributions.

Benjamin Sellers	Susan Deavours
Vernon Edwards	Kim Briggs
Lisa Novak	Patricia Chehovin
Marek Kaszubski	Barbara Barnes

In Memory of my long-time friend and mentor Mr. W. Gregor Macfarlan, Gentleman, Scholar, and Educator a true giant in the field of contract management.

ABOUT THE AUTHOR

Gregory A. Garrett is the Managing Director and leader of the Government Contractor Services practice of Navigant Consulting, Inc. He is a best-selling and award-winning, author, dynamic speaker, and industry leader who has provided services to world-class corporations and government organizations on six continents in more than 40 countries. He has successfully led more than $30 Billion of complex high technology contracts and projects worldwide. Formerly, he has served as the Chief Operating Officer of Acquisition Solutions Inc., and the Chief Compliance Officer, U.S. Federal Government Programs, Lucent Technologies, Inc. He also is President and Chief Executive Officer, Garrett Consulting Services.

Mr. Garrett previously served as Executive Director of Global Business for ESI International. He has led numerous global teams of business professionals in planning, developing, and implementing a wide range of high technology products, services, and customized solutions for multinational organizations, including: ABB, AT&T, BellSouth, Inter-American Development Bank, IBM Corporation, Lucent Technologies, Inc., Motorola, Inc., NCR Corporation, Nippon Telephone and Telegraph, Panama Canal Commission, TASC, Inc., the United Nations, U.S. Department of Defense, and the U.S. Trade and Development Agency.

Mr. Garrett has served as a Lecturer for The George Washington University Law School and the School of Business and Public Management. Previously, he served as a highly decorated military officer in the United States Air Force, where he led the contract management of more than $15 billion in high technology satellite communication, advanced aircraft, and electronic programs. He has personally taught or consulted with more than 25,000 business professionals in both public and private business.

Mr. Garrett is a Certified Professional Contracts Manager, a fellow and a member of the Executive Advisory Council of the National Contract Management Association. He has received four national awards from NCMA: the National Achievement Award, the Charles J. Delaney Memorial Award for the most outstanding article in the Contract Management Magazine, the Blanche Witte Memorial Award for outstanding service to the contracting profession and the National Education Award for work in contract management education. He is a Certified Project Management Professional, of the Project Management Institute and he has earned two international business awards from PMI: The Eric Jenett Project Management Excellence Award and the David I. Cleland Project Management Literature Award. He has authored 19 books and more than 100 published articles on a wide range of business topics including: capture management, contract management, cost estimating, contract pricing, contract negotiations, managing subcontracts, government contract cost accounting, contract administration, project management, and leadership topics.

INTRODUCTION

WHY THIS BOOK IS FOR YOU

This book goes beyond the hype to the business partnerships, people, processes, tools, and best practices needed to be successful.

BEST PRACTICES OF WINNING COMPANIES

Winning companies, like ABB, Exxon-Mobile, Home Depot, IBM, Lockheed-Martin, Microsoft, Hewlett-Packard, and Wal-Mart, just to mention a few of those cited by the *World Trade Magazine* as among the top 100 best companies, all realize the strategic value of building successful partnerships.

While all companies experience periods of highs, lows, and transitions in their respective performance and in stock prices, truly successful companies build lasting partnerships that sustain and provide long-term value to all partners, employees, and shareholders. This book contains more than 100 best practices of winning companies.

HOW THE BOOK IS ORGANIZED

World-Class Contracting is organized in a simple, easy-to-follow format, focusing on business partnerships, people, processes, tools, and best practices. Chapters 1 and 2 discuss what actions winning companies are taking to build successful partnerships, manage expectations, and build trust between organizations. Chapters 3 through 6 describe the contract management process, roles and responsibilities of team members, contracts and legal issues, e-procurement, and a variety of contracting methods. Chapters 7 through 10 discuss in detail the three phases of the contract management process and contract pricing arrangements. Chapters 11 and 12 provide a discussion of common contracting misconceptions, key best practices of contract management, and the value of the program management discipline to deliver the results agreed to in the contract. Chapters 13 and 14 provide two very unique tools to help organizations improve their buying and/or selling performance, namely the Contract Management Maturity Model and the Contract Management Risk and Opportunity Assessment Tool. Chapter 15 provides a valuable discussion of the need for enterprise contract management process and a fair, balanced, and independent review of six of the leading contract management software systems/tools/applications and how they can help you improve performance. Chapters 16 and 17 focus on U.S. federal government contracts, namely how to build contractor teaming arrangements in the federal marketplace and how to successfully manage government subcontracts.

A special feature is the discussion of more than 100 best practices from leading global companies involved in contracting for a wide range of goods and services. The best practices are discussed in each phase of the contract management process. Additional features include:

- More than 25 sample forms that can be used in everyday contract management situations (Appendix A)
- United Nations Convention on Contracts for the International Sale of Goods (Appendix B)
- The Uniform Commercial Code
- Glossary of contract management terminology
- Extensive bibliography of resource materials

CHAPTER

1

BUILDING SUCCESSFUL PARTNERSHIPS IN THE E-BUSINESS AGE

Today, the goals of most winning companies include, but are not limited to, the following: exceeding customer expectations, capturing ever-increasing global market share, beating the competition to the market, reducing cost of revenue, reducing business risks, and securing long-term mutually profitable partnerships. While all of these goals are important, securing long-term mutually profitable (buyer-seller) partnerships is clearly the most important strategic goal.

So, how do winning companies build successful partnerships in the e-business age?

Winning companies are taking four common actions to build successful partnerships:

- Unleashing corporate buying and selling power
- Changing buying and selling processes
- Developing an integrated supply chain
- Learning and applying the best practices and e-tools from industry leaders

UNLEASHING CORPORATE BUYING AND SELLING POWER

Never before has anyone seen anything like this. What is occurring is a rapid revolution of how companies buy and sell products, services, and solutions. Nearly everything is or can be done electronically via intranets, local area networks, wide area networks, extranets, or the Internet.

Incredibly, large amounts of data can be sent at the speed of light nearly anywhere in the world via broadband networks, composed of state-of-the-art fiber optic and/or wireless technology.

The communication technologies revolution has fueled the e-business age and the explosive growth of the e-procurement market. The older generation of client/server procurement systems, designed to help individual organizations purchase off-the-shelf goods and services more effectively from many suppliers, has all but been replaced by rapid migration to Web-based solutions and Internet marketplaces. The new Internet marketplaces quickly bring many buyers together with many sellers to help all parties get the best deal in the shortest amount of time.

ONE

Speed is the mantra of the e-business or digital age. The need for speed is driving e-procurement to become a much larger and more diversified pursuit, going well beyond self-service purchasing from electronic catalogs of off-the-shelf products to procurement of integrated complex products, services, and solutions.

Business Web sites that contain dynamic pricing features—such as e-auctions and reverse auctions, where the price goes down as the bidding progresses—are becoming very popular. In some markets, the e-auction's price competition is supported by companies offering a wide variety of professional services to assist with providing or sourcing related goods and services.

As communication technologies continue to allow more data to be transmitted faster, and in a more secure manner, e-procurement grows. Likewise, the e-procurement business environment requires a smaller but more skilled procurement workforce.

Most companies that extensively use e-procurement have been able to reduce both their acquisition cycle time and their personnel expenses, because fewer sales managers, contract managers, lawyers, and purchasing agents are required. As a result of the e-procurement revolution, the roles of sales managers, buyers, contract managers, or purchasing agents have all evolved to require more broadly skilled business managers.

The evolution of the role of the buying and selling professional in today's e-business age is helping to unleash tremendous corporate buying and selling power, which is contributing to the continued growth of our global economy. The new breed of buying and selling business professionals is developing highly innovative ways for companies to form business relationships and outsource both goods and services on a massive scale. These include strategic sourcing agreements, back-sourcing arrangements, joint-equity partnerships, preferred supplier agreements, and most favored customer agreements, just to mention a few.

Clearly, the new communication technologies have unleashed tremendous corporate buying and selling power of both people and information systems. However, the full potential of buying and selling power can only be realized if we change the underlying processes that control or limit results.

CHANGING BUYING AND SELLING PROCESSES

Winning companies are all focused on speed to market, cost reduction, and customer satisfaction—whether buying or selling goods, services, and solutions. Today, many leading companies are changing their selling processes and tools, including the following actions:

- Expanding self-service sales via Web-based sales catalogs of products and related services available to buyers
- Creating customized electronic interfaces between themselves and their strategic customers to facilitate rapid order receipt and order processing. Typically, sellers provide their most favored customers/buyers with preferred pricing/large discounts.
- Offering multinational companies global pricing policies for products and services with economic-related adjustments, i.e., variations due to labor rates in specific countries or regions, inflation/deflation, value-added taxes, etc.
- Developing standard statements of work (SOW), Performance Work Statements (PWS), acceptance criteria, and standards intervals for consistent on-time delivery worldwide
- Understanding the buyer's business needs and budget in order to develop customized solutions priced to fit the buyer's desired business case
- Providing financing to buyers to help them purchase products when required
- Offering extended payment terms to customers, well beyond the usual net–15 days or net–30 days to net–90 days or net–180 days
- Developing Web portals to facilitate rapid and direct communications between sellers and their strategic partners
- Providing countertrade, offsets, or counterpurchases in order to secure large purchases

These actions are just a few of the many innovative process changes, tools, or unique business arrangements that sellers are using to build successful partnerships with their best buyers and to improve their quote-to-cash process.

Likewise, many winning companies are changing their procurement processes and tools to take maximum advantage of the marketplace. The following diagram illustrates the typical request-to-remit process used by many companies today. The request-to-remit process contains four key elements, each of which provides opportunities to reduce the cost of the products or services purchased and the cost associated with the purchasing process itself.

Form 1-1 Typical Purchasing Process
Request
Requirement
Buy
Supply
Remit

More and more companies are expanding their use of e-procurement to reduce their purchasing lead-time and purchasing process costs. However, e-procurement applications cannot produce maximum results unless companies also change their procurement processes as shown below.

Table 1-1 Maximizing e-Procurement Success	Procurement Today: Managed per Transaction	e-Procurement: Managed by Exception
Online product selection	Search large catalogs	Personalized views; named shopping carts
Requisition approval	One to 12 levels of manual approval	Transactions automatically approved based on rules
P.O. transmission	Fax, e-mail, EDI direct to supplier; supplier retypes the order	Order is sent through a supplier clearinghouse
Payment authorization	Dependent on three-way match of P.O. with invoice and receipts	Immediate; based on shipment notice
Analysis	Sporadic; not linked to supplier performance	Continuous; integrated in real time; drives optimization of process

In addition to changing their internal purchasing processes and tools, many winning companies are choosing to outsource some or nearly all of their procurement function to companies that specialize in providing professional procurement services using an integrated supply chain.

DEVELOPING AN INTEGRATED SUPPLY CHAIN

In the 1980s and 1990s, almost the entire professional procurement community hailed supply chain management as the panacea to solving most purchasing challenges. Supply chain management advocates told buyers that they needed to (1) use fewer suppliers vs. many suppliers, (2) negotiate long-term contracts vs. short-term contracts, (3) conduct more detailed progress or milestone tracking of suppliers and their subcontractors, (4) obtain lower pricing via preferred buyer/customer terms and conditions, and (5) analyze every action/link in the supply chain between the buyer and lowest level vendor. Supply chain management has helped many companies worldwide reduce their procurement costs and their procurement cycle time.

However, more and more companies in the new e-business age have realized that supply chain management as a procurement concept is good—but is not good enough. In order to create a truly integrated supply chain, a new global hub or trade exchange for each industry must be created that will allow all players to connect their internal systems to the internal systems of other companies through the Internet. Real integration means providing enterprise resource planning (ERP) to core business transaction functionality to all participants in the industry.

Buyers can achieve an integrated supply chain only if they develop trusted partnerships with sellers, who, in-turn, serve as value-added business service providers.

Today, large vertical trade exchanges, built cooperatively by industry participants, are changing the nature of competition. Many winning companies have decided that, because the Internet is so accessible and so efficient, competing on the basis of connectivity throughout the supply chain is no longer good business. As a result, many competitors are cooperating to build efficient Internet connections and competing on how they can use these new capabilities to better achieve customer satisfaction.

LEARNING AND APPLYING THE BEST PRACTICES AND E-TOOLS FROM INDUSTRY LEADERS

E-business is forcing businesses worldwide to reexamine how they do business. Today, the questions that CEOs have to answer are more about "How do I design, manufacture, or outsource and distribute products, services, and solutions to meet or exceed my customer's needs?" rather than "What quantity of my off-the-shelf products do I have to sell in order to make my quarterly or annual revenue target?"

Winning companies realize that they must help their buyers reduce their internal direct and indirect procurement costs. The following are a few recent best practices and successful e-tools from several industry leaders.

Microsoft's Best Practices: Working in the e-Business Age

Clearly, one of the leading companies of the e-business age is Microsoft. Microsoft Chairman Bill Gates has created his best practices or new rules of how to function in the new digital business infrastructure.

Table 1-2 Bill Gates' New Rules	
1.	Insist that communications flow through e-mail
2.	Study sales data online to share insights easily
3.	Shift knowledge workers into high-level thinking
4.	Use digital tools to create virtual teams
5.	Convert every paper process to a digital process
6.	Use digital tools to eliminate single-task jobs
7.	Create a digital feedback loop
8.	Use digital systems to route customer complaints immediately
9.	Use digital communication to redefine boundaries
10.	Transform every business process into just-in-time delivery
11.	Use digital delivery to eliminate middleman
12.	Use digital tools to help customers solve problems for themselves

Cisco Systems' Best Practices: Internet Strategy and Solutions

By employing its own Internet strategy and solutions, Cisco Systems has successfully maintained its agility, culture of empowerment, and competitive advantage. All of Cisco's business operations, including finance, supply-chain management, and employee communications are Internet-based. Today, Cisco transacts nearly 90 percent of orders and 82 percent of customer support inquiries over the Web.

Using outsourcing and the Internet has allowed Cisco to create a virtual manufacturing system that seamlessly manages 37 global plants as one.

Cisco's Internet technology and global real-time project level accounting allow the company to conduct a virtual close on their financial books each fiscal quarter within 24 hours.

Hormel Foods' Best Practices: Oracle Internet Procurement e-Tool

Hormel Foods has recently completed the installation of Oracle Internet Procurement at all of its 50 locations. Employees at all of these sites are now able to create purchasing requisitions for non-production items and have them automatically routed for approval, as well as track and access information on a real-time basis.

Self-guiding online catalogs allow workers to search for goods and services from approved suppliers.

Most of the savings associated with the implementation of Oracle Internet Procurement is a result of Hormel's procurement personnel no longer having to spend considerable amounts of time dealing with routine purchases. Additional savings will be realized through the elimination of non-contract purchases. Hormel also values the fact that its procurement personnel now have more time to devote to the more professional tasks of creating, managing, and leveraging partnerships with its suppliers.

Lockheed Martin's Best Practices: SAP Business-to-Business Procurement e-Tool

The Missiles and Fire Control Division of Lockheed Martin located in Dallas, Texas selected the Business-to-Business (B2B) procurement system developed by SAP to replace an out-dated, paper-based indirect procurement process.

Lockheed Martin leveraged the capabilities of the SAP business workflow component to implement consistent business rules to ensure user's purchases were appropriate, priced within limits, and ordered from approved suppliers.

As a result of SAP's focus and rapid implementation, ease-of-use, and flexibility, Lockheed Martin was able to control the use of their indirect procurement expenses achieving dramatic cost reductions.

SUMMARY

The power of e-business has been unleashed by the advent of new communication technologies. However, to achieve high performance results year after year, companies must form successful long-term partnerships. In order to do this, winning companies are taking four common actions to build successful partnerships: (1) unleashing corporate buying and selling power, (2) changing buying and selling processes and tools, (3) developing an integrated supply chain, and (4) learning and applying the best practices and e-tools from industry leaders. Although speed is the mantra of the e-business age, after recent buying and selling scandals worldwide, achieving excellence with integrity is now the most important aspect of business.

CHAPTER 2

BUILDING TRUST: MANAGING EXPECTATIONS AND HONORING COMMITMENTS

One of the biggest challenges in creating and maintaining a successful long-term business partnership is building trust. Trust is like quality; it is difficult to describe accurately, but you know it when it's there.

Trust is typically earned by doing what you say you are going to do on a repeated basis; in other words, by honoring commitments. A company can also instill trust when it comes to the rescue of another company in a time of urgent business need.

Building trust in business partnerships can take years to accomplish, but sometimes can be lost very quickly.

One of the key elements of building trust is how a company, whether buyer or seller, manages the expectations of its business partner(s). Expectations are assumptions or beliefs about future events. They are usually hopeful and optimistic. Sometimes expectations are pessimistic "plans for the worst."

In our current dynamic high-speed world of e-business, expectations are incredibly high. Too often, people leap to expect the impossible to be achieved without knowing all the facts or details. Of course, sometimes companies can create virtual miracles but, in many cases, fall well short of their customers' unrealistic expectations.

No one in business can avoid setting expectations. Everything companies say or do—or don't say or don't do—sets some form of expectation in the minds of others. Most companies try to set expectations through their advertising and marketing. However, companies' real market expectations are typically set by their actual performance in comparison to their promises, commonly referred to by results-oriented business leaders as the Hype-to-Results index. The real key to successfully managing expectations and honoring commitments is understanding the process.

The process of managing expectations is primarily a communication process. The following diagram depicts a variety of simple ways to describe the essential elements. Understanding the managing expectations process is good; applying it is even better. Unfortunately, because of the speed of business today, companies frequently react to partial information based upon inaccurate assumptions, rather than truly listening and understanding their customers' needs and desires. Often, sellers do not properly distinguish the real difference between a buyer's needs vs. a buyer's desires.

Figure 2-1 The Managing Expectations Process

Aligning expectations to reality is a critical step in the managing expectations process. Aligning expectations does not mean reducing objectives or requirements to the lowest level. Aligning expectations is about negotiating a challenging but achievable set of objectives for all parties, based upon the realities of the situation (i.e., technology maturity, schedule, budget, scope of work, mutual priorities, and resource availability).

In order to meet or exceed customer expectations, a company must first agree upon, preferably in writing, what is required. These requirements, often referred to as acceptance criteria, include price, schedule, quality, quantity, etc. It is clearly in the best interest of both parties to ensure that the agreed-to products, services, or solutions will meet or exceed the documented acceptance criteria.

Frequent, open, and honest communication is vital to building successful partnerships between companies. When meeting with customers to provide status reports on the business partnership, whether on a contract or program basis, business professionals must learn to deliver the truth, both good and bad. No business partnership goes perfectly, but communicating the good, the bad, and at times the ugly goes a long way to building trust. What a company does to overcome business obstacles and successfully communicate those actions with customers can be vital to building trust even when the final results are not the best.

BUILDING TRUST: LESSONS LEARNED

The following checklist contains 20 techniques or actions that are a simple but effective means of managing expectations and building trust between business partners.

Table 2-1 Building Trust for Successful Partnerships: Checklist
❑ Listen to the customer
❑ Understand the customer's needs vs. desires
❑ State the obvious
❑ Be accessible
❑ Return phone calls, vmails, and emails in a timely manner
❑ Provide regular communication on contract, program, and partnership status
❑ Develop a project plan for every deal (scope of work, integrated schedule, work breakdown structure, responsibility assignment matrix, and acceptance criteria)
❑ Develop a risk management plan
❑ Disclose problems early and mitigate negative impacts
❑ Back up all verbal agreements and conversations with written documentation
❑ Develop a changes management process
❑ Provide frequent communication via multiple media
❑ Be prepared to deliver both good and bad news at multiple levels, both internally and with customers
❑ Be flexible; develop alternatives
❑ Set challenging but achievable objectives
❑ Demonstrate passion in honoring commitments
❑ Recognize that trust is the most important thing in a successful business relationship
❑ Learn from mistakes and openly communicate lessons learned
❑ Celebrate joint successes
❑ Document and share best practices

Building Partnerships that Last: Best Practices

To build successful partnerships, businesses typically look for one or more of three key ingredients: complementary strength, common customer base, and chemistry.

Often businesses seek to find a partner or partners that have strength in areas in which they are weak. For example, a manufacturer might form a partnership with an online distributor to help facilitate the delivery of goods over a wider geographic area. In a similar deal, **AOL** and **Wal-Mart** announced an agreement that will boost Wal-Mart's online presence while getting AOL CD-ROMs into the hands of millions of Wal-Mart shoppers.

A second ingredient for forming a lasting business partnership is sharing a common customer base. A case in point is **Starbucks** and **KOZMO.COM**, in which Starbucks has agreed to have KOZMO boxes placed in its stores to allow for the return of goods purchased on KOZMO.COM. Starbucks and KOZMO.COM are taking advantage of their common customer base—one that is largely urban and on the go.

A third crucial element for building a successful partnership is chemistry. Most companies want to partner with a company or companies that have an excellent industry reputation; share a common leadership vision, including their commitments to their people and their customers; and have the financial strength to deliver on their commitments. A good example is **GE** and **Sun Microsystems**, which over the past few years have built a strong business relationship based upon trust. Both companies have outstanding reputations in their industries as well as financial strength, and their respective CEOs have the same vision for their employees and their customers.

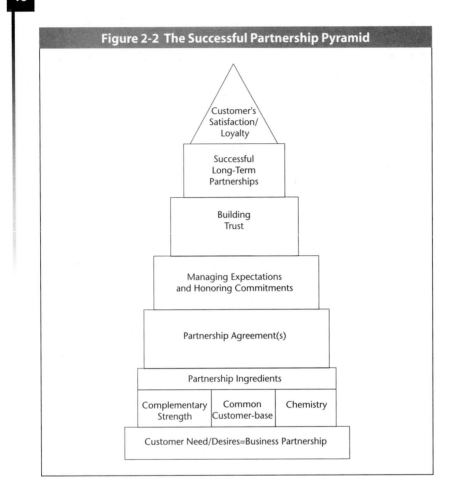

Figure 2-2 The Successful Partnership Pyramid

Customer's Satisfaction/ Loyalty

Successful Long-Term Partnerships

Building Trust

Managing Expectations and Honoring Commitments

Partnership Agreement(s)

Partnership Ingredients

Complementary Strength | Common Customer-base | Chemistry

Customer Need/Desires=Business Partnership

SUMMARY

The Successful Partnership Pyramid shown above illustrates the key points of this chapter. Customers' needs and desires fuel the business necessary to form partnerships. Business partnerships are typically linked to complementary strength, common customer base, and/or chemistry. Once a partnership agreement is formed, its ultimate success is principally determined by how each party manages expectations and honors commitments, thus building trust.

In order to make a business partnership work, companies must develop effective and efficient joint processes to facilitate the buying and selling of goods, services, and solutions to each other and their respective customers.

CHAPTER 3

THE CONTRACT MANAGEMENT PROCESS

As a business professional who manages contracts, you will encounter contracts in two ways. As a seller (the provider of goods or services in return for compensation), contracts will be sources of business opportunities. As a buyer (the purchaser of goods or services), contracts will be the means of obtaining the goods and services needed to conduct your business. You will face uncertainty and risk in both types of encounters, so managing contracts effectively will be essential. That process is called contract management: the art and science of managing a contractual agreement throughout the contracting process.

Business organizations must strive for the most efficient use of their resources—labor, capital, and money. In an age of ever greater specialization, buyers must make strategic decisions about how best to obtain the goods and services they need. Often, procuring materials, components, parts, finished goods, and services from other companies proves more practical than making or providing them in-house. This practice of obtaining goods and services from outside the organization is commonly called outsourcing. These make-or-buy decisions are an important part of design and production planning and general business operations.

Outsourcing has become a hot topic in business management today, with more and more companies using contracts to help reduce costs, capitalize expenses, improve quality, and increase profitability. The decision to buy goods or services rather than produce them in-house can be a fateful one, however. The buyer will depend on the seller, an entity not entirely under the buyer's control. Therefore, the buyer will face an element of uncertainty and risk. What if the seller cannot deliver on time, within budget, and according to specifications? To what extent does the seller depend on other companies (subcontractors) to deliver the goods and services needed by the buyer?

Market-based societies developed the legal concept of a contract in response to this critical problem of seller-related risk. Thus, contracts became tools for managing uncertainty and risk. Contracts enable buyers and sellers to enforce their agreements through the power of government, thereby reducing (but not eliminating) the risks associated with commercial transactions of goods and services. But because the idea of a contract as both social convention and legal construct has developed over hundreds of years in many different societies and legal systems, contracting concepts are quite complex.

Remember that contracts are first and foremost about developing and maintaining a professional business partnership between the buyer and the seller. Secondarily, contracts are the written documents that confirm and communicate the agreement between the buyer and seller. Thus, to understand contracts fully can take years of specialized study and professional practice. However, as a business professional who manages contracts, you cannot take years to become an expert in contract law; you must learn quickly to operate in the world of contracts as an intelligent layperson.

Think about approaching contract management this way: although not every project involves a contract, almost every contract can be considered a project. Aside from routine retail transactions, virtually all contracts satisfy the four criteria for being a project:

- They are goal-oriented
- They involve the coordinated undertaking of related activities
- They are of finite duration, with a beginning and an end
- They are unique—each different from the next

In managing contracts as projects, it is essential to break down the process into smaller steps that can be handled easily. Thus, the contract management process comprises three common phases, and the phases comprise six major steps for the buyer and six major activities for the seller. This process is summarized in Figure 3-1 and discussed briefly in the remaining sections of this chapter.

Figure 3-1 Contract Management Process

CONDUCTING THE PREAWARD PHASE

The contract management preaward phase includes procurement planning, market research, requirements determination, the make-or-buy decision, solicitation, bid/no-bid decision making, and bid or proposal preparation. This phase is vital in creating successful business relationships.

The preaward phase has three major activities or steps for the buyer:

■ Step 1: Procurement planning
■ Step 2: Solicitation planning
■ Step 3: Solicitation

Three major activities or steps are also involved for the seller:

■ Step 1: Presales activity
■ Step 2: Bid/no-bid decision making
■ Step 3: Bid or proposal preparation

Figures 3-2 and 3-3 illustrate the contract management process steps for the buyer and the seller, respectively.

Figure 3-2 Contract Management Process: Buyer's Steps

Contract Management (Buyer)

1. Procurement Planning

Input
- Scope statement
- Product description
- Procurement resources
- Market conditions
- Other planning output
- Constraints
- Assumptions

Tools and Techniques
- Make-or-buy analysis
- Expert judgment
- Contract type selection
- Risk management process
- Contract terms and conditions

Output
- Procurement management plan
- Statement of work

2. Solicitation Planning

Input
- Procurement management plan
- Statement of work
- Other procurement planning output

Tools and Techniques
- Standard forms
- Expert judgment

Output
- Procurement documents
- Evaluation criteria
- Statement of work updates

3. Solicitation

Input
- Procurement documents
- Qualified seller lists

Tools and Techniques
- Bidders' conferences
- Advertising

Output
- Proposals

4. Source Selection

Input
- Proposals
- Evaluation criteria
- Evaluation standards
- Organizational policies

Tools and Techniques
- Contract negotiation
- Weighting system
- Screening system
- Independent estimates

Output
- Contract

5. Contract Administration

Input
- Contract
- Work results
- Change requests
- Invoices and payments
- Contract administration policies

Tools and Techniques
- Contract analysis and planning
- Preperformance conference
- Performance measuring and reporting
- Payment system
- Change control system
- Dispute management system

Output
- Documentation
- Contract changes
- Payment
- Completion of work

6. Contract Closeout or Termination

Input
- Completion of work
- Contract documentation

or
- Termination notice

Tools and Techniques
- Compliance verification
- Contract documentation
- Contract closeout checklist

or
- Termination

Output
- Product or service completion
- Acceptance and final payment
- Contract closeout or termination documents
- Documented lessons learned

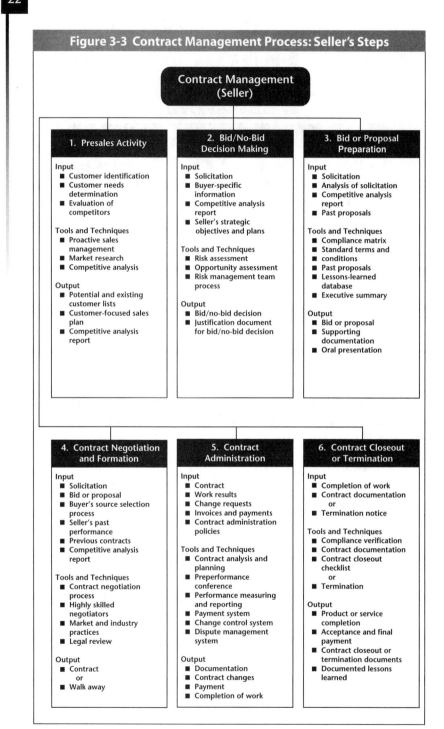

Figure 3-3 Contract Management Process: Seller's Steps

Contract Management (Seller)

1. Presales Activity

Input
- Customer identification
- Customer needs determination
- Evaluation of competitors

Tools and Techniques
- Proactive sales management
- Market research
- Competitive analysis

Output
- Potential and existing customer lists
- Customer-focused sales plan
- Competitive analysis report

2. Bid/No-Bid Decision Making

Input
- Solicitation
- Buyer-specific information
- Competitive analysis report
- Seller's strategic objectives and plans

Tools and Techniques
- Risk assessment
- Opportunity assessment
- Risk management team process

Output
- Bid/no-bid decision
- Justification document for bid/no-bid decision

3. Bid or Proposal Preparation

Input
- Solicitation
- Analysis of solicitation
- Competitive analysis report
- Past proposals

Tools and Techniques
- Compliance matrix
- Standard terms and conditions
- Past proposals
- Lessons-learned database
- Executive summary

Output
- Bid or proposal
- Supporting documentation
- Oral presentation

4. Contract Negotiation and Formation

Input
- Solicitation
- Bid or proposal
- Buyer's source selection process
- Seller's past performance
- Previous contracts
- Competitive analysis report

Tools and Techniques
- Contract negotiation process
- Highly skilled negotiators
- Market and industry practices
- Legal review

Output
- Contract
  or
- Walk away

5. Contract Administration

Input
- Contract
- Work results
- Change requests
- Invoices and payments
- Contract administration policies

Tools and Techniques
- Contract analysis and planning
- Preperformance conference
- Performance measuring and reporting
- Payment system
- Change control system
- Dispute management system

Output
- Documentation
- Contract changes
- Payment
- Completion of work

6. Contract Closeout or Termination

Input
- Completion of work
- Contract documentation
  or
- Termination notice

Tools and Techniques
- Compliance verification
- Contract documentation
- Contract closeout checklist
  or
- Termination

Output
- Product or service completion
- Acceptance and final payment
- Contract closeout or termination documents
- Documented lessons learned

Buyer Step 1: Procurement Planning

Procurement planning is determining what to procure and when. The first contract management problem for the buyer is to decide which goods and services to provide or perform in-house and which to outsource. This *make-or-buy decision or outsourcing decision* requires consideration of many factors, some of which are strategically important. The decision to buy creates a project that will be implemented in cooperation with an outside organization that is not entirely within the buyer's control. As a result, an element of uncertainty and risk will be introduced for the buyer.

The relationship between buyer and seller is as legal, if not economic, equals. The contract binds them to one another but does not place one under the other's managerial control. Sometimes the seller's economic position may be so powerful, however, that the *terms and conditions* (Ts and Cs) of the contract are ineffective in protecting the interests of the buyer.

For the seller, the contract will present an opportunity to succeed, but it also will pose great risks. The seller may find that the buyer has specified its needs inadequately or defectively; the seller's marketing department has oversold its products, services, or capabilities; faulty communication has transpired between the two parties during contract formation; or more likely, some combination of all three has occurred. In any of these cases, performance may be much more demanding than originally contemplated and may even be beyond the seller's capabilities. In addition, the buyer may wield great economic power, which effectively outweighs the contract Ts and Cs designed to protect the seller from the buyer's potentially unreasonable demands.

All the communication breakdowns, misunderstandings, conflicts, and disputes that can occur within virtually every organization also can occur between organizations, often with greater virulence and more disastrous effect. Although the contract is intended to provide a remedy to the injured party if the other fails to fulfill its contractual obligations, it is not a guarantee. Legal remedies may be uncertain and, even if attained, may not fully compensate the injured party for the other party's failure.

The make-or-buy decision can be a critical one for any organization. After the decision to contract for goods or services is made, the buyer must plan carefully and implement the decision properly.

Buyer Step 2: Solicitation Planning

In the course of planning, the buyer must–

- Determine how to specify its requirements or deliverables
- Identify potential sources
- Analyze the sources of uncertainty and risk that the purchase will entail
- Develop the Ts and Cs of the contract
- Choose the methods for selecting a seller and for proposal evaluation, negotiation, and contract formation
- Arrange for effective administration of the contract

Developing a statement of work (SOW) and the specifications that are usually included in it is one of the most difficult challenges in procurement planning. First, the buyer must understand its own requirements–quite a difficult task. Second, the buyer must be able to communicate those requirements, typically in the form of either specific deliverables or some form of a level of effort, to others outside the buyer's organization–an even more difficult task. Because developing and communicating requirements is one of the most critical functions in contract management, it will be discussed extensively in Chapter 11 - Global Contract Management-Misconceptions and Best Practices.

Buyer Step 3: Solicitation

Buyers may request bids, quotes, tenders, or proposals orally, in writing, or electronically through procurement documents generally called *solicitations*. Solicitations can take the following forms: request for proposals, request for quotations, request for tenders, invitation to bid, invitation for bids, and invitation for negotiation.

Solicitations should communicate the buyer's needs clearly to all potential sellers. Submitting a high-quality solicitation is vital to the buyer's success. Better solicitations from the buyer generally result in having better bids, quotes, proposals, or tenders submitted by the seller in a more timely manner. Poorly communicated solicitations often result in delays, confusion, fewer bids or proposals, and lower-quality responses. Increasingly, buyers are using electronic data interchange and electronic commerce to solicit offers from sellers of products and services worldwide.

Seller Step 1: Presales Activity

Presales activity is the proactive involvement of the seller with prospective and current buyers. Presales activities include identifying prospective and current customers, determining their needs and plans, and evaluating competitors. The most successful of these activities include proactive sales management and the extensive use of market research, benchmarking, and competitive analysis as proven tools and techniques to improve customer focus, gain insight, and provide advantage over competitors.

Seller Step 2: Bid/No-Bid Decision Making

Making the bid/no-bid decision should be a two-part process: evaluating the buyer's solicitation, the competitive environment, and your company and assessing the risks against the opportunities for a prospective contract. This step is critical to the contract management process; however, far too many companies devote too little time and attention to properly evaluating the risks before they leap into preparing bids and proposals.

Effectively managing this risk is one of the keys to the success of sellers in today's highly competitive global business environment. Several world-class companies have developed tools and techniques to help their business managers in evaluating the risks versus the opportunities of potential contracts. The tools they use involve risk identification, risk analysis, and risk mitigation.

Seller Step 3: Bid or Proposal Preparation

Bid or proposal preparation is the process of developing offers in response to oral or written solicitations or based on perceived buyer needs. Bid and proposal preparation can range from one person writing a one- or two-page proposal to a team of people developing a multivolume proposal of thousands of pages that takes months to prepare.

Conducting the Award Phase

Based on the solicitation, the buyer must evaluate offers (bids, proposals, tenders), select a seller, negotiate Ts and Cs, and award the contract. Buyers commonly call this step *source selection.* The seller negotiates the Ts and Cs with the buyer and helps form the contract.

Buyer Step 4: Source Selection

Clearly, seller selection is one of the most important decisions a buyer will make. Contract success or failure will depend on the competence and reliability of one or more key sellers and their subcontractors. Procurement planners must identify potential sources of goods and services, analyze the nature of the industry and market in which they operate, develop criteria and procedures to evaluate each source, and select one for contract award. No single set of criteria or procedures is appropriate for all procurements; thus, to some extent, original analyses must be made for each contract.

Source selection may be as simple as determining which competing set of bid prices is the lowest. On the other hand, it may involve weeks or even months of proposal analysis, plant visits, prototype development, and testing. The selection may be accomplished by one person, or it may require an extended effort by a panel of company managers.

Today, companies are spending more time planning and conducting source selection than ever before. The industry trend is toward more comprehensive screening and selection of fewer suppliers for longer duration contracts.

Seller Step 4: Contract Negotiation and Formation

After a source is selected, the parties must reach a common understanding of the nature of their undertaking and negotiate the Ts and Cs of contract performance. The ideal is to develop a set of shared expectations and understandings. However, this goal is difficult to attain for several reasons. First, either party may not fully understand its own requirements and expectations. Second, in most communication, many obstacles prevent achieving a true "meeting of the minds." Errors, miscues, hidden agendas, cultural differences, differences in linguistic use and competence, haste, lack of clarity in thought or expression, conflicting objectives, lack of good faith (or even ill will), business exigencies—all these factors can and do contribute to poor communication.

In any undertaking, uncertainty and risk arise from many sources. In a business undertaking, many of those sources are characteristic of the industry or industries involved. Because one purpose of a contract is to manage uncertainty and risk, the types and sources of uncertainty and risk must be identified and understood. Then buyer and seller must develop and agree to contract Ts and Cs that are designed to express their mutual expectations about performance and that reflect the uncertainties and risks of performance. Although tradition and the experiences of others provide a starting point for analysis, each contract must be considered unique.

The development of appropriate Ts and Cs is an important aspect of contract negotiation and formation. (Common Ts and Cs include period of performance, limitation of liabilities, warranties, intellectual property rights, payments, acceptance/completion criteria, terminations, and change management.) Some organizations spend a lot of time, perhaps months, selecting a source, but they hurry through the process of arriving at a mutual understanding of the contract Ts and Cs. A "let's get on with it" mentality sets in. It is true that contracts formed in this way sometimes prove successful for all concerned. However, when both sides involve large organizations, difficulties can arise from the different agendas of the functional groups existing within each organization's contracting party.

Some world-class companies have developed internal electronic systems to help their contract managers in negotiating, forming, and approving their contracts.

Conducting the Postaward Phase

The steps in the postaward phase are the same for both buyer and seller: contract administration and contract closeout or termination.

Buyer and Seller Step 5: Contract Administration

Contract administration is the process of ensuring compliance with contractual Ts and Cs during contract performance and up to contract closeout or termination.

After award, both parties must act according to the Ts and Cs of their agreement; they must read and understand their contract, do what it requires of them, and avoid doing what they have agreed not to do.

Best practices in contract administration include–

- Reading the contract
- Ensuring that all organizational elements are aware of their responsibilities in relation to the contract
- Providing copies of the contract to all affected organizations either paper or electronic copies
- Establishing systems to verify conformance with contract technical and administrative requirements
- Conducting preperformance (or kickoff) meetings with the buyer and the seller
- Assigning responsibility to check actual performance against requirements
- Identifying significant variances
- Analyzing each such variance to determine its cause
- Ensuring that someone takes appropriate corrective action and then follows up
- Managing the contract change process
- Establishing and maintaining contract documentation: diaries and telephone logs, meeting minutes, inspection reports, progress reports, test reports, invoices and payment records, accounting source documents, accounting journals and ledgers, contracting records, change orders and other contract modifications, claims, and routine correspondence

Periodically, buyer and seller must meet to discuss performance and verify that it is on track and that each party's expectations are being met. This activity is critical. Conflict is almost inescapable within and between organizations. The friction that can arise from minor misunderstandings, failures, and disagreements can heat to the boiling point before anyone on either side is fully aware of it. When this happens, the relationship between the parties may be irreparably damaged, and amicable problem resolution may become impossible. Periodic joint assessments by contract managers can identify and resolve problems early and help to ensure mutually satisfactory performance.

Some world-class companies use electronic systems to assist them with contract monitoring, performance measurement, progress reporting, and contract compliance documentation.

Buyer and Seller Step 6:
Contract Closeout or Termination

After the parties have completed the main elements of performance, they must settle final administrative and legal details before closing out the contract. They may have to make price adjustments and settle claims. The buyer will want to evaluate the seller's performance. Both parties must collect records and prepare them for storage in accordance with administrative and legal retention requirements.

Unfortunately, contracts are sometimes terminated due to the mutual agreement of the parties or due to the failure of one or both of the parties to perform all or part of the contract. After a termination notice is received, the parties must still go through the same closeout actions as for a completed contract.

SUMMARY

Like projects, contracts must be managed effectively to be successful. Business professionals are responsible for managing contracts–how you will be affected by a particular contract and how you will manage it will depend on whether you are acting as the buyer or the seller of the product or service.

The contract management process is a complex one, with six specific steps required by the buyer and six by the seller. However, even the most effective process can work only if the senior management and all team members commit to making it happen. Chapter 4 will discuss the importance of people, the nature of teamwork, and the roles and responsibilities involved in the contract management process.

CHAPTER

TEAMWORK– ROLES AND RESPONSIBILITIES

Within a business organization, contract managers (CMs), financial managers, sales managers (SMs), and project managers (PMs) often must work together to successfully purchase or provide quality products, services, or solutions on time, on budget, and to the total satisfaction of their customers. Indeed, most companies have found that an effective, efficient working relationship between team members is vital in achieving strategic business objectives.

It is essential to enhance recognition and understanding of the important relationship between CMs and PMs–and of how it can be improved. Here, the connection between the certification programs and the official bodies of knowledge of the key professional associations that represent the CM and PM fields is discussed. Then the chapter examines the potential overlap of on-the-job responsibility between the two professions and the importance of clearly establishing "who's in charge." Finally, seven best practices are presented for improving the CM/PM working relationship, as demonstrated by one of the world's leading information technology companies.

EXAMINING CONTRACT MANAGER AND PROJECT MANAGER COMMONALITIES

What do CMs and PMs have in common in terms of knowledge, skills, responsibilities, and professional interests? The answer to that question is found in part by examining the certification programs and official bodies of knowledge of the two fields' independent, not-for-profit professional associations.

Contract management is principally represented by the three professional associations: National Contract Management Association (NCMA), founded in 1959, focuses on U.S. government contracting and commercial contract management both buying and selling, with about 20,000 members worldwide, the Institute for Supply Management (ISM), founded in 1915, which focuses mainly on commercial purchasing and supply chain management with about 40,000 members worldwide, and the newest, International Association of Contract and Commercial Management (IACCM). Most NCMA and ISM members are from within the United States, but each association has chapters worldwide. IACCM was founded in 1999 and now has membership that includes more than 2,000 public and private sector organizations from over 100 countries.

FOUR

Project management is principally represented by the Project Management Institute (PMI) and the International Project Management Association (IPMA). PMI has more than 320,000 members from more than 150 countries worldwide. IPMA's members are predominantly European.

NCMA, ISM, IACCM, and PMI have professional certification programs with rigorous examinations based on well-defined bodies of knowledge deemed requisite to professional competence in the field. When those certification programs and bodies of knowledge are compared, a strong relationship between the two professions becomes clear.

Those who want to be recognized by NCMA as Certified Professional Contracts Manager (CPCM) must have five years of business experience, 120 Certified Professional Education (CPE) units in contract or business-related training, a bachelor's degree from a college or university that is accredited regionally or by the Distance Education and Training Council (DETC), and must successfully complete a rigorous multi-choice examination based upon best practices in both commercial and government contract management. For an individual to become a Certified Federal Contracts Manager (CFCM) he must have one year of business experience, 80 CPE units in contract or business-related training, a bachelor's degree from a college or university, as stated above, and successfully complete a rigorous multi-choice examination based upon the U.S. Federal Acquisition Regulation. Likewise, an individual may become a Certified Commercial Contract Manager (CCCM) by having one year of business experience, 80 CPE units in contract or related-business training, a bachelor's degree from a college or university, as stated above, and successfully complete a rigorous multi-choice examination based on commercial contracting and general business knowledge. Further, NCMA has created, in partnership with the Federal Contracting Institute, a new certification program called the Certified Schedules Contract Manager (CSCM), which shows that an individual possesses detailed knowledge in Federal Supply Schedules and Multiple Award Schedule contracting done by the U.S. Federal Government. This certificate is earned by completing five required training courses and passing a standardized test. To learn more about NCMA go to *www.ncmahq.org*.

ISM formerly offered a Certified Purchasing Manager (CPM) program worldwide, but is no longer offering this professional credential. Since, 2008 ISM offers the Certified Professional Supply Manager (CPSM) designation, which requires skills in finance, supplier relationship management, organizational global strategy, and risk compliance. Those who want to become a CPSM must have three years of experience in supply management, a bachelor's degree from a regionally accredited institution or international equivalent, and successfully pass 3 CPSM exams or if he is a C.P.M. in good standing, pass the Bridge exam. To learn more about ISM go to *www.ism.ws.*

IACCM has a well-established web-based skills assessment tool and unique set of professional certification programs. The certification programs offered by IACCM are supported by a growing portfolio of web-based learning modules, addressing the needs of both buyers and sellers. The IACCM Management Learning Program is also unique in its capabilities, combining each recorded module with a wide array of texts, research results and recommended readings. Since IACCM currently has no chapters, magazines, or journals, it provides web-based information transfer via message boards, mentoring, member surveys, and webcasts worldwide. Thus, IACCM effectively provides virtual membership globally using the power of the internet.

Like NCMA and ISM, IACCM offers conferences worldwide and a wide-array of classroom training for those that want on-site, live programs to enhance the web-based materials. To learn more about IACCM go to *www.iaccm.com.*

Those who want to be recognized by PMI as certified Project Management Professionals (PMP) must have three years of experience in project management, earned 60 Professional Development Units (PDUs) in project management and related training courses, and successfully complete a challenging 4-hour examination of 200 multiple-choice questions as part of the qualifications. The exam is now offered electronically at Sylvan Learning Centers throughout the United States and at numerous international locations. The exam covers PMI's Project Management Body of Knowledge (PMBOK). One of these areas of knowledge is project procurement management (see Figure 4–1.) Further, PMI has expanded its certification programs to include: Certified Associate in Project

Management (CAPM), a PMI Scheduling Professional (PMI-SP), and PMI Risk Management Professional (PMI-RMP), and the Program Management Professional (PgMP). To learn more about PMI and its numerous professional credentials go to *www.pmi.org.*

In 1991, when NCMA created special topic committees (STCs) to give NCMA members with similar interests the opportunity to share lessons learned, one STC established was program/project management. The charter of this STC was to promote a greater awareness of the importance of the CM/PM relationship and the need to understand the role each plays in supporting the organization's customers. NCMA no longer offers Special Topic Committees. Instead, NCMA has created a few Communities of Interest (COIs).

Figure 4-1 Overview of Project Management Knowledge Areas

DETERMINING WHO'S IN CHARGE

If the overlap between CM and PM competencies and responsibilities becomes evident in looking at the profession's respective certification programs and bodies of knowledge, it becomes obvious when examining the day-to-day interactions between members of the two professions. In addition, there is coordination with sales managers, financial managers, and others. In many organizations, so much on-the-job overlap exists that it becomes a source of tension and conflict—to the point that the question "who's in charge?" arises.

Who has the final say in tailoring the organization's standard contract Ts and Cs? Who drafts and who approves the SOW and specifications? Who determines what pricing method to use? Who actually selects the seller? Who leads the negotiation? Who controls contract administration and subcontract management?

These questions exemplify some of the contract-related activities that can, in a project context, cause conflict. The degree and focus of the conflict will vary, depending on how the organization is structured and how it allocates authority and responsibility between PMs and CMs. In other words, the answer to the question of "who's in charge?" is "it depends."

In commercial companies, PMs typically are responsible for ensuring the coordinated undertaking of goal-oriented projects. Often they work in a matrix organization characterized by multifunctional teams composed of product line, professional services, functional area (engineering, manufacturing, systems integration), and geographical area (country, region, plant) representatives. For their part, CMs may work in such a matrix organization—supporting many projects—or they may be part of a functional purchasing or contract management organization that supports all contracting requirements companywide.

In most companies, PMs serve as multifunctional team leaders on one or more projects, shouldering the responsibility for achieving the desired results for these projects. What may vary, however, is the extent of their authority over the resources needed to accomplish this feat. When it comes to contracting, PMs in most companies lack the authority to sign, modify, or cancel contracts that legally bind companies to buy or sell products or services.

Yet PMs in some companies have the express authority to sign contracts and modifications or cancellations of contracts.

CMs, however, seldom are in charge of the day-to-day project planning or operation. Yet, as individuals authorized to enter into legally binding contractual arrangements, they may shoulder the responsibility for having critical resources available as needed under tight, often conflicting or unrealistic time frames. Alternatively, they may be placed in an advisory or support role to PMs who have contracting authority, or they may share responsibility and authority for many tasks typically thought of as contract management tasks, including precontract award actions, contract negotiation, and postcontract award actions.

Sales managers typically serve as the seller's primary interface with the buyer. In many companies the sales manager also serves as the company's lead negotiator. Sales managers often have a reputation of promising anything and everything in order to get the contract.

Figure 4-2 illustrates the typical and desirable assignments of the key team members during the life of a contract.

Figure 4-2 PM, CM, and SM Assignments in the Contract Life Cycle

Who should be in charge of such contract management tasks? Again, the answer must be "it depends." Each company must make its own determination based on corporate structure and culture, contract and project management capabilities, and other factors. What matters most is that "who's in charge" is clear. Having multiskilled individuals who can accomplish various tasks is valuable. However, ensuring that all involved in project activities know who has the authority to bind the company legally and who does not, as well as who holds ultimate responsibility for all steps in the seller selection and contract administration processes, is essential.

DEFINING CONTRACTUAL AUTHORITY

Most business organizations, whether they are operating as buyers of products or services or as sellers, empower one or more individuals with the authority to bind their organization legally in contractual obligations. This employee (usually a contract manager) is typically referred to in contract law as the *agent*. The source of authority is typically referred to as the *principal* or *agency*. When a principal, such as a buyer or seller, delegates authority to an individual to represent the principal, the authorized person is an agent. The legal concept of agency exists between the principal and the agent. Agency is that relationship based on the delegation of authority by the principal to the agent, to act on the principal's behalf.

The two major types of authority are *actual* and *apparent*. Actual authority is granted intentionally to the agent and can be either *express* (in writing) or *implied* (not stated in writing but based on a person's position within the purchasing department or agency). Apparent authority, although not actually granted, may nonetheless rest with the agent if the principal or agency allows the agent to exercise such authority and the other party believes that the agent indeed possesses such authority. If, however, the agent acts without authority or knowingly exceeds the scope of authority granted and the principal or agency does not approve of such acts, the law makes the agent liable for any loss sustained by third parties. Some agents operate with express limits to their authority—that is, dollar amount, type of contract, nature of product or service, and so on— and other agents have no specified limits to their authority.

Project managers, engineers, implementation managers, and others must realize that although they hold important positions, they usually do not have the authority to direct any changes to the contract. In turn, contract managers in charge of buying products or services usually have no authority to direct the subcontractor in any manner of performance (however, more buying organizations are requesting the right of approval of subcontractors).

Promoting Teamwork

In all companies that seek to fulfill customer requirements through cross-functional management teams, business professionals regardless of job titles will find themselves working together to some extent in one arrangement or another. So the question arises: "What can be done to ensure that the working relationship is optimally productive and in line with the company's business objectives?"

Following NCR's Lead: Best Practices

One company that has addressed this often overlooked issue directly is NCR Corporation, a global company dedicated to being the world's best at bringing computing and communications solutions together to provide people easy access to information and to each other–anytime, anywhere. NCR provides customer-focused solutions that help businesses better understand and serve their customers by more effectively getting, moving, and using customer information. Achieving this goal places great pressure on the company's project management and contract management organizations.

The company has hundreds of PMs worldwide who collectively manage thousands of information technology projects. These projects range from relatively common installations of off-the-shelf computer hardware to highly complex multinational systems integration and professional services undertakings. The company also has hundreds of CMs who support PMs as members of project teams. CMs maintain all contractual authority. They serve as agents who legally bind the company to buy or sell goods and services.

Recently, NCR has developed and implemented various ways to foster effective interaction among its CMs and PMs. The following seven best practices may prove helpful to other organizations seeking to enhance such interaction in their own work environments.

- *GlobalPM®:* NCR empowered its PMs by creating and implementing a state-of-the-art project management methodology called GlobalPM®. GlobalPM® practices and techniques provide PMs and CMs worldwide with a clear, concise, consistent set of organizational, conceptual, and documentation tools.
- *Customer-focused teams:* The company formed several hundred customer-focused business teams to implement a new customer-focused business model. A customer-focused team

is a cross-functional unit dedicated to understanding a specific customer's needs and interests and to delivering solutions fitting the customer's unique organizational profile. Each team has a leader and consists of representatives from a variety of functional areas, including contract management.

- All team members focus on helping the customer reach its business goals and objectives. The team has the decision-making authority, responsibility, and accountability needed to be fully responsive to the customer's business issues. Its goal is to work together with shared values and a common bond to please the customer.

- *Early involvement of the PM in the contracting process:* The company learned that early involvement of its PMs in precontract award activities was a proactive means of mitigating risk. Often PMs can give CMs and marketing managers critical insights into the value of certain requirements and the realistic opportunities of achieving the results the customer desires. PMs can, for example, assess whether cost and schedule estimates are realistic, analyze the risks and opportunities the project provides, and recommend special Ts and Cs for tailoring the contract to the project goals.

- *Empowered CMs:* The NCR legal department designed a program that places CMs closer to their customers. This new program gives CMs greater authority to negotiate contracts as long as they work within broad guidelines. For example, CMs now have more flexibility to modify specific contract Ts and Cs to meet the needs of their customers. The program enables CMs to serve as pragmatic experts who are responsive to customer needs and are able to support the company's PMs effectively.

- *Simplified contracts that ease contract management:* A key to successful contract administration is a clear and concise contract that is easily understood by all parties concerned. The company rewrote many of its standard contract forms to be shorter and easier to read and understand. Because PMs are often responsible for contract administration tasks, PMs and CMs both benefit, as does the customer.

- *Shared lessons learned:* To learn from the past, the project management and contract management organizations must work together to document the successes and failures of their endeavors. The company recognized that it must consistently improve its efforts to share lessons learned. In addition, CMs and PMs are encouraged to engage in process improvement continually.

■ *Professional development programs:* The company promotes and provides professional development programs for its business managers globally. It has sent hundreds of its managers through a comprehensive professional development program offered by The George Washington University and ESI International.

GETTING RESULTS

In most companies that seek to compete successfully in today's global markets, SMs, CMs and PMs all play key roles. Those roles, and the levels of authority and types of responsibility they entail, vary from company to company. Despite what the roles are, the professionals who fill them are most effective when the roles are clearly delineated and the company recognizes the importance of effective interaction between employees of the two professions.

The competitiveness of today's global markets demands responsiveness to customers through smart solutions, swift turnarounds, and best value. Companies must foster the professionalism of their sales management, contract management and project management employees and find ways to develop strong working relationships among those employees. The companies that follow these practices will be in the best position to develop and implement the sophisticated competitive strategies that are critical to success.

SUMMARY

People make every process work or fail. The process itself can make the work easier or more difficult, but ultimately, the people make the difference. Good people can and routinely do overcome bad processes. However, good people working within a well-defined, effective process with clearly stated roles and responsibilities can achieve outstanding results.

Clearly defining all team members' roles and responsibilities is crucial for working together in a unified effort to meet business objectives. NCR has taken steps to address this issue. Its seven best practices can serve as a model for fostering teamwork among contract management and project management professionals.

CHAPTER 5

GLOBAL CONTRACTING CONCEPTS AND PRINCIPLES

Although business professionals who manage contracts need not be experts in contract law, they must understand its basic legal concepts and principles to practice effective contract management. As more organizations expand their operations overseas, their business professionals also must be knowledgeable about the legal systems in the countries where they do business. This chapter provides a basic understanding of contract law in the United States and alerts business professionals to some problems that may arise because of the different contracting concepts and principles used around the globe.

DETERMINING CONTRACTING OBJECTIVES

The first step in developing a contractual relationship is usually to set contracting objectives. In the United States, objectives are stated in concrete business terms such as quantities, dates, and monetary values. When the transaction is outside the United States, objectives sometimes have to begin with more basic questions. For effective contracting, parties must first understand why they seek to form a contract, then what a contract is and how and when to form one.

Why Do Parties Form Contracts?

When asked in the United States, the answer is usually "to promote understanding between the parties, to avoid litigation in the event of dispute, and to protect parties in the event of litigation." When asked outside the United States, the answer is more frequently "to get business done" or "to do the deal."

These different attitudes affect the way we contract. In the United States, formal dispute resolution is an integral part of the contract. We strive to resolve all potential disputes before they arise by using the contract terms. Outside the United States, a dispute resolution process is often not part of the contract document. Rather, if a dispute arises, the contract document is abandoned and the parties begin negotiation to resolve the dispute. Experienced international business people often describe U.S. contracts as the final or end point of the negotiation and most international contracts as the starting point.

For many people, this difference is a very frustrating aspect of global business. Bridging the gap in objectives can be time consuming

FIVE

and tedious and is sometimes impossible. Any attempt to bridge the gap requires understanding the underlying legal and cultural reasons for the difference in perspective.

What Is a Contract?

Underlying the difference in why we contract is the differing perception of what a contract is. The term *contract* has two meanings.

First, a contract is a relationship between buyer and seller defined by an agreement about their respective rights and responsibilities. Contracts define an agreed-on relationship between a buyer and a seller. Relationships involve expectations, and that is what contracts are about. When a buyer contracts with a seller to provide products or services, the buyer is essentially melding the seller into its organization. Both buyer and seller have expectations embodied in the contract Ts and Cs. The contract itself is manifested in the oral expressions and other behavior of the contracting parties.

Second, a contract is a document that describes an agreement about rights and responsibilities. In any jurisdiction, a contract is "an agreement governed and restricted by law," and the applicable law shapes the nature of the contract.

In the United States, the law places great emphasis on the written manifestation of the agreement; we tend to think of the contract as the written document. In fact, under common law as adopted by most U.S. jurisdictions, contracts can be oral (spoken agreements), written, implied, or created by operation of law. Nonetheless, most commercial contracts fall under a rule that requires them to be in written form to be enforceable. Thus, our entire commercial system revolves around the written document.

Outside the United States, many legal systems place less emphasis on the written document that evidences an agreement. They tend to define the contract as the entire contractual relationship in all its nuances. In general, commercial sales contracts do not have to be in writing to be enforceable. Therefore, contracting parties tend to view the written document with less emphasis and finality.

When Does a Negotiation Become a Contract?

Under any legal system, rules determine exactly when a negotiation reaches the point of becoming an enforceable agreement. Because of the emphasis on the written document in the United States, that point often relates to the signing of the document. In other systems, the point of contracting relates to the behavior of the parties, which may or may not include a signature. This distinction is a source of much international conflict. For example, the U.S. corporation may dissolve a transaction before signing the contract document, believing that no contract exists. Yet the non-U.S. corporation believes that the elements of an agreement under its system were met, and thus a contract was formed. Parties operating in global business should understand all contract formation rules that may apply to them to avoid inadvertently entering into a contract. In short, it is a good business practice to agree at the outset with your international partners that no contract will result from any transaction unless a final written document is prepared.

Contract documentation allows people who did not participate in forming the contract to carry out the agreement made by the people who did. This capability is essential if organizations are going to make contracts. However, it increases the potential for misunderstanding, because words are imprecise communication tools, and because many people do not use them well. People who were not present during agreement negotiation frequently misinterpret the written words of those who were. Adjectives and adverbs are inherently ambiguous words, and the use of English pronouns can be confusing.

TAKING A GLOBAL PERSPECTIVE

To understand how one system differs from another, you must thoroughly understand the different systems. Each individual operates using a set of assumptions based on language, culture, and the legal system in which he or she learned to do business. For effective global contracting, you must identify and understand your own assumptions, then learn how your partners' assumptions differ.

UNDERSTANDING THE LEGAL FRAMEWORK

There is no universal law of contracts. Some countries have adopted a statutory or civil law system; others, including England and its former colonies, are governed by common law. In the United States, 49 states are governed by common law. Louisiana is the only civil law state in the Union.

Many core ideas are shared by the two systems of law; however, common law and civil law are not identical. *Civil law* is that body of law created by acts of legislature. Therefore, civil law countries rely solely on statutes, called *codes*, to regulate their contractual relations. In contrast, common law comprises the body of those principles and rules of action that derive their authority not from legislative enactments but from usages and customs or from judgments and decrees of the courts recognizing, affirming, and enforcing such usages and customs.

Currently, commercial sales are governed by statutes even in most common law countries. A *sale* is a contract pursuant to whose terms goods are transferred from seller to buyer. Although the law of sales is based on the same principles applicable to other contracts, it has developed certain specialized aspects concerning the rights and obligations arising from the transfer of goods. For instance in the United States, a contract for the sale of goods will be subject to the statute enacted by all states called the Uniform Commercial Code (UCC).

U.S. Common Law

The U.S. legal system was based on the English common law system in effect more than 200 years ago. The U.S. Constitution's authors held intact the basic way that courts in England resolved legal disputes. In fact, they adopted as U.S. law the existing law of England to the extent that it did not conflict with the new Constitution.

The most fundamental principle of a common law system is the value of precedent. This concept exists in the context of a hierarchical court system, as shown in Figure 5–1. When a higher court resolves a legal issue, all lower courts are bound by that decision and must apply a similar rule in similar situations. When an appellate court decides a case, it reports the facts of the case and the rules of law applied given those facts. When a lower court faces a similar set of facts, it must apply the same rules of law. If another court subsequently does not apply the same rules of law, the outcome of the case may be appealed to a higher court.

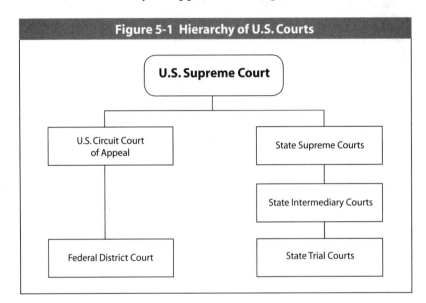

Figure 5-1 Hierarchy of U.S. Courts

The hierarchy of U.S. courts is set out in the Constitution, with the hierarchical structure based on parallel court systems. Federal laws are prosecuted and appealed through the federal courts, and state laws are prosecuted and appealed through the state courts. However, if a state court decision involves a constitutional issue, ultimately it too may be appealed to the U.S. Supreme Court.

According to the Constitution, federal courts address all federal issues (issues arising from federal statutory law). All other law is created by individual states. Except for federal government contracting, all contracting law is state law and, therefore, differs among states.

If parties to an international contract choose U.S. contract law to apply to their contract, they must be careful to choose the law of a particular state. No general U.S. contract law exists.

Diversity Jurisdiction

A commonly misunderstood aspect of U.S. contract law, based on the UCC, is *diversity jurisdiction*. If disputing parties are diverse (they come from different states or from a state and another country), and the amount in controversy exceeds $50,000, the case may be tried in federal court (the court has jurisdiction). However, the court will apply state law.

For example, if a company outside the United States sues a Virginia company over a contractual dispute of $400,000, the case may be tried in the Federal District Court for the Eastern District of Virginia, and the court will apply Virginia law (or, in certain circumstances, the law of another state).

Civil Law

Unlike common law systems, civil law systems do not give precedence to previous court decisions. The theory of a pure civil law system is that one comprehensive code (written statute) governs all disputes. Thus, each case begins with a fresh look at the statutory law (the code).

For parties from common law jurisdictions, the usual practice is to draft contract language with the understanding that it will be interpreted as it has always been interpreted by the courts. For example, a contract a U.S. company is a party to may say that each party is excused from delay resulting from "weather." The U.S. party agreeing on the language of the contract did not mean *any* weather. It intended the meaning that U.S. courts have always given that phrase—unusually severe weather for that location at that time of year. In using the contract for global business, out of the reach of U.S. courts, the word *weather* loses that case law interpretation.

All contracts should be scrutinized to determine whether the meaning of the language is clear or whether the drafter is relying on the full interpretation of the language applied previously by U.S. courts.

COMMUNICATING NEEDS

What should be clear from these descriptions is that the existence of a contract manifests itself through communication by words and deeds. It is difficult for one person to know what is in the mind of another; thus the subjective intentions of the parties are not as important as what they actually communicated to one another when they made their agreement. Human behavior and language, slippery media at best, are the means of establishing the content of the agreement between the parties.

Herein lie two potential problems for contract managers. The first problem has to do with how clear an idea each party has of its expectations for the new relationship. (Indeed, does either party have *anything* clearly in mind?) The second problem has to do with how successful each party is in communicating its ideas to the other party and obtaining acceptance of those ideas.

Inadequate forethought and poor communication can result in relationships that are contracts in the legal sense but ambiguous as a practical matter. If the parties do not successfully resolve these issues during contract formation, the contract document may reflect their ambiguity about the nature of their relationship and its objectives. Conversely, a genuine agreement reached by the parties may not be accurately reflected in the contract document. In either event, the project objectives will not be well defined. This problem can lead to crises in quality, cost, and schedule.

These problems are highly intractable for two reasons. First, many people do not think clearly at times or may not develop their ideas fully. Second, many people are not skillful when using their own language or the language of those with whom they must communicate. For either reason, people may be unable to communicate their ideas to others.

RECOGNIZING THE SOURCES OF RISK

Uncertainty and risk in contracting arise from five main sources:

- Lack of buyer understanding of its requirements
- Shortcomings of human language and differing interpretations
- Behavior of the parties
- Haste
- Deception

Lack of Buyer Understanding of Its Requirements

If the buyer does not have a clear understanding of its requirements or cannot express that understanding effectively in terms of specific deliverables or level of effort, an agreement cannot be reached with another party to fulfill those requirements.

Many buyers have only a vague notion of their requirements, as revealed in the language of their specifications or statements of work. Broad, ambiguous expressions that obligate a seller to do something "as required" or "as necessary" are often used because the buyer does not know the requirements or needs but wants to put the seller in the position of having to do whatever it is whenever the buyer finds it out. How can the seller estimate the cost of meeting such obligations?

Ironically, some buyers overcompensate by specifying their needs down to the smallest detail. If these details have been well researched, the specification may indeed reflect the buyer's needs. But such detailed requirements are often specified by people who are not familiar with the technology available, or soon to become available in the marketplace, or with industry methods or market practices. As a result, the specification may describe processes discarded by the industry or product features not yet available, no longer available, or not available in combination with other specified features.

These difficulties arise because many, if not most, buyers are uninformed about goods and services they must purchase from an industry other than their own. Rare is the buyer who knows as much about a product or service as the companies that design, produce, and market it for a living. This fact is the source of much difficulty in writing and interpreting specifications and of performance crises for the project manager who must fulfill contractually specified requirements.

Shortcomings of Human Language and Differing Interpretations

A party to a contract may mean one thing but say another. An inability to express ideas clearly may result in a contract document that does not accurately reflect the intended agreement. Meaning may be clear in the language of one country but become obscured during translation. Unfortunately, these scenarios are all too common in the world of contracting.

Behavior of the Parties

The actions of one or both of the parties after the contract is signed may give meaning to the words of the contract that the parties did not originally intend. For example, the seller may choose not to enforce a late payment penalty clause when an important buyer consistently pays late. Thus, the seller establishes a precedence of performance, or lack thereof, which is inconsistent with the language in the contract.

Haste

In business, haste causes many problems. Because of an impatience with the bureaucratic contracting process, project managers often promote haste in contract formation. In the rush to "get on contract," many ideas are not fully developed or discussed by the parties. As a result, the expectations of both parties may never be fully understood, by themselves or by each other. Unrealistic expectations go unchallenged. Realistic expectations go uncommunicated. These expectations do not disappear, however, and will rise to haunt both contract managers and project managers after the project is under way.

Deception

Deception, with both ill and benign intent, is a reality of the business world–thus the warning "caveat emptor," or "let the buyer beware." Deception is a deliberate defect in the communication process. As discussed previously, buyers often do not fully understand the nature of the goods and services they buy, the methods of the industry producing them, or the practices of the market selling them. Buyers may have only a vague idea of the results they hope to obtain from those goods and services, an idea limited to the expectation that "things will be better."

In trying to give expression to their vague ideas and unrealistic expectations, buyers may develop faulty specifications. In these circumstances, sales representatives and proposal writers may find acceding to such requirements more convenient than educating the buyer. They adopt the strategy of winning the contract first and educating the buyer after contract award.

Although the strategy may involve outright fraud, it is probably more commonly based on the belief (or hope) that "once they have it, they'll be satisfied" or "if they really knew what they wanted, they would want what we plan to give them." A remarkable degree of self-deception can exist on the parts of both buyer and seller involved in such a strategy. Even when the intention is ultimately to make the buyer happy, the method is deceptive and often leads to trouble.

CONFRONTING THE CHALLENGES OF RISK

Although intended to reduce uncertainties and risks associated with business transactions, contracts can introduce new risk. For example, the agreement may prove to be incomplete (essential aspects of the relationship left unaddressed or unresolved and subject to dispute), or the parties to a contract may dispute the precise interpretation of the contract document. Either circumstance will cause problems for both parties.

Furthermore, one party may be unwilling or unable to keep its promises, the threat of litigation notwithstanding, but will be able to prevent or evade enforcement or will be unable to comply with a court order for compensation or restitution. One party may also inadvertently breach the contract (fail to comply with the contract without a legal excuse), exposing itself to sanctions or allowing the other party to avoid its obligations.

Unfortunately, a trouble-proof, loophole-free contract has never been written and will never be written as long as human beings are involved in the process. Merely having a signed contract does not ensure that the parties have a fully formed agreement, and it is certainly no guarantee against trouble.

Part of managing a contract is working out the relationship on a day-to-day, issue-by-issue basis. Differences between the contracting parties will arise and must be resolved in a businesslike manner, professionally and without rancor. If the parties discover that their agreement did not anticipate all contingencies, ad hoc settlements must be negotiated. Such circumstances do not mean that the contract terms should be ignored; they simply indicate that a signed contract is just the beginning of the contract manager's and project manager's work.

Having a contract does not eliminate business risk; at best, it exchanges one set of risks for another. The contracting parties must make an effort to administer the contract properly to minimize these and other risks that may arise. That effort is itself a project, and all the project management principles apply.

Understanding Basic Terminology

Most contracts you will see will be in writing. The contract document will contain words, numerals, symbols, and perhaps drawings to describe the relationship that will exist between the contracting parties.

Clauses

A contract consists of a series of statements called *clauses*. The following is a fairly standard contract clause:

Governing Law

> Any dispute, controversy, or claim arising out of or in connection with this Agreement, or the breach, termination, or invalidity thereof, shall be finally settled by arbitration based on the laws of the state of New York, United States of America.

This clause is short and easy to understand. But other clauses, especially when the contracting parties are from different legal systems, may be several pages in length and require careful reading to grasp their meanings.

Terms and Conditions

Collectively, clauses form the terms and conditions of the contract, and they define the rights and responsibilities of the parties to the contractual agreement. If called upon to enforce the contract in arbitration or a lawsuit, the arbitrator or court will look to these Ts and Cs in resolving the dispute.

A *term* is simply a part of the contract that addresses a specific subject. In most contracts, terms address payment, delivery, product quality, warranty of goods or services, termination of the agreement, resolution of disputes, and other subjects. Terms are described in clauses. The "Governing Law" clause is a contract term.

A *condition* is a phrase that either activates or suspends a term. A condition that activates a term is called a *condition precedent;* one that suspends a term is called a *condition subsequent.* Understanding the effect of conditions is critical to properly documenting and administering a contract. For example, the following sentence might appear in a "Specifications and Inspections" clause:

> Buyer may charge Seller for the cost of an above-normal level of inspection if rejection of the shipment based on the Buyer's normal inspection level endangers production schedules and if the inspected products are necessary to meet production schedules.

In other words, if the buyer rejects the seller's products based on a normal level of inspection, and if that causes those products to be unavailable for production, and if the products in question are necessary to meet a production schedule that will be endangered because of their unavailability, then the seller must pay the buyer the cost of performing inspections made at above-normal levels in order to meet that production schedule.

When experience teaches that certain clauses should always be included in contracts of a given type, those clauses may be preprinted in standard form. Such preprinted clauses are often called *standard terms and conditions*, which are useful when a business regularly enters many contracts and wants to reduce the administrative costs of its purchasing or sales operation. Standard Ts and Cs eliminate the need to hire an attorney to write a new contract every time a firm wants to buy or sell something.

In addition to reducing the administrative costs of contracting, standard Ts and Cs also reduce the risks of contract ambiguity. Contract managers, project managers, buyers, and sellers can become familiar with standard clauses and their proper interpretation, which will greatly reduce the potential for misunderstandings and disputes.

Certain clauses appear in virtually every kind of contract. Take, for example, the following clause:

> ABC Company is not liable for failing to fulfill its obligations due to acts of God, civil or military authority, war, strikes, fire, failure of its suppliers to meet commitments, or other causes beyond its reasonable control.

Clauses of this type are often called *force majeure,* a French term for "major or irresistible force." They appear in nearly all large contracts. Another commonly used clause requires suppliers to–

> ... comply with all federal, state, and local laws, regulations, rules, and orders. Any provision which is required to be a part of this Agreement by virtue of any such law, regulation, rule, or order is incorporated by reference.

Of course, neither party is familiar with all such provisions, but the idea is to relieve the buyer of any responsibility for the indiscretions of the seller.

Other clauses may give the buyer the right to purchase additional quantities of goods or extend the performance of services at agreed-on prices. Indemnification clauses often require one party to protect the other from certain types of losses, liabilities, judgments, and so forth. The indemnified party is given security of financial reimbursement by the indemnifying party for any loss described in the clause.

A common misunderstanding is that price is separate and distinct from the Ts and Cs, but that is not so. Nearly all Ts and Cs affect price, either increasing or decreasing costs or liabilities to the parties. In world-class companies, senior management ensures that all business managers involved with contracts are aware of and fully understand the cost, risk, and value of Ts and Cs and how they affect price.

APPLYING CONTRACTING PRINCIPLES

Although contracting law in the United States is different from state to state, some basic principles are common to all states. With or without formal legal training, most U.S. business professionals who manage contracts absorb the following principles while doing business. Many principles you may take for granted, however, are not valid in civil law countries. When contracting globally, examining your basic assumptions to determine whether your trading partners are operating on the same ones is essential.

FIVE

Some common legal principles and concepts are described in the following paragraphs. Differences in civil law are noted below the common law descriptions.

Formation

In common law, to form an enforceable contract, there must be an offer, acceptance, exchange of consideration, competent parties, and legality of purpose.

Offer

An offer must be unequivocal, and it must be intentionally communicated to another party. An offer is presumed revocable unless it specifically states that it is irrevocable. An offer once made will be open for a reasonable period of time and is binding on the offeror unless revoked by the offeror before the other party's acceptance.

> *Civil law:* An offer is usually irrevocable for a reasonable period of time, unless the offer unequivocally states that it is revocable.

Acceptance

Acceptance means agreement to the terms offered. An acceptance must be communicated, and it must be the mirror image of the offer. If the terms change, it is a *counteroffer* that then must be accepted. The UCC changes this mirror image rule by stating that definite and seasonable expression of acceptance that is sent within a reasonable time operates as an acceptance even though it states terms additional to or different from those offered under §2-207(1).

> *Civil law:* Many jurisdictions lack a mirror image rule. Rather, the acceptance must merely be to the significant terms of the offer.

Consideration

For a common law contract to be enforceable, the parties must exchange something of value (consideration). Consideration can be something of monetary value, or it can be promising to do something not required by law or promising to refrain from doing something permitted by law.

Civil law: There is no concept of consideration.

Competent Parties

Both civil and common law countries require that in order to form (create) an enforceable contract, the party must possess legal capacity to contract, that is, it must be competent. Generally for physical persons (humans), competency is paramount with attaining the so-called legal age. On the other hand, such entities as corporations, partnerships, and so on (legal persons) gain legal capacity either by an act of government (issuance of Certificate of Incorporation) or by an act of the party itself (execution of the partnership agreement).

Legality of Purpose

Another element in the process of forming an enforceable contract is the requirement that the underlying purpose of the deal be legal (as viewed by the law of the contract). The requirement of legality of purpose is shared by both civil and common law countries.

Contract Privity

One key concept of contract law is contract privity, which is the legal connection or relationship that exists between the contracting parties.* Such privity must exist between the plaintiff and defendant with respect to a matter being contested. A major exception to this principle that only the contracting parties can sue each other was created with the enactment of warranty statutes. For example, any person who is in the buyer's family or household may now sue for the breach of a seller's warranty.

Bilateral and Unilateral Contracts

If an offer states that an acceptance is sufficient if the accepting party promises to perform, a *bilateral* contract is created. If the

---

*   For example, when a buyer contracts with a seller and the seller contracts with a third party to perform part of the project work, the seller is called the *prime contractor* and the third party is a *subcontractor.* Under ordinary circumstances, privity of contract exists between the buyer and the prime contractor and between the prime contractor and the subcontractor, but not between the buyer and the subcontractor. This principle holds true even though the subcontractor and the buyer have contact with one another on a day-to-day basis during contract performance.

offer states that the only way to accept is by performing, then a *unilateral* contract is created (for example, offering a reward for finding a lost pet).

> *Civil law:* Unilateral contracts are relatively rare in the United States, but are used with some frequency in several civil law jurisdictions.

Executed and Executory Contracts

Executed contracts are those contracts that are formed and performed at the same time, such as the purchase of clothing at a department store. *Executory contracts* are those contracts that are formed at one time and performed later, such as most commercial contracts.

Statute of Frauds

The *statute of frauds* is named for an old English statute designed to alleviate fraudulent claims. It provides that any contract that cannot be fully performed in less than a year and any contract for more than $500 must be in writing to be enforceable.

> *Civil law:* Few jurisdictions require that a sales contract be in writing. However, almost all civil law countries require that a sales contract involving real estate be in writing.

Signature of the Party to Be Charged

For a written contract to be admissible evidence in court, it must have the signature of the party to be charged (the defendant).

> *Civil law:* Because a contract does not have to be in writing, few formal rules govern the form of a contract. A written contract transmitted back and forth between the parties may be admitted as evidence of an oral agreement, whether or not there is a signature.

Apparent and Actual Authority

Actual authority may be express or implied. Express actual authority arises when an agent has clear direction to act on behalf of the principal. Implied actual authority derives from the position held by the agent, as where the actions in question are reasonably necessary for the agent carry out his express authority. Apparent authority arises when it appears to third parties that an agent has the authority to bind the principal (under a "reasonable person" standard).

> *Civil law:* In parts of Europe and in some Asian countries, corporate law provides for specific officers who are authorized to bind the corporation. The holders of the authorized positions are kept in an official court registry. If a person is not registered to bind the corporation, no action, no matter how deceptive, can serve to bind the corporation.

Waiver

A *waiver* is the voluntary and unilateral relinquishment by some act or conduct of a person of a right that he or she has. In common law countries, any contractual right of a party can be waived explicitly or implicitly by the party benefiting from the right. Similarly, any contractual obligation can be waived explicitly or implicitly by the party to whom the obligation is owed.

> *Civil law:* Like the United States, every sovereign jurisdiction has specific areas sensitive to public policy based on the culture and economy of a nation. Frequently, in areas that touch on public policy, there are statutory rights that cannot be waived in a contract. Each jurisdiction must be examined to determine what, if any, nonwaivable rights the trading partner may have.

Forbearance

Forbearance is an intentional failure of a party to enforce a contract requirement, usually done for an act of immediate or future consideration from the other party. Sometimes forbearance is referred to as a nonwaiver or as a one-time waiver, but not a relinquishment of rights.

Specific Performance vs. Damages

Most contractual disputes are remedied with *damages* (money) to make the aggrieved (wronged) party "whole." In certain limited circumstances, a party may be forced to actually perform the contract, known as *specific performance.*

Liquidated and Compensatory vs. Punitive Damages

After determining that a party is wronged and is entitled to damages, a determination must be made regarding the appropriate amount of damages. Using the evidence presented by the parties and rules of law, the court will find an exact amount due *(compensatory damages)*. In certain situations, parties may agree in advance that if a party is wronged in a specific way, then a specific amount of damages will be due the other party, thereby liquidating the damages in advance. Thus, if the parties include a *liquidated damages* clause in their contract, the court will determine only whether a party was in fact wronged and entitled to damages. Both common law and civil law allow the parties to the contract to agree on future damages. Note, however, that in common law, liquidated run-in damages must have reasonable relation to the probable actual damages; they cannot be a mere penalty. *Punitive damages,* unlike compensatory damages, are those damages awarded to the plaintiff over and above what will barely compensate for his or her loss. Punitive damages are based on actively different public policy consideration, that of punishing the defendant or of setting an example for similar wrongdoers.

Parol Evidence Rule

The best evidence of a written contract is the document itself. If a contract is unambiguous, the court will not allow the introduction of evidence other than the written contract (*parol* to the contract) to alter the contract terms.

> *Civil law:* The rule does not exist. Oral evidence is usually admissible to vary the contract terms. Some civil courts will even accept oral contract amendments in the face of a clause that states that all amendments must be in writing, provided that if someone testifies that both parties agreed to ignore the clause and make an oral amendment.

Table 5–1 summarizes some differences between common law and civil law.

The Uniform Commercial Code

As stated previously, despite the fact that each jurisdiction has its own laws, commercial sales are governed in the United States by a fairly uniform set of rules called Uniform Commercial Code. The UCC is a model law developed to standardize commercial contracting law among the states. It has been adopted by 49 states (and in significant portions by Louisiana). The UCC comprises articles that deal with specific commercial subject matters, including sales and letters of credit. Article 2 ("Sales") governs most trade in goods.

Most of the UCC merely puts into uniform statutory form the common law of contracts. Sometimes however, the UCC has moved the United States more toward civil law concepts. If parties choose U.S. law to govern their contracts, they usually are choosing the UCC. Both the United States and its international business partner should understand the implications. The following sections describe some UCC provisions that are sometimes misunderstood.

Battle of the Forms

In modern business, it has become common for a company to make offers on standardized documents, such as purchase orders, that had numerous Ts and Cs preprinted on the reverse side. Another company would then acknowledge the order on a preprinted form, the reverse of which would include many conditions different from the first form (the battle of the forms). Under common law, the acceptance with the differing terms was not the mirror image of the offer; therefore, no binding contract was formed. In fact, it was a counteroffer. The UCC changed this mirror image rule by stating that a *definite and reasonable expression of acceptance* (which is sent within a reasonable time) *operates as an acceptance* even though it states terms additional or different from those offered. If the material terms on the faces of the forms match, a contract is formed; any nonmaterial additional terms are added to the terms of the buyer's or seller's form.

Table 5-1 Differences Between Common Law and Civil Law		
Concept or Principle	**Common Law**	**Civil Law**
Acceptance	The material aspects of an acceptance must be the mirror image of the offer; otherwise it is a counteroffer. The concept is significantly modified by UCC.	No mirror image rule exists. Acceptance must merely be to the significant terms of the offer.
Apparent and actual authority	If a principal sets up a situation in which it appears that an agent has the authority to bind the principal, then the principal is bound by the acts of the agent.	In some jurisdictions, corporate law provides for specific officers who are authorized to bind the corporation. Others cannot bind the corporation.
Bilateral and unilateral contracts	Bilateral contracts (where the accepting party promises to perform) are common. Unilateral contracts (where the only way to accept is by performing) are the exception.	Unilateral contracts are used frequently.
Consideration	For a contract to be enforceable, the parties must exchange something of value (consideration).	No concept of consideration exists.
Interpretation of language	Missing terms are filled in by the court. Ambiguities are construed against the drafter.	Neither rule exists. Some jurisdictions tend to follow these principles, some do not.
Offer	An offer is presumed revocable unless stated otherwise.	An offer is presumed irrevocable for a reasonable time unless stated otherwise.
Parol evidence rule	If a written contract is unambiguous, the court will not allow the introduction of evidence other than the written contract to alter the contract terms.	Oral evidence is usually admissible.
Signature of the party to be charged	For a written contract to be admissible in court, it must have the signature of the defendant.	A signature is not required.
Statute of frauds	Any contract that cannot be fully performed in a year and any contract for more than US$500 must be in writing.	Few jurisdictions require that a sales contract be in writing. However, almost all civil law countries require that a sales contract involving real estate be in writing.
Waiver	A contractual right can be waived by the party benefiting from it, and a contractual obligation can be waived by the party to whom the obligation is owed.	Some statutory rights cannot be waived, depending on the jurisdiction.

Warranties

The UCC is the source of the now well-known "Warranty of Merchantability" and the "Warranty of Fitness for a Particular Purpose." The UCC states specifically how these warranties can and cannot be waived. These warranties are incorporated into European Union uniform laws and are rapidly being adopted around the world.

Statute of Frauds

The statute of frauds was adopted into the UCC.

Signature

One significant change in the UCC is how it defines *signature.* Under common law, signature of the party to be charged meant the handwritten signature of the party's name. Under the UCC, signature means any affixation of the party's name or symbol to the document by hand, type, or other means, by the party to be charged. Such significance can include initials, letterhead, logos, stamps, or preprinted forms.

Comity

Comity is the concept of deferring to the law of another jurisdiction that has a greater connection (nexus) to the case. Comity exists in both common and civil law jurisdictions and manifests itself in several ways. Initially, when an action is brought, a court may transfer the case to a more convenient forum (for instance, where all the witnesses live). Then, while a case is tried, a court may apply the law of another forum that is more closely connected to the case. Finally, if another court has already rendered a final decision on the same case, the court will defer to the decision of the other court.

Choice-of-Law Rules

To determine whether comity demands application of the law of another jurisdiction, courts have sets of rules that, given the facts of the case and the residency of the parties, determine which jurisdiction has the greatest connection to the case. Courts in the United States may apply the law of a different state or a different country, if appropriate. For example, a New York court may apply the law of Virginia or the law of France.

FIVE

Choice-of-Law Clauses

Caution should be exercised when using choice-of-law clauses. Some examples follow:

> This contract shall be governed by U.S. law.

Contract law in the United States is state law. No U.S. contract law exists. Even the UCC is state law. Without choosing a state, the contract does not effectively choose the governing law.

> This contract shall be governed by the law of the state of New York.

The law of the state of New York includes its choice-of-law rules. Therefore, this clause does not guarantee that New York law will be applied.

> This contract shall be governed by the law of the state of New York, without regard to its choice of law rules.

Here the parties have chosen New York law. Note, however, that this clause is still not an ironclad guarantee of New York law in the event of a dispute. Any court can decide as a matter of public policy not to enforce such a clause. In addition, not all jurisdictions will enforce choice-of-law clauses. Particularly if an action is brought outside the United States, the clause may not be enforced.

Global Perspective of Contracts

Many people outside the United States view U.S. commercial contracts as overly technical, wordy, and legalistic. In our legal traditions, each party drafts a "one-sided," highly protective document, and the resulting contract is usually a compromise version of the two drafts. As a result, U.S.-generated drafts are often considered to be difficult to understand and comply with by parties from other countries. A good business practice is not to assume that the other party will produce an equally one-sided, adversarial document. It may choose instead not to do business with you.

Summary

The contract is the means of describing the buyer's and seller's obligations and of documenting and enforcing the responsibilities of each party. All managers of contracts, both buyers and sellers, must understand the basic concepts and principles of the contracts they work with and support. Both parties must ensure that their contracts are clear and concise and that they facilitate, not inhibit, communication.

Buyer and seller should be aware that an agreement about how the project should be conducted does not exist just because the parties have agreed that there should be a contract. The basis of a contract is an agreement, and communication is essential to achieving an agreement. Whatever procedure is used to form the contract, the parties should provide time for thoroughly discussing objectives, expectations, and terms and conditions.

CHAPTER 6

E-PROCUREMENT AND CONTRACTING METHODS

To obtain products, services, or business solutions, a buyer must seek information about the relevant attributes of the specific sources available, including their reliability and responsiveness. Before e-procurement, this process was primarily accomplished formally—via written and mailed communications soliciting information, qualifications, and references—or informally—via market research, questionnaires, sales presentations, or visits to potential sellers' facilities. The old procurement process was slow, labor-intensive, and costly.

In today's brave new world of e-procurement, everything is done at a much more rapid pace, but still not as fast as most business executives would like. Today, buyers of commodity products, services, and even some customized business solutions are able to conduct market research, solicit bids or proposals, analyze offers, place orders, submit invoices, and transmit payment for purchases electronically via numerous methods, including net marketplaces, web portals, private exchanges, vertical exchanges, and horizontal exchanges.

Still, the specific method of obtaining information depends on the size and complexity of the procurement, the practices of the industry and market, and the resources available to the buyer. After obtaining information about potential sources, the buyer must make the evaluation, select the best alternative, and reach an agreement with the selected source. Before e-procurement, the source selection process was often a very time-consuming and expensive task, even for purchasing simple off-the-shelf items.

Many winning companies are performing these activities in one continuous process, with the source selection and contract formation steps merged into a single procedure. Many contracting methods are available to select sources and form contracts, some of which are more formal and time-consuming than others.

Today, nearly every contracting method uses aspects of e-procurement, ranging from older electronic data interchange (EDI) batch-processed simple transactions to more recent net marketplaces involving multiple buyers and sellers exchanging transactions via the Internet, to accelerate both delivery to the buyer and payment to the seller.

There are two main approaches to contracting: *competitive methods,* such as purchase cards, imprest funds, auctioning, net market-places, vertical exchanges, horizontal exchanges, web portals, sealed bidding, private exchanges, two-step sealed bidding, and competitive negotiations, and *noncompetitive methods,* such as purchase agreements and sole-source or single-source negotiations (see Table 6-1).

Table 6-1 Two Approaches to Contracting		
	Competitive	**Noncompetitive**
Simplified	Purchase cards	Purchase agreements
	Imprest funds or petty cash	
	Auctioning	
	Net marketplaces	
	Vertical exchanges	
	Horizontal exchanges	
	Web portals	
Formal	Sealed bidding	Sole-source negotiation
	Private exchanges	
	Two-step sealed bidding	Single-source negotiation
	Competitive proposals	
	Competitive negotiations	

USING COMPETITIVE CONTRACTING METHODS

Many competitive contracting methods to obtain products and services exist, ranging from simple to highly complex; all involve aspects of e-procurement.

Simplified Competitive Contracting Methods

Simplified competitive contracting methods include:

■ *Purchasing or procurement cards (P-cards):* An organization's credit card commonly used to purchase low-price, off-the-shelf products and services. The degree of competition depends on the guidelines that the procurement organization provides to the individuals empowered to use the P-card. Most companies set predetermined spending limits on employee usage and track purchases to ensure that purchases are for business purposes only.

- *Imprest funds or petty cash:* A small amount of money used to pay for small purchases of common products or services. Source selection depends on the company's or organization's purchasing guidelines.

- *Auctioning and reverse auctions:* A widely practiced head-to-head bidding method, typically done face-to-face or via teleconferences, that is used to increase direct competition and that can be applied to the purchase of any product or service.

- *Net marketplaces:* Two-sided Internet-based exchange where buyers and sellers negotiate prices, usually with a bid-and-ask system, and where prices move both up and down.

- *Vertical exchanges:* A form of net marketplace that is specific to a single industry.

- *Horizontal exchanges:* A form of net marketplace that deals with goods and services that are not specific to one industry.

- *Web portal:* A public exchange, which may be a vertical exchange or a horizontal exchange, in which a company or group of companies lists products and services for sale and/or shares other business information.

Formal Competitive Contracting Methods

Formal competitive contracting methods are controlled bidding processes that keep pressure on competitors throughout the source selection process. Most of that pressure bears on price. Thus, from the buyer's point of view, competitive bidding is a highly effective technique for keeping prices low.

However, several disadvantages are associated with competitive bidding. First, it can be a costly process to administer because of the need to evaluate multiple formal proposals, and it can occupy a buyer's personnel for an extended time. Second, it can stifle communication between the buyer and seller during contract formation because of the need to protect confidential information in the competitors' proposals. This increases the risk of misunderstandings and disputes during contract performance. Third, the pressure to keep prices low can drive them below the point of realism, increasing cost risk and the attendant risk of poor seller performance and disputes. Competitive bidding, more so than other approaches, may create an adversarial relationship between buyer and seller, especially when the process takes on the characteristics of sealed bidding.

Nevertheless, competitive bidding can be effective, especially for purchasing commodities and for simple projects in which price is the most important factor. Most contracts for construction projects are still awarded through competitive bidding, as are most government contracts worldwide.

Sealed Bidding

Competitive bidding usually takes the form of *sealed bidding,* in which price is the only criterion for selecting a source from a set of competing, prequalified sources. This technique entails soliciting, typically electronically, firm bids. The solicitation describes what the seller must do or deliver, the performance terms and conditions (Ts and Cs), and the deadline and location for submitting the bids. The bids usually state nothing more than the offered price. Sometimes bidders state their own Ts and Cs.

After the deadline passes, the buyer reviews the bids and evaluates them by comparing the prices offered. Buyers usually select the lowest bidder, but not always. The buyer may reject the lowest bids because they are too risky or because the bidder is not qualified. In the commercial world, the parties may negotiate after bid opening to reach agreement on details. Some buyers negotiate prices even after soliciting low bids, but this technique is ill-advised because bidders will anticipate the practice in the future and adjust their bids accordingly.

To use sealed bidding, the buyer must have a specification that clearly and definitively describes the required product or service. For bid price comparison to be meaningful, all bidders must be pricing the same requirement. Otherwise, the bids will not be truly comparable. In addition, the specification must be free of errors, ambiguities, and other defects. If a bidder thinks that the buyer will change the specification during contract performance, that bidder may submit a below-cost bid to win the competition, anticipating the opportunity to increase the cost while negotiating for the change. This practice is called *buying in.*

In addition, because sealed bidding makes sense only for the award of firm-fixed-price contracts, performance cost uncertainty must be low. Otherwise, selecting the lowest bid will be a decision to select the proposal with the highest cost risk, which as already discussed, can have serious consequences. In a firm-fixed-price contract awarded by sealed bidding, an adversarial relationship is likely to develop between buyer and seller.

When using sealed bidding, the buyer must prequalify bidders or provide another way to ensure that the low bidder is competent to perform the work satisfactorily. Most buyers have a standard procedure by which potential sources can get on the *bidders' mailing list* or *qualified suppliers' list.* Many buyers will not entertain a bid from a source that is not prequalified by the quality and purchasing departments. Some buyers wait until after bids are reviewed and the low bidder is identified to determine its competence to perform, but this procedure is a wasteful one that frequently delays contract award.

Private Exchanges

Today many companies have developed private exchanges to procure goods and services from prequalified or preauthorized sellers. A private exchange is hosted by a single company and is located behind or inside the company's firewall. A private exchange typically operates using either a sealed bidding process or an e-auction process. More and more companies are using private exchanges to get the benefit of competition, but are doing it in a controlled and secure electronic environment.

Two-Step Sealed Bidding

The *two-step sealed bidding* method requires sellers to first submit their technical proposal, typically electronically, and all other management and company qualification information, including past performance information. The buyer evaluates all the technical and other data—everything except pricing information—to determine whether the potential seller is a qualified supplier of the needed products or services.

The buyer then requests that the qualified sellers submit their respective pricing information for evaluation. Typically, the buyer then awards the contract to the qualified seller with the lowest price. Figure 6-1 compares sealed bidding and two-step sealed bidding.

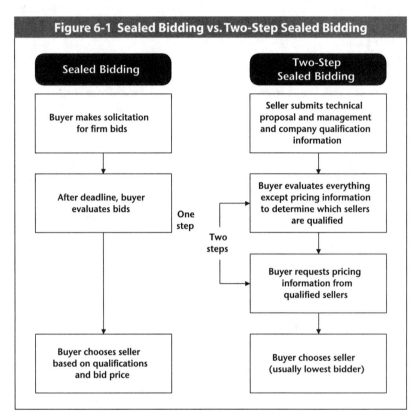

Figure 6-1 Sealed Bidding vs. Two-Step Sealed Bidding

Competitive Negotiations

Sometimes buyers will use *competitive negotiations*, in which they solicit formal proposals from, and have discussions with, several competitors simultaneously. They may request formal *best and final offers* before making a source selection decision. This approach is used commonly in government work and, in recent years, with increasing frequency in the commercial world at large. In these competitions, technical considerations, such as system design, are often more important than price, and the award is often made to someone other than the lowest bidder.

Competitive negotiations, even with electronic transmission of documents, can be time-consuming, labor-intensive, and costly for both buyers and competitors. Competing businesses must often prepare voluminous proposals full of technical detail, make oral presentations, and prepare numerous proposal revisions and written responses to buyer inquiries. Proposal preparation costs can be high.

Competitive bidding and competitive negotiations have the common trait of merging source selection and contract formation. Combining these steps is accomplished through the buyer's solicitation (invitation for bids, tender, or request for proposals), which not only asks for proposals but also specifies what the buyer wants included as contract Ts and Cs. The proposal, which is accompanied by other information intended to persuade the buyer that the firm submitting the proposal is the best qualified, is usually a promise to comply with the Ts and Cs in the buyer's solicitation.

If the source has not taken exception to any Ts and Cs in the solicitation and if the buyer is willing to accept all aspects of the proposal, selecting the best-qualified source is tantamount to accepting that firm's proposal. If the source has taken exception or if the buyer does not like all aspects of the source's proposal, the parties must negotiate to reach an agreement.

USING NONCOMPETITIVE CONTRACTING METHODS

Simplified Noncompetitive Contracting Methods

When a buyer has selected a seller and wants to establish a successful, long-term contract relationship involving repetitive transactions, buyer and seller will commonly use simplified noncompetitive contracting methods to facilitate the process.

These methods include oral contracts, oral contract modifications, and written agreements known as basic ordering agreements, purchase agreements, sales agreements, general agreements, master agreements, distributor agreements, and universal agreements, among other things. These written agreements establish standard Ts and Cs by which the parties can reduce administrative costs and cycle time and increase customer satisfaction.

Noncompetitive contracting methods can be applied to either single-source or sole-source negotiation.

Formal Noncompetitive Contracting Methods: Single-Source vs. Sole-Source Negotiation

Single-source negotiation occurs when the buyer selects a single company or seller to provide the product or service. In single-source situations, the buyer has the opportunity to select other sellers but has a preference for a specific seller. Sole-source negotiation occurs when there is only one seller that can provide the needed product or service. Thus, a sole-source seller has a monopoly in its market and tremendous leverage with most buyers.

Increasingly, buyers are reducing their use of competitive bidding and relying on negotiation with only one company as a means of awarding contracts. This process entails a more rigorous separation between source selection and contract formation than does competitive bidding.

Source selection is carried out through relatively informal processes of inquiry. Market research provides a short list of potential sources. The companies on this list are contacted usually electronically and asked to complete questionnaires or prepare information packages, or the buyer may simply use the Web and search for specific goods or services via supplier electronic catalogs without preparing a formal request for proposal. The buyer may visit the sources to evaluate their facilities and capabilities in person or virtually via videoconferencing, net-meeting, or video tapes.

The buyer may shorten the list to two or three companies to contact for more extensive discussions. When enough information is gathered, the buyer evaluates it and selects a single source for negotiation, leading to contract award. The parties may communicate several times before the source finalizes its proposal. When the source submits its proposal to the buyer, much of it will not be new but will merely confirm agreements reached during preliminary discussions.

After receiving the proposal, typically electronically, and conducting a preliminary analysis, the buyer may engage in *fact finding*, seeking to understand all elements before deciding whether to bargain for better terms. With all the facts in hand, the buyer performs a thorough cost and technical evaluation of the proposal. During this evaluation, the buyer identifies every aspect of the proposal that must be modified through bargaining.

If the buyer decides to bargain, the negotiator develops a *negotiation objective* and presents it to company superiors for approval. If the objective is approved, the negotiator communicates with the source and bargains until the parties reach an agreement or a stalemate. The parties then prepare a document describing the Ts and Cs of their agreement and sign it to complete the source selection and contract formation processes.

Figure 6-2 compares competitive bidding, competitive proposals and negotiations, and single- and sole-source negotiation.

Figure 6-2 Comparison of Contracting Methods

SIX

These proven successful contracting methods may be used in either a paper/written mode or electronically. Competitive contracting methods are used most frequently for the transaction of products and services globally. However, today most of the money is exchanged on large-dollar, multi-year, complex contracts that integrate products, services, and solutions through noncompetitive contracting methods.

SUMMARY

The explosion of e-procurement is continually reducing the buying/selling cycle time. Speed is a fundamental aspect of the strategy of all winning companies. The electronic preparation, submission, evaluation, and revision of bids or proposals have dramatically reduced the time and expense of transacting goods and services globally.

Likewise, the electronic transmission of contracts, contract modifications, contract-related communications via e-mail, and electronic funds transfer or payment has improved the timeliness of communications and increased the frequency of communications after contract award.

Unfortunately, e-procurement is not a panacea. It cannot totally prevent a buyer or seller from doing something stupid–like buying the wrong product or service, selecting the wrong company to partner with, or selling a product or service for too low of a price.

However, the rapidly growing use of net marketplaces, including vertical exchanges, horizontal exchanges, web portals, and private exchanges, has given buyers more opportunity to increase competition, reduce prices through reverse auctions, and reduce their procurement lead-time via e-procurement. In the world of buying and selling, the advantage is rapidly moving to the buyer.

CHAPTER

THE
PREAWARD
PHASE

Contracts can involve serious risks because of uncertainties inherent in the contracting process and because failure to meet the other party's expectations can have legal consequences. Remember four key actions during the preaward: do not enter a contract without–

- Clearly stating your objectives
- Identifying the sources and nature of uncertainties about achieving those objectives
- Defining and assessing the risks
- Making decisions about an appropriate course of action

Preaward is the first phase of the contract management process and comprises all buyer and seller actions from procurement planning through submitting a bid or proposal. Figure 7-1 depicts these steps.

Figure 7-1 Contract Management Process: Preaward Phase

PARTICIPATING FROM THE BUYER'S PERSPECTIVE

Preaward must focus on clearly expressing the requirements and getting realistic guarantees of the buyer's satisfaction. The buyer must–

- Decide what products and services to procure from others, describe those requirements unambiguously, and estimate cost and schedule requirements

- Identify the sources and nature of uncertainties about quality, cost, and schedule
- Define and assess the consequences of seller failure to achieve performance objectives
- Develop contract Ts and Cs that address and distribute performance risk in ways that are technically, commercially, and financially sound
- Develop effective procedures for seller selection, negotiation, and contract formation

For the buyer, these preaward activities typically involve three major steps: procurement planning, solicitation planning, and solicitation.

Buyer Step 1: Procurement Planning

Procurement planning is the process of identifying which business needs can be best met by procuring products or services outside the organization. This process involves determining whether to procure, how to procure, what to procure, how much to procure, and when to procure. Procurement planning also should include consideration of potential subcontracts, particularly if the buyer wants to exercise some degree of influence or control over subcontracting decisions.

Input

The input to procurement planning consists of the following items:

- *Scope statement:* The scope statement describes the current business boundaries. It provides important information about buyer needs and strategies that must be considered during procurement planning.

- *Product description:* The description of the project's product or service provides important information about any technical issues or concerns that must be considered during the procurement planning step. The product description is generally broader than a statement of work. A product description describes the ultimate end-product of the project; an SOW is a tasking document that describes the portion of that product to be provided by a seller to the buyer.

- *Procurement resources:* If the organization does not have contract management resources, the business team managing the contract process must supply both the resources and the expertise to support procurement activities.

- *Market conditions:* The procurement planning process must include consideration of what products and services are available in the marketplace, from whom, and under what terms and conditions.

- *Other planning output:* To the extent that other planning output is available, it must be considered during procurement planning. Examples might include preliminary cost and schedule estimates, quality management plans, cash flow projections, work breakdown structure, identified risks, and planned staffing.

- *Constraints:* Constraints are factors that limit the buyer's options. One common project constraint is funds availability.

- *Assumptions:* Assumptions are factors that, for planning purposes, are considered to be true, real, or certain. Assumptions made should always be documented.

Tools and Techniques

The following tools and techniques are used for procurement planning:

- *Outsource analysis:* The decision to outsource must be made in cooperation with a multifunctional team, the precise size and identity of which depends on the nature of the undertaking and on the buyer's business and organization. The purchasing or contracting department should be consulted for obvious reasons, but other interested or affected functional organizations could include research and development, marketing and sales, finance, production, human resources, security, and legal, to name a few.

The decision to outsource or buy is essentially a decision to meld the seller's organization with the buyer's. However, the decision casts the business professional's usual challenges of communication and control in an unusual light, because he or she must communicate and exercise control through the special medium of the contract.

Outsource analysis must reflect the perspective of the performing organization as well as the immediate business needs. For example, purchasing a capital item (anything from a construction crane to a personal computer) rather than renting it is seldom cost-effective. However, if the performing organization has an ongoing need for the item, the portion of the purchase cost allocated to the project may be less than the cost of the rental.

■ *Expert judgment:* Assessing the input to the procurement planning process often requires expert judgment. Such expertise may be provided by any group or individual with specialized knowledge or training and is available from many sources, including other units within the performing organization, consultants and educators, professional and technical associations, and industry groups.

■ *Contract type selection:* Different types of contracts are appropriate for different types of purchases. (See Chapter 8, "Contract Pricing Arrangements.")

■ *Risk management process:* ESI International developed a risk management process that includes two major elements and seven steps. The process, as shown in Figure 7-2, is so simple to understand and implement that many companies throughout the world are successfully using it to improve their business results.

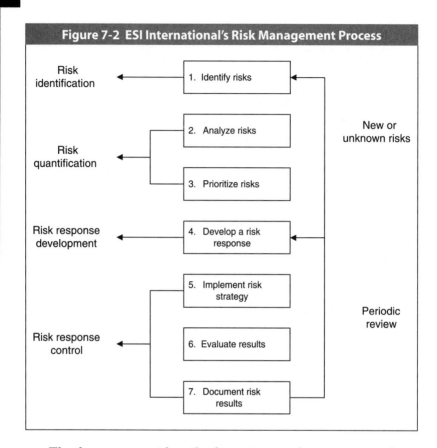

Figure 7-2 ESI International's Risk Management Process

The buyer must identify the sources of uncertainty about contract performance and the risks associated with those uncertainties to write a contract that will address those risks and fairly distribute them between buyer and seller. This process is a critical planning function, because the contract is a device for effectively managing risk. Inadequate risk analysis will result in a contract that is not suitable for the conditions of performance and that might increase rather than reduce the potential for conflict and project failure.

Risk, which is exposure to harm, is associated with contingent *events.* An event is an occurrence or a nonoccurrence. Risk can take the form of either uncertainty about an event or undesirable consequences associated with the event. If an event must happen for the project to succeed, but that event's occurrence is uncertain, then risk is associated with that event. If an event must not happen for the contract to succeed, but the nonoccurrence of the event is uncertain, then risk is associated with that event also. However, if you are certain that a desirable event will not happen or that an undesirable event will happen, then risk is evident because you either know what you must do to avoid the consequences, if avoidable, or you can prepare yourself for the worst, if unavoidable. Problems arise when you are not sure what to do because you are not sure what will happen. When risks are understood, intelligent decisions can be made about how to avoid them and about the costs and benefits of taking specific actions.

The buyer must analyze the potential project and identify contingent events of critical importance to the project. Some degree of uncertainty will exist for every planned event, as well as some measure of consequences, but some risks are not serious enough to merit a response. The buyer must make reasonable judgments about what is important and what is not. This process will entail estimating the event's probability and nature and the extent of the consequences that will be suffered if things go badly. It also will entail estimating and trading off the costs and benefits of taking action to avoid or mitigate the risks.

When risks are significant, the buyer must decide how to handle them and then devise contract terms to express those decisions. On a construction project that requires extensive excavation, for example, the buyer might be uncertain about whether earth or rock lies beneath the surface. That information would affect the methods and types of equipment the seller would use to excavate and, thus, the cost and time required for project completion. The risk associated with this element of performance would depend on the degree of uncertainty about subsurface conditions and the possible effects of the various events on cost and schedule.

If the risk is great, the buyer might decide to spend money to perform extensive preconstruction site investigations to reduce the uncertainty about subsurface conditions. The buyer could then include that information in the contract specifications. If the risks are minor, the buyer might decide to do nothing more than include a differing site conditions clause in the contract, which would require the seller to bear the cost risk of a differing site condition while the buyer bears the schedule risk.

■ *Contract terms and conditions:* Law and custom, company experience and policy, and project-specific analyses will determine what contract Ts and Cs the buyer will prefer. Governments and large companies usually have regulations or manuals that prescribe boilerplate clauses for the most common types of contracts. In these organizations, the contract manager writes the contract by simply checking off the appropriate clauses from a list (perhaps automated) for inclusion in the solicitation or contract document. (See Form 1 in Appendix A.)

In smaller organizations and in larger organizations for contracts of an unusual nature, the Ts and Cs may have to be developed. In such cases, the contract clauses may have to be written or reviewed by lawyers with experience in such matters. In some industries, books are available that include samples of recommended contract clauses.

Today many companies have developed or purchased automated tools using Lotus Notes or other database management software to help them in developing appropriate Ts and Cs.

Output

The output from procurement planning consists of the following items:

■ *Procurement management plan:* This plan should describe how the remaining procurement processes (from solicitation planning through contract closeout) will be managed. The following are examples of questions to ask in developing the procurement management plan:

❑ What types of contracts will be used?
❑ If independent estimates will be needed as evaluation criteria, who will prepare them and when?
❑ What actions can the project management team take on its own?
❑ If standardized procurement documents are needed, where can they be found?
❑ How will multiple providers be managed?
❑ How will procurement be coordinated with other business aspects such as scheduling and performance reporting?

A procurement management plan may be formal or informal and highly detailed or broadly framed, based on business needs.

■ *Statement of work:* The SOW describes the buyer's requirements in sufficient detail to allow prospective sellers to determine whether they can provide the product, service, or solution. "Sufficient detail" may vary depending on the nature of the item, the needs of the buyer, or the expected contract form. The current trend is toward developing performance-based SOWs that describe what is needed, not how to accomplish it.

Identifying and analyzing requirements should follow a systematic procedure. First, the buyer must determine the function to be performed by the required product or service and the relationship of that function to others. For example, if the buyer needs an item of hardware or software or needs a task performed, how does that item or task relate to other parts of the project? Second, the buyer must determine the specific types and levels of performance that must be attained. Third, the buyer may have to determine a specific design, that is, the physical form the item must take or the specific method or procedure by which the task must be performed.

These three categories of requirements—function, performance, and design—move from general to specific. Function is described by verbs that relate what the product or service must *do*. Performance and design are described by adjectives and adverbs that relate the *attributes* of the product or service, that is, *how well* the product or service must perform the function and the specific form that the product or service must take.

The SOW development team should include in the process people who will use the product or service, if they are not already part of the business team. The process must be rational and systematic. It is iterative, achieving ever greater refinement of the buyer's ideas and descriptions with each iteration.

Buyer Step 2: Solicitation Planning

Input	Tools & Techniques	Output
Procurement management plan	Standard forms	Procurement documents
Statement of work	Expert judgement	Evaluation criteria
Other procurement planning output		Statement of work updates

Solicitation planning involves preparing the documents needed to support the solicitation.

Input

The input to solicitation planning consists of the following items:

■ *Procurement management plan:* This plan, which describes how the procurement process will be conducted throughout contract management, should be reviewed at the start of solicitation planning.

■ *Statement of work:* The SOW is a key ingredient in solicitation planning and in the solicitation document to be developed.

■ *Other procurement planning output:* Other output, which may have been modified since procurement planning, should be reviewed. In particular, solicitation planning should be closely coordinated with the project schedule.

Tools and Techniques

Following are descriptions of the tools and techniques used for solicitation planning:

■ *Standard forms:* These forms may include standardized versions of contracts, standardized descriptions of procurement items, or standardized versions of all or part of the needed bid documents. Organizations doing substantial amounts of procurement should have many of these documents standardized and automated.

- *Expert judgment:* As in procurement planning, expert judgment is a vital tool. Individuals with specialized knowledge or training, both in-house and outside the organization, should be consulted.

Output

Solicitation planning results in the following output:

- *Procurement documents:* Procurement documents, or solicitations, request proposals from prospective sellers. The terms *bid* and *quotation* are generally used when the source selection decision will be price driven (as when buying commercial items), whereas the term *proposal* or *tender* is generally used when nonfinancial considerations, such as technical skills or approach, are paramount (as when buying professional services). However, the terms are often used interchangeably and care should be taken not to make unwarranted assumptions about the implications of the term used. Types of procurement documents include the request for proposals (RFP), request for quotations (RFQ), request for tenders (RFT), invitation to bid (ITB), invitation for bids (IFB), and invitation for negotiation (IFN).

  Procurement documents should be structured to facilitate accurate and complete responses from prospective sellers. They should always include the relevant SOW, a description of the desired form of response, and any required contract Ts and Cs (for example, a copy of a model contract's nondisclosure provisions). Some or all of the content and structure of procurement documents, particularly for those prepared by a government agency, may be defined by regulation.

  Procurement documents should be rigorous enough to ensure consistent, comparable responses but flexible enough to allow consideration of seller suggestions for better ways to satisfy the requirements.

- *Evaluation criteria:* Evaluation criteria are used to rate or score proposals. They may be objective (for example, "the proposed project manager must be a certified project management professional") or subjective (for example, "the proposed project manager must have documented previous experience with similar projects"). Evaluation criteria are often included as part of the procurement documents. (See "Evaluation Criteria" in Chapter 9.)

- *Statement of work updates:* Modifications to one or more SOWs may be identified during solicitation planning.

Buyer Step 3: Solicitation

Input	Tools & Techniques	Output
Procurement documents Qualified seller lists	Bidders' conferences Advertising	Solicitation that leads to proposal or bid submission

Solicitation consists of obtaining information (bids and proposals) from prospective sellers on how project needs can be met. Prospective sellers expend most of the effort in this process, normally at no cost to the buyer.

Input

The input to solicitation includes the following items:

- *Procurement documents:* Procurement documents, or solicitations, include RFPs, RFQs, ITBs, and so on.

- *Qualified seller lists:* Some buyers maintain lists or files with information on prospective sellers. These lists generally have information on relevant experience, past performance, and other characteristics of the prospective sellers.

  If such lists are not available, new sources must be developed. General information is widely available from library directories, Dun and Bradstreet Corporation, relevant local associations, trade catalogs, industry associations, and other similar organizations or publications. Detailed information on specific sources may require more extensive effort, such as site visits or contact with previous customers.

Tools and Techniques

Following are the tools and techniques used for solicitation:

- *Bidders' conferences:* These conferences (also called contractor, vendor, or prebid conferences) are meetings with prospective sellers before they prepare their proposals. They may be conducted in person, via video conference, teleconference, or Net meetings. The meetings ensure that all prospective sellers have a clear, common understanding of the procurement (both technical requirements and contract requirements). Responses to questions may be incorporated into the procurement documents as amendments.

- *Advertising:* Existing lists of potential sellers can often be expanded by placing advertisements in general circulation publications, such as newspapers, or in specialty publications, such as professional journals. Some government jurisdictions require public advertising of certain types of procurement items; most government jurisdictions require public advertising of subcontracts on a government contract.

Output

The output from solicitation consists of bids or proposals, which are the written or oral offers to perform services or provide products to another party. Proposals range from simple to highly complex.

PARTICIPATING FROM THE SELLER'S PERSPECTIVE

From the seller's perspective, the preaward phase involves identifying potentially successful contract opportunities and capturing and performing such contracts. A potentially successful contract is one that can be performed at a price that will enable the seller to meet the needs of the buyer and earn a reasonable profit or gain another benefit, such as future business. The seller must—

- Identify contract opportunities such as revenue, basic gross profit, measured operating income, and future business

- Determine the potential profit or other business potential of the contract, the cost to pursue and win it, the chances of winning, and the likelihood of successful contract performance
- Define and assess the consequences of failure
- Develop a winning strategy, proposal, and performance plan

For the seller, these preaward activities typically incorporate three major steps: presales activity, bid/no-bid decision making, and bid or proposal preparation.

Seller Step 1: Presales Activity

Input	Tools & Techniques	Output
Customer identification	Proactive sales management	Potential and existing customer lists
Determination of customer needs	Market research Competitive analysis	Customer-focused sales plan
Evaluation of competitors		Competitive analysis report

Presales activity is the process of identifying business opportunities, determining customer needs and plans, and evaluating the competitive environment. Presales activity is critical to the success of a seller.

Input

The input to presales activity consists of the following activities:

- *Customer identification:* Identifying and pursuing new business is an ongoing marketing function. The seller's sales representatives must obtain information about potential buyers and their needs continually. Sales personnel must learn who buys the types of products their company sells and must make contact with those buyers. Initial contacts with potential buyers must establish a basis for continuing the communication process and increasing the potential buyer's confidence in the seller and its products or services. These contacts also must create interest in the products or services of the seller over those of its competitors. To achieve these goals, the seller must stay up-to-date in the technologies relevant to its products and services, the needs of its buyers, the strategies and activities of its competitors, and the dynamics of the market. All these factors will influence the seller's marketing strategy.

- *Determination of customer needs:* After identifying potential buyers, the seller must intensify its efforts to determine what the buyer needs and how it plans to fulfill those needs. This task is not a passive process of receiving information from the buyer. The seller must actively help the buyer clarify and focus its thinking.

During this step, the seller learns about the buyer's business, organization, history, people, culture, and plans, including attempting to ascertain the buyer's budgets and schedules as they pertain to specific requirements. In addition, the seller identifies its competitors. This knowledge will be the starting point for collecting competitive intelligence.

Widely known for its proactive early involvement with customers, the International Business Machines Corporation (IBM) is one of the world's best companies at determining customer needs and plans. IBM uses customer managers, engagement managers, project managers, and others in highly integrated teams to determine the needs and plans of its customer early in the process to gain a competitive advantage.

- *Evaluation of competitors:* Any effort to win the buyer's business must be based on an objective analysis of the competitive environment, which includes the buyer and the seller, as well as the seller's competitors.

In its analysis of the buyer, the seller must focus on the specific piece of business it wants to obtain. What is the sales potential, short term and long term? What is the profit potential? What will be required to win the business?

In turning a critical eye on itself, the seller must analyze whether its products and services measure up to the competition's. How do its prices compare? What is its market share? What are its strengths and weaknesses? What is its reputation? This analysis should focus on the differences between the seller and its competitors in the context of the buyer's needs. The seller must then determine how best to present those differences to the buyer as strengths, with weaknesses eliminated or neutralized.

Finally, in analyzing its competitors, the seller must ask the following questions: Who are they? What are the features of their products and services? What are their capabilities, strengths, and weaknesses? What are their prices? What are their market shares? What are their reputations, both generally and in the eyes of the buyer?

Tools and Techniques

The following tools and techniques are used for presales activity:

- *Proactive sales management:* Early and frequent involvement with current and potential customers is essential to winning new business opportunities. Marketing and sales personnel must know the customers' processes, needs, desires, budgets, and key decision makers.

- *Market research:* Market research involves obtaining information that may be of value in improving internal processes, products, and services. Market research involves intelligence gathering within one or more marketplaces.

- *Business Case analysis:* Winning business costs money. Before spending significant sums in pursuit of a buyer, the seller must analyze its competitive position and prospects for a win. A competitive analysis matrix can help in this activity. (See Appedix A Form 2.) The seller must understand how it differs from its competitors and decide whether those differences provide the basis for a successful proposal. It also must estimate the time and money needed to win the job and determine the risks of performance. Only then should the seller measure the potential benefits and decide whether they are worth the costs and risks. Based on this evaluation, the seller can determine whether to pursue the business. If the answer is yes, the seller can establish a budget and outline its strategy to win the contract.

Output

The output for the presales activity consists of the following items:

- *Potential and existing customer lists:* Lists of potential and existing customers should be developed to include information on the products or services needed and any other pertinent data about the customer. These lists should be prioritized by the importance of the customer to your business–although all customers are important, some are more important than others.

- *Customer-focused sales plan:* The sales plan should be a formal, written plan of action to obtain or retain a customer, with sales efforts focused on customer needs and desires.

- *Competitive analysis report:* This report is a formal, written plan that compares the seller's strengths and weaknesses to those of competitors.

- *Business case:* A complete financial analysis of the opportunity including an assessment of expected costs, both direct and indirect, expected revenue, cost of money, desired margin, expected rate of return, and estimated realized revenue.

Seller Step 2: Bid/No-Bid Decision Making

Input	Tools & Techniques	Output
Solicitation	Risk assessment	Bid/no-bid decision
Buyer-specific information	Opportunity assessment	Justification document for bid/no-bid decision
Competitive analysis report	Risk management team process	
Seller's strategic objectives and plans		

The bid/no-bid decision requires analyzing the risks versus the opportunities of a potential business deal, then deciding whether to proceed.

Input

Input for bid/no-bid decision making consists of the following items:

- *Solicitation:* Solicitations, or procurement documents, include RFPs, RFQs, ITBs, and so on.

- *Buyer-specific information:* Relevant data about the buyer could include budget, schedule, and strategic and long-term plans.

- *Competitive analysis report:* This report provides a written comparison of the seller's strengths and weaknesses to those of its competitors.

- *Seller's strategic objectives and plans:* Ideally, the buyer's needs should align with the strategic market objectives and plans of the seller. Otherwise, the seller must carefully weigh the opportunities against the risks of stretching the company beyond its current boundaries.

Tools and Techniques

The following tools and techniques are used for bid/no-bid decision making:

- *Risk assessment:* Sellers must identify, analyze, and prioritize the risks associated with a potential project. Many world-class companies have developed practical risk assessment tools—surveys, checklists, models, and reports—containing both qualitative and quantitative information. Software programs are increasingly being developed to help managers assess risks.

- *Opportunity assessment:* Sellers must identify and analyze the opportunities that are potentially viable. Many successful companies have developed standard forms, surveys, checklists, or models to help managers assess opportunity.

- *Risk management team process:* Sound business management requires a solid understanding of risks and the methods to identify, analyze, and mitigate them. Successful companies follow a designated risk management team process, not just a best-guess individual assessment.

Output

The following output results from bid/no-bid decision making:

- *Bid/no-bid decision:* The final decision on whether to bid on the project is made after rigorous analysis and evaluation.

- *Justification document for bid/no-bid decision:* The justification document describes the seller's reasons for its decision on whether to bid on a particular project.

Seller Step 3: Bid or Proposal Preparation

Input	Tools & Techniques	Output
Solicitation	Compliance matrix	Bid or proposal
Analysis of solicitation	Standard terms and conditions	Supporting documentation
Competitive analysis report	Past proposals	Oral presentation
Past proposals	Lessons-learned database	
	Executive summary	

The seller's bid or proposal may be presented orally, in writing, or electronically. It may be delivered in a single presentation or over time. Whatever the mode of presentation, the proposal should be prepared as a sales presentation, not just a technical document. Its purpose is to persuade the buyer to enter into a contract.

As the final step in the preaward phase of contract management, developing and preparing the proposal must reflect all the work and decisions that have gone before. It must articulate and substantiate the themes that give voice to the seller's competitive strategy, and it must reflect the seller's strengths, how it has resolved or overcome any past weaknesses, and what differentiates the seller from its competitors.

Input

Input for bid or proposal preparation consists of the following items:

- *Solicitation:* Solicitations, or procurement documents, include RFPs, RFQs, ITBs, and so on.

- *Analysis of solicitation:* Ultimately, the proposal must be grounded in the needs of the buyer, as stated in the buyer's solicitation or oral request. All the words, numbers, and graphics in the proposal must focus on the buyer's need and on attributes that will satisfy that need in ways that are superior to the competition's. Needs, attributes, and benefits provide the underlying logic and structure of every successful sales presentation.

  Many successful companies perform a detailed analysis of the buyer's solicitation and develop a compliance matrix showing where they meet, exceed, or fail to meet the buyer's stated requirements.

- *Competitive analysis report:* When analyzing competitors, some experts use the acronym DOAG to remind them of basic proposal tactics. DOAG stands for *discriminators, oh-oh's, ah-ha's, and ghosts.* Discriminators are statements that describe beneficial differences between the seller and its competitors, for which competitors have no effective response. Oh-oh's are seller weaknesses that must be eliminated or effectively neutralized and that must not be allowed to undermine the seller's efforts to substantiate its themes. Ah-ha's are the seller's strengths and the ultimate bases for its theme statements. Ghosts are statements that spotlight the competition's weaknesses in ways that neutralize the competition's strengths. Documenting DOAG in a competitive analysis report can provide valuable insight for proposal preparation.

- *Past proposals:* Using past proposals as a tool to share lessons learned is a proven best practice.

Tools and Techniques

The following tools and techniques are used for bid or proposal preparation:

- *Compliance matrix:* Using a compliance matrix ensures that all sections of the solicitation document were addressed. (See Appendix A Form 3.)

- *Standard terms and conditions:* Reviewing standard Ts and Cs provides a basis for developing Ts and Cs tailored to a particular solicitation.

- *Past proposals:* A team review of the best and worst aspects of past proposals–both winning and losing ones–provides an excellent tool for bid and proposal preparation. Individuals from outside the team also can provide valuable insight.

- *Lessons-learned database:* Learning from experience is critical to winning new business. Documenting and sharing bid and proposal preparation practices is vital to reducing non-value-added bid and proposal development costs.

- *Executive summary:* A brief summary is an effective way to communicate the key aspects of a detailed proposal.

Output

The bid or proposal preparation effort results in the following output:

- *Bid or proposal:* Effective proposal development and presentation is a team effort and will require the effective participation of individuals from many parts of the seller's organization. Unfortunately, personnel often view participation in proposal preparation as a nuisance–a distraction from their main responsibilities and interests. However, because it is a key factor in obtaining new business, proposal preparation must be taken seriously. Every participant should be encouraged to give it a best effort.

  As with any project, proposal preparation must be managed effectively if it is to achieve its objectives. Proposal efforts must be coordinated, planned, implemented, and controlled, and the final product must be objectively evaluated by personnel outside the proposal team before submittal to the potential buyer.

- *Supporting documentation:* Supporting documentation includes any information used to develop the bid or proposal.

- *Oral presentation:* Many companies are either supplementing or replacing their written proposals with oral presentations, which allow for real-time discussions, demonstrations, and feedback. Oral presentations are increasingly being used by organizations to reduce cycle time and increase the quality of the products or services offered by providing more information for better decision making.

Best Practices: 25 Actions to Improve Results

Buyer

- Decide what products, services, or solutions you need
- Conduct market research and benchmarking of industry practices
- Identify risks in quality, cost, and schedule (outsource analysis)
- Develop a solicitation that clearly and concisely communicates your needs in terms of performance
- Develop effective procedures for seller selection, negotiation, and contract implementation
- Obtain expert judgment internally or externally to help in solicitation planning
- Determine the appropriate type of contract or pricing arrangement, considering the risks to each party
- Use a risk management process to mitigate risks
- Create standard Ts and Cs that favor you
- Develop qualified seller lists
- Conduct bidders' conferences—in person, video conference, or via Net meeting
- Use draft solicitations and obtain feedback from sellers before final solicitation

Seller

- Identify potential customers early
- Evaluate competitors and create a competitive analysis report
- Conduct proactive sales management—know your customers and influence their needs
- Conduct market research and benchmarking of industry practices
- Develop customer-focused sales plans
- Assess risks and opportunities early—prepare a Business Case
- Apply a risk management team process for bid/no-bid decision making
- Develop and use a compliance matrix to evaluate your capabilities versus the solicitation requirements
- Create standard Ts and Cs that favor you

- Develop clear, concise, and accurate bids or proposals in response to solicitations, including executive summaries and value-based pricing
- Develop and use a proposal lessons-learned database
- Provide oral presentations of your proposals
- Conduct proposal reviews before submission

SUMMARY

The preaward phase of the contract management process is critical to the successful transaction of business involving products and services. The buyer must make an informed outsourcing decision and, if the decision is to buy, clearly and effectively communicate its needs to potential sellers.

Sellers must make an intelligent bid/no-bid decision based on a well-thought-out risk vs. opportunity assessment, and Business Case. After making a decision to bid, the seller must develop an effective win strategy and then successfully communicate its strengths and capabilities to the buyer through a bid or proposal.

CHAPTER 8

CONTRACT
PRICING
ARRANGEMENTS

Business professionals who manage contracts must be aware of the many types of contract pricing arrangements available in order to choose the best type for each situation. Over time, three general pricing arrangements categories have evolved: fixed-price, cost-reimbursement (CR), and time-and-materials (T&M). These categories and the contract types within each category are described in this chapter, along with information on determining contract price and using pricing arrangements to balance the risk between contracting parties. In today's complex business world, a solid understanding of contract pricing options is essential for meeting business objectives.

ASSESSING REQUIREMENTS TO DETERMINE COSTS

Contract cost is determined by the contract requirements, which fall into two main categories: technical and administrative.

Technical Requirements

The solicitation specifications and statement of work contain technical requirements. These documents describe what the buyer wants to buy–the products that must be delivered and the services that must be rendered by the seller. The seller must consume resources–labor, capital, and money–to provide products and services to the buyer.

Administrative Requirements

Contract clauses describe other terms and conditions that will require the seller to consume resources, although the Ts and Cs relate only indirectly to the technical requirements. The following clause excerpt provides such an example:

Company-Furnished Property

> . . . orders from ABC Company shall be held at the Seller's risk and shall be kept insured by the Seller at the Seller's expense while in Seller's custody and control in an amount equal to the replacement cost thereof, with loss payable to ABC Company.

The insurance requirement will cost money, but it is only indirectly related to the technical requirements of the project. Contracts contain many such administrative requirements.

PRICING CONTRACTS

Contract pricing begins with determining the cost of performing the contract. To determine contract cost, a business professional who manages contracts must thoroughly analyze a prospective buyer's solicitation and develop a work breakdown structure based on the technical and administrative performance requirements. Next, he or she decides how the work will be implemented—that is, the order in which it will be performed and the methods and procedures that will be used to accomplish it. Based on these plans, the business professional estimates performance costs so that a price can be proposed. After the company has agreed on a contract price, it will be obligated to complete the work at that price unless a different arrangement can be negotiated.

To estimate performance costs, the following questions must be answered: What resources (labor, capital, money) will be needed to do the work? In what quantities will they be needed? When will they be needed? How much will those resources cost in the marketplace?

Estimating techniques do not necessarily require developing detailed answers to those questions. Parametric estimates, for instance, are used at a very high level and do not involve the type of analysis implied by the four questions. Nevertheless, some level of response to those questions is implicit in every cost estimate.

Uncertainty and Risk in Contract Pricing

The business professional's cost estimate will be a judgment, that is, a prediction about the future, rather than a fact. When the project manager says, "I estimate that the contract will cost $500,000 to complete," that statement really means, "I *predict* that when I have completed the project according to the specifications, statement of work, and other contract terms and conditions, I will have consumed $500,000 worth of labor, capital, and money."

The problem with this prediction, as with all predictions, is that no one will know whether it is true until all the events have occurred. Predictions are based largely on history; they assume that cause-and-effect relationships in the future will be similar to those in the past. However, people frequently have an incorrect or incomplete understanding of the past. In addition, they may carry out even the best-laid plans imperfectly because of error or unexpected events. All these factors can cause the future to materialize differently than predicted.

Thus, the business professional's estimate may be incorrect. If it is too high, the company's proposal may not be competitive. If it is too low, the contract price may not be high enough to cover the project costs, and the company will suffer a financial loss.

However sound the cost estimate, the contract *price* must be negotiated. Every negotiated price is a compromise between the extremes of an optimistic and a pessimistic prediction about future costs. The range between these two extremes is called the *range of possible costs*. The compromise results from negotiation between a risk-avoiding buyer and a risk-avoiding seller.

The risk-avoiding buyer wants to minimize the risk of agreeing to a higher price than necessary to cover the seller's costs plus a reasonable profit. Thus, the buyer tends to push the price toward the more optimistic end of the range of possible costs. The risk-avoiding seller wants to avoid the risk of agreeing to a price that may not cover its actual performance costs or allow a reasonable profit. Thus, the seller tends to push the price toward the more pessimistic end of the range of possible costs.

The consequence of uncertainty about the future is risk, or the possibility of injury. A seller who undertakes a contractual obligation to complete a project for a fixed price but has estimated too low will suffer financial loss, unless it can shift the excess costs to the buyer or avoid them altogether. The effort made to avoid the injury will be proportional to its magnitude and related to its cause and direction.

Cost Overrun vs. Cost Growth

In both *cost overruns* and *cost growth*, actual costs exceed estimated costs, but in each case, they do so for different reasons. Cost overruns occur when the work has not changed, but it costs more than anticipated. This circumstance may occur for any number of reasons, including misfortune, mismanagement, faulty estimating, or poor planning, project design, or execution. Cost growth occurs when the parties change the work, adding to the cost of the project. This circumstance may occur because of changes in the buyer's objectives or in marketable technology.

Although the causes are different, the result may be the same—actual costs exceed estimated costs. Usually, the parties will acknowledge cost growth and make appropriate adjustments to the contract price to compensate the seller for cost increases that arise from project changes. However, for cost overruns, neither party may be willing to take responsibility.

Effects of Cost Risk on Contract Performance

The initial injury from a cost overrun will befall the seller, because the seller is performing the work and incurring the costs. If the injury is small, the seller may choose to do nothing and pay the extra costs out of profit. If the injury is large, the seller will try to discover the source and nature of the overrun.

The more serious the cost overrun, the more desperate the seller will be to find a remedy. The first step is to determine who is at fault. If the seller is responsible, it has no recourse but to suffer the loss, unless it can find ways to cut project costs to compensate for the overrun. Cutting costs can be accomplished by not doing things or by doing things less expensively than planned. If the seller takes either approach, the buyer will have a legitimate concern that the quality of goods or services will suffer.

Alternatively, the seller may argue with the buyer's interpretation of the contract's terms and conditions, seeking to avoid costly obligations. The seller may assert that various buyer requirements are "extras" or may claim that actions of the buyer were contrary to the terms of the contract, thus entitling the seller to more money. If the overrun is serious enough to threaten its survival, the seller may be unable or unwilling to continue to perform and may default.

Frequently the buyer is the cause of cost overruns. This circumstance can occur when the buyer wheedles extra work from an overly responsive sales manager or when a project manager accedes to erroneous interpretations of the contract.

Obviously, risk affects behavior. Accordingly, when the parties to a contract recognize that the cost uncertainties of performance are great—so great that the attendant risks may result in behaviors that threaten the project's objectives—the parties should adopt pricing arrangements that equitably distribute that risk between them.

DEVELOPING PRICING ARRANGEMENTS

Over the years some standard pricing arrangements have evolved. These arrangements fall into three categories: *fixed-price, cost-reimbursement,* and *time-and-materials* contracts (PMI also designates unit-price contracts as a separate category.) These contract categories have developed as practical responses to cost risk, and they have become fairly standard formal arrangements. Incentives can be added to any of the contracts types in these three categories and are discussed in detail later in this chapter. Table 8-1 lists several common contract types in these categories.

Table 8-1 Contract Categories and Types			
	Fixed-Price	Cost-Reimbursement or Unit Price*	Time-and-Materials
Types of Contracts	Firm-fixed-price	Cost-reimbursement	Time-and-materials
	Fixed-price with economic price adjustment	Cost-plus-a-percentage-of-cost	Unit-price
	Fixed-price incentive	Cost-plus-fixed fee	
		Cost-plus-incentive fee	
		Cost-plus-award fee	

*PMI designates this as a separate category.

These pricing arrangements, however, are manifested in the specific terms and conditions of contracts, that is, in the contract clauses. No standard clauses for their implementation exist. Therefore, the contracting parties must write clauses that describe their specific agreement.

Fixed-Price Category

Fixed-price contracts are the standard business pricing arrangement. The two basic types of fixed-price contracts are *firm-fixed-price (FFP)* and *fixed-price with economic price adjustment (FP/EPA)*. Firm-fixed-price contracts are further divided into *lump-sum* and *unit-price* arrangements.

Firm-Fixed-Price Contracts

The simplest and most common business pricing arrangement is the FFP contract. The seller agrees to supply specified goods or deliverables in a specified quantity or to render a specified service or level of effort (LOE) in return for a specified price, either a lump sum or a unit price. The price is fixed, that is, not subject to change based on the seller's actual cost experience. (However, it may be subject to change if the parties modify the contract.) This pricing arrangement is used for the sale of commercial goods and services.

Some companies include a complex clause in their FFP contracts. Such a clause may read in part as follows:

Prices and Taxes

The price of Products shall be ABC Company's published list prices on the date ABC Company accepts your order less any applicable discount. If ABC Company announces a price increase for Equipment, or Software licensed for a one-time fee, after it accepts your order but before shipment, ABC Company shall invoice you at the increased price only if delivery occurs more than 120 days after the effective date of the price increase. If ABC Company announces a price increase for Services, Rentals, or Software licensed for a periodic fee, the price increase shall apply to billing periods beginning after its effective date.

Note that this clause was written by the seller, not the buyer, and reflects the seller's point of view and concerns. Nevertheless, the pricing arrangement it describes is firm-fixed-price, because the contract price will not be subject to adjustment based on ABC Company's actual performance costs.

Clauses such as "Prices and Taxes" frequently form part of a document known as a *universal agreement.* Such a document is not a contract, it is a precontract agreement that merely communicates any agreed-to Ts and Cs that will apply when an order is placed by the buyer. After an order is accepted by the seller, the company's published or announced list prices become the basis for the contract price according to the terms of the universal agreement. (This agreement is discussed later in this chapter in "Purchase Agreements.")

Firm-fixed-price contracts are appropriate for most commercial transactions when cost uncertainty is within commercially acceptable limits. What those limits may be depends on the industry and the market.

Fixed-Price with Economic Price Adjustment

Fixed-price contracts sometimes include various clauses that provide for adjusting prices based on specified contingencies. The clauses may provide for upward or downward adjustments, or both. Economic price adjustments are usually limited to factors beyond the seller's immediate control, such as market forces.

This pricing arrangement is not *firm*-fixed-price, because the contract provides for a price adjustment based on the seller's actual performance costs. Thus, the seller is protected from the risk of certain labor or material cost increases. The EPA clause can provide for price increases based on the seller's *costs* but not on the seller's decision to increase the *prices* of its products or services. Thus, there can be a significant difference between this clause and the "Prices and Taxes" clause discussed previously.

The shift of risk to the buyer creates greater buyer intrusion into the affairs of the seller. This intrusion typically takes the form of an audit provision at the end of the clause, particularly when the buyer is a government.

EPA clauses are appropriate in times of market instability, when great uncertainty exists regarding labor and material costs. The risk of cost fluctuations is more balanced between the parties than would be the case under an FFP contract.

Cost-Reimbursement Category

Cost-reimbursement contracts usually include an estimate of project cost, a provision for reimbursing the seller's expenses, and a provision for paying a fee as profit. Normally, CR contracts also include a limitation on the buyer's cost liability.

A common perception is that CR contracts are to be avoided. However, if uncertainty about costs is great enough, a buyer may be unable to find a seller willing to accept a fixed price, even with adjustment clauses, or a seller may insist on extraordinary contingencies within that price. In the latter case, the buyer may find the demands unreasonable. Such high levels of cost uncertainty are often found in research and development, large-scale construction, and systems integration projects. In such circumstances, the best solution may be a CR contract–but only if the buyer is confident that the seller has a highly accurate and reliable cost accounting system.

The parties to a CR contract will find themselves confronting some challenging issues, especially concerning the definition, measurement, allocation, and confirmation of costs. First, the parties must agree on a definition for acceptable cost. For instance, the buyer may decide that the cost of air travel should be limited to the price of a coach or business-class ticket and should not include a first-class ticket. The buyer will specify other cost limitations, and the parties will negotiate until they agree on what constitutes a reimbursable cost.

Next, the parties must decide who will measure costs and what accounting rules will be used to do so. For example, several depreciation techniques are in use, some of which would be less advantageous to the buyer than others. Which technique will the buyer consider acceptable? How will labor costs be calculated? Will standard costs be acceptable, or must the seller determine and invoice actual costs? What methods of allocating overhead will be acceptable to the buyer? How will the buyer know that the seller's reimbursement invoices are accurate? Will the buyer have the right to obtain an independent audit? If the buyer is also a competitor of the seller, should the seller be willing to open its books to the buyer?

If these issues remain unsettled, the buyer is accepting the risk of having to reimburse costs it may later find to be unreasonable. This issue is the central problem with cost-reimbursement contracting, and it has never been resolved entirely.

Clearly, the CR contract presents the parties with difficulties they would not face under a fixed-price contract. The parties must define costs and establish acceptable procedures for cost measurement and allocation, the buyer takes on greater cost risk and must incur greater administrative costs to protect its interests, and the seller faces greater intrusion by the buyer into its affairs. Nevertheless, many contracting parties have found a CR contract to be a better arrangement than a fixed-price contract for undertakings with high cost uncertainty.

Types of CR contracts include *cost, cost-sharing, cost-plus-a-percentage-of-cost (CPPC)*, and *cost-plus-fixed fee (CPFF)*.

Cost Contracts

The cost contract is the simplest type of CR contract. Governments commonly use this type when contracting with universities and nonprofit organizations for research projects. The contract provides for reimbursing contractually allowable costs, with no allowance given for profit.

Cost-Sharing Contracts

The cost-sharing contract provides for only partial reimbursement of the seller's costs. The parties share the cost liability, with no allowance for profit. The cost-sharing contract is appropriate when the seller will enjoy some benefit from the results of the project and that benefit is sufficient to encourage the seller to undertake the work for only a portion of its costs and without fee.

Cost-Plus-a-Percentage-of-Cost Contracts

The CPPC contract provides for the seller to receive reimbursement for its costs and a profit component, called a *fee*, equal to some predetermined percentage of its actual costs. Thus, as costs go up, so does profit. This arrangement is a poor one from the buyer's standpoint; it provides no incentive to control costs, because the fee gets bigger as the costs go up. This type of contract was used extensively by the U.S. government during World War I but has since been made illegal for U.S. government contracts, for good reason. It is still occasionally used for construction projects and some service contracts in the private sector.

The rationale for this pricing arrangement was probably "the bigger the job, the bigger the fee," that is, as the job grows, so should the fee. This arrangement is similar to a professional fee, such as an attorney's fee, which grows as the professional puts more time into the project. This arrangement may have developed as a response to the cost-growth phenomenon in projects that were initially ill-defined. As a seller proceeded with the work, the buyer's needs became better defined and grew, until the seller felt that the fees initially agreed to were not enough for the expanded scope of work.

Cost-Plus-Fixed Fee Contracts

Cost-plus-fixed fee is the most common type of CR contract. As with the others, the seller is reimbursed for its costs, but the contract also provides for payment of a fixed fee that does not change in response to the seller's actual cost experience. The seller is paid the fixed fee on successful completion of the contract, whether its actual costs were higher or lower than the estimated costs.

If the seller completes the work for less than the estimated cost, it receives the entire fixed fee. If the seller incurs the estimated cost without completing the work and if the buyer decides not to pay for the overrun costs necessary for completion, the seller receives a portion of the fixed fee that is equal to the percentage of work completed. If the buyer decides to pay overrun costs, the seller must complete the work without any increase in the fixed fee. The only adjustment to the fee would be a result of cost growth, when the buyer requires the seller to do more work than initially specified.

This type of contract is on the opposite end of the spectrum from the FFP contract, because cost risk rests entirely on the shoulders of the buyer. Under a CR contract, a buyer might have to reimburse the seller for the entire estimated cost and part of the fee but have nothing to show for it but bits and pieces of the work.

Classification of Contract Incentives

The fundamental purpose of contract incentives is to motivate desired performance in one or more specific areas. Contract incentives are generally classified as either objectively based and evaluated or subjectively based and evaluated. Further, both classifications of contract incentives are typically categorized as either positive incentives (rewards–get more money) or negative incentives (penalties–get less money) or some combination thereof.

Those incentives that use predetermined formula-based methods to calculate the amount of incentive, either positive or negative, in one or more designated areas are objectively based and evaluated. Facts and actual events are used as a basis for determination–individual judgment and opinions are not considered in an evaluation of performance.

Objectively based and evaluated contract incentives commonly include the following designated performance areas:

■ Cost performance
■ Schedule or delivery performance
■ Quality performance

Subjectively based and evaluated contract incentives are those incentives that use individual judgment, opinions, and informed impressions as the basis for determining the amount of incentive, either positive or negative, in one or more designated areas. These incentives can and often do contain some objective aspects or factors. However, subjective contract incentives are ultimately determined by one or more individuals making a decision based on their experience, knowledge, and the available information–a total judgment.

Subjectively based and evaluated contract incentives typically include the following:

■ Award fees
■ Other special incentives

Figure 8–1 summarizes the link between rewards and penalties and contract incentives as described in the following paragraphs.

Figure 8-1 Contract Incentives			
Types of Incentives	Positive (rewards)	No Reward or Penalty	Negative (penalties)
Objective incentives			
Cost performance	Under budget	On budget	Over budget
Schedule or delivery performance	Early delivery	On-time delivery	Late delivery
Quality performance	Exceed requirements	Achieve contract requirements	Do not achieve requirements
Subjective incentives Award fee Other special incentives	Exceed requirements	Achieve award fee plan	Do not achieve requirements

Objective Incentives

Incentives Based on Cost Performance

Cost is the most commonly chosen performance variable. For fixed-price (cost) incentive contracts, the parties negotiate a *target cost* and a *target profit* (which equals the *target price*), and a *sharing formula* for cost overruns and cost underruns. They also negotiate a *ceiling price*, which is the buyer's maximum dollar liability. When performance is complete, they determine the final actual costs and apply the sharing formula to any overrun or underrun. Applying the sharing formula determines the seller's final profit, if any.

Consider an example in which the parties agree to the following arrangement:

> *Target cost:* $10,000,000
> *Target profit:* $850,000
> *Target price:* $10,850,000
> *Sharing formula:* 70/30 (buyer 70 percent, seller 30 percent)
> *Ceiling price:* $11,500,000

Assume that the seller completes the work at an actual cost of $10,050,000, overrunning the target cost by $50,000. The seller's share of the overrun is 30 percent of $50,000, which is $15,000. The target profit will be reduced by that amount ($850,000 – 15,000 = $835,000). The seller will then receive the $10,050,000 cost of performance plus an earned profit of $835,000. Thus, the price to the buyer will be $10,885,000, which is $615,000 below the ceiling price. The $35,000 increase over the target price of $10,850,000 represents the buyer's 70 percent share of the cost overrun.

Had the seller overrun the target cost by $100,000, raising the actual cost to $10,100,000, the seller's share of the overrun would have been 30 percent or $30,000. That amount would have reduced the seller's profit to $820,000.

Basically, at some point before reaching the ceiling price, the sharing arrangement effectively changes to 0/100, with the seller assuming 100 percent of the cost risk. This effect is implicit in fixed-price incentive arrangements because of the ceiling price and is not an explicit element of the formula. The point at which sharing changes to 0/100 is called the *point of total assumption (PTA)*, which represents a cost figure. Indeed, the PTA is often appropriately referred to as the *high-cost estimate*. Figure 8–2 depicts these relationships and outcomes in graphical form. (Note that the graph describes a first-degree linear equation of the form $Y = A - BX$, with cost as the independent variable X, and profit as the dependent variable Y. B, the coefficient of X, is equal to the seller's share.)

Figure 8-2 Illustration of Fixed-Price Incentive Arrangement

The PTA can be determined by applying the following formula:

$$\text{PTA} = \left(\frac{\text{Ceiling price - Target price}}{\text{Buyer share ratio}} \right) + \text{Target Cost}$$

In the event of an underrun, the seller would enjoy greater profit. If the final cost is $9,000,000 (a $1,000,000 underrun), the seller's share of the underrun is 30 percent, which is $300,000. Thus, the price to the buyer would include the $9,000,000 cost and the $850,000 target profit plus the seller's $300,000 underrun share (total profit of $1,150,000). Thus, $9,000,000 actual cost plus $1,150,000 actual profit equals $10,150,000 actual price, reflecting precisely the buyer's 70 percent share of the $1,000,000 underrun [$10,850,000 target price – 70 percent of the $1,000,000 underrun ($700,000) = $10,150,000].

Incentives Based on Schedule or Delivery Performance

For many years, construction, aerospace, and numerous service industries have used schedule or delivery performance incentives to motivate sellers to provide either early or on-time delivery of products and services.

Liquidated damages is a negative incentive (penalty) for late delivery. Typically, a liquidated damages clause stated in the contract terms and conditions designates how much money one party, usually the seller, must pay the other party, usually the buyer, for not meeting the contract schedule. Often the amount of liquidated damages payable is specified as an amount of money for a specific period of time (day, week, month). A key aspect of liquidated damages is that the penalty is to be based on the amount of damages incurred or compensable in nature, not an excessive or punitive amount.

A proven best practice for buyers is to require negative incentives (or penalties) for late delivery and late schedule performance. Likewise, a proven best practice for sellers is to limit their liability on liquidated damages by agreeing to a cap or maximum amount, and seeking positive incentives (or rewards) for early delivery and early schedule performance.

Incentives Based on Quality Performance

Quality performance incentives is one of the most common topics in government and commercial contracting. Surveys in both government and industry have revealed widespread service contracting problems, including deficient statements of work, poor contract administration, performance delays, and quality shortcomings.

When a contract is based on performance, all aspects of the contract are structured around the purpose of the work to be performed rather than the manner in which it is to be done. The buyer seeks to elicit the best performance the seller has to offer, at a reasonable price or cost, by stating its objectives and giving sellers both latitude in determining how to achieve them and incentives for achieving them. In source selection, for example, the buyer might publish a draft solicitation for comment, use quality-related evaluation factors, or both. The statement of work will provide performance standards rather than spelling out what the seller is to do. The contract normally contains a plan for quality assurance surveillance. And the contract typically includes positive and negative performance incentives.

Few people disagree with the concept that buyers, who collectively spend billions of dollars on services annually, should look to the performance-based approach, focusing more on results and less on detailed requirements. However, implementing performance-based contracting (using cost, schedule, and/or quality performance variables) is far easier said than done. The sound use of performance incentives is key to the success of the performance-based contracting approach.

Problems with Applying Objective Incentives

The objective-incentive schemes described have some merit, but they also involve some serious practical problems. First, they assume a level of buyer and seller competence that may not exist. Second, they assume effects that may not occur. Third, they create serious challenges for contract administration.

To negotiate objective incentives intelligently, the parties must have some knowledge of the range of possible costs for a project. They also must have some knowledge of the likely causes and probabilities of different cost outcomes. If both parties do not have sufficient information on these issues, they will not be able to structure an effective incentive formula.

It is important that the parties share their information. If one party has superior knowledge that it does not share with the other, it will be able to skew the formula in its favor during negotiation. If that happens, the whole point of the arrangement, which is to equitably balance the risks of performance, will be lost. The buyer is usually at a disadvantage with respect to the seller in this regard.

An objective incentive assumes that the seller can effect a performance outcome along the entire range of the independent variable. However, such may not be true. For instance, the seller may actually exercise control along only a short sector of the range of possible costs. Some possible cost outcomes may be entirely outside the seller's control because of factors such as market performance. In reality, the seller's project manager may have little control over important factors that may determine the cost outcome, such as overhead costs. In addition, short-term companywide factors, especially those involving overhead, may, on some contracts, make incurring additional cost rather than earning additional profit more advantageous for the seller.

In addition, objective cost incentives are complicated and costly to administer, with all the cost definition, measurement, allocation, and confirmation problems of CR contracts. The parties must be particularly careful to segregate the target cost effects of cost growth from those of cost overruns; otherwise, they may lose money for the wrong reasons. As a practical matter, segregating such costs is often quite difficult.

When using other performance incentives, the parties may find themselves disputing the causes of various performance outcomes. The seller may argue that schedule delays are a result of actions of the buyer. Quality problems, such as poor reliability, may have been caused by improper buyer operation rather than seller performance. The causes of performance failures may be difficult to determine.

One reason for using such contracts is to reduce the deleterious effects of risk on the behavior of the parties. Thus, if a pricing arrangement increases the likelihood of trouble, it should not be used. The decision to apply objective incentives should be made only after careful analysis.

Best Practices: 15 Actions to Improve Your Use of Contract Incentives

These best practices should be followed when using incentive contracts:

- *Think creatively:* Creativity is a critical aspect in the success of performance-based incentive contracting
- Avoid rewarding sellers for simply meeting contract requirements
- Recognize that developing clear, concise, objectively measurable performance incentives will be a challenge, and plan accordingly
- Create a proper balance of objective incentives—cost, schedule, and quality performance
- Ensure that performance incentives focus the seller's efforts on the buyer's desired objectives
- Make all forms of performance incentives challenging yet attainable
- Ensure that incentives motivate quality control and that the results of the seller's quality control efforts can be measured
- Consider tying on-time delivery to cost and or quality performance criteria
- Recognize that not everything can be measured objectively— consider using a combination of objectively measured standards and subjectively determined incentives
- Encourage open communication and ongoing involvement with potential sellers in developing the performance-based SOW and the incentive plan, both before and after issuing the formal request for proposals
- Consider including socioeconomic incentives (non-SOW-related) in the incentive plan
- Use clear, objective formulas for determining performance incentives
- Use a combination of positive and negative incentives
- Include incentives for discounts based on early payments
- Ensure that all incentives, both positive and negative, have limits

Subjective Incentives

Award Fee Plans

In an award fee plan, the parties negotiate an estimated cost, just as for CPFF contracts. Then they negotiate an agreement on the amount of money to be included in an *award fee pool*. Finally, they agree on a set of criteria and procedures to be applied by the buyer in determining how well the seller has performed and how much fee the seller has earned. In some cases, the parties also negotiate a *base fee*, which is a fixed fee that the seller will earn no matter how its performance is evaluated.

The contract performance period is then divided into equal *award fee periods*. A part of the award fee pool is allocated to each period proportionate to the percentage of the work scheduled to be completed. All this information is included in the award fee plan, which becomes part of the contract. In some cases, the contract allows the buyer to change the award fee plan unilaterally before the start of a new award fee period.

During each award fee period, the buyer observes and documents the seller's performance achievements or failures. At the end of each period, the buyer evaluates the seller's performance according to the award fee plan and decides how much fee to award from the portion allocated to that period. Under some contracts, the seller has an opportunity to present its own evaluation of its performance and a specific request for award fee. The buyer then informs the seller how much of the available award fee it has earned and how its performance could be improved during ensuing award fee periods. This arrangement invariably involves subjectivity on the part of the buyer; precisely how much depends on how the award fee plan is written.

Pros and Cons of the Award Fee Arrangement

The cost-plus-award fee (CPAF) contract is a cost-reimbursement contract, with all its requirements for cost definition, measurement, allocation, and confirmation. For the buyer, the CPAF contract requires the additional administrative investment associated with observing, documenting, and evaluating seller performance. However, this disadvantage may sometimes be overemphasized, because the buyer should already be performing many of these activities under a CR contract.

The disadvantages for the buyer are offset by the extraordinary power it obtains from the ability to make subjective determinations about how much fee the seller has earned. The buyer may have difficulty establishing objective criteria for satisfactory service performance.

The power of subjective fee determination tends to make sellers extraordinarily responsive to the buyer's demands. However, the buyer must be careful, because that very responsiveness can be the cause of cost overruns and unintended cost growth.

The buyer's advantages are almost entirely disadvantages from the viewpoint of the seller, because the seller will have placed itself within the power of the buyer to an exceptional degree. Subjectivity can approach arbitrariness or even cross the line. The seller may find itself dealing with a buyer that is impossible to please or that believes that the seller cannot earn all the award fee because no one can achieve "perfect" performance.

Other Special Incentives

There is a growing recognition by buyers and sellers worldwide, in both the public and private sectors, that contract incentives can be expanded and that they are indeed valuable tools to motivate the desired performance. Increasingly, when outsourcing, buyers are motivating sellers to subcontract with local companies, often with special rewards for subcontracting with designated small businesses.

Likewise, many sellers are providing buyers with special incentives for early payment, such as product or services discounts or additional specified services at no change.

Award Term Arrangement

Similar in nature to an award fee, the buyer may unilaterally decide to extend the period of performance of a contract, if the contractor's performance met or exceeded the original contract requirements.

Incentive Contracts

Cost-Plus-Incentive Fee Contracts

Cost-plus-incentive fee (CPIF) contracts allow overrun or underrun sharing of cost through a predetermined formula for fee adjustments that apply to incentives for cost category contracts. Within the basic concept of the buyer's paying all costs for a cost contract, the limits for a CPIF contract become those of maximum and minimum fees.

The necessary elements for a CPIF contract are maximum fee, minimum fee, target cost, target fee, and share ratio(s).

Fixed-Price Incentive Contracts

In an FPI contract, seller profit is linked to another aspect of performance—cost, schedule, quality, or a combination of all three. The objective is to give the seller a monetary incentive to optimize cost performance.

Fixed-price incentive contracts may be useful for initial production of complex new products or systems, although the parties may have difficulty agreeing on labor and material costs for such projects because of a lack of production experience. However, the cost uncertainty may not be great enough to warrant use of a CR contract.

Cost-Plus-Award Fee Contracts

Cost-plus-award fee contracts include subjective incentives, in which the profit a seller earns depends on how well the seller satisfies a buyer's subjective desires. This type of contract has been used for a long time in both government and commercial contracts worldwide. The U.S. Army Corps of Engineers developed an evaluated fee contract for use in construction during the early 1930s, based on its contracting experience during World War I. The U.S. National Aeronautics and Space Administration has used CPAF contracts to procure services since the 1950s. Other U.S. government agencies have also used these contracts extensively, including the Department of Energy and the Department of Defense. A small but growing number of commercial companies now use award fees to motivate their suppliers to achieve exceptional performance.

Cost-plus-award fee contracts are used primarily to procure services, particularly those that involve an ongoing, long-term relationship between buyer and seller, such as maintenance and systems engineering support. Objective criteria for determining the acceptability of the performance of such services are inherently difficult to establish. The award fee arrangement is particularly well suited to such circumstances, at least from the buyer's point of view. However, this type of contract also is used to procure architecture and engineering, research and development, hardware and software systems design and development, construction, and many other services.

Use of Award Fees and Incentive Fees in DOD

In December 2005, the Government Accountability Office (GAO) issued their report entitled "Defense Acquisitions: DOD Has Paid Billions in Award and Incentive Fees Regardless of Acquisition Outcomes," GAO Report (GAO-06-66). In this report, GAO found "the power of monetary incentives to motivate excellent contractor performance and improve acquisition outcomes is diluted by the way DOD structures and implements incentives." Further, the GAO report stated, "As a result, DOD has paid out an estimated $8 Billion in award fees to date on contracts in our study population regardless of outcomes." GAO believes these practices, along with paying significant amounts of fee for "acceptable, average, expected, good, or satisfactory" performance, undermine the effectiveness of fees as a motivational tool and marginalize their use in holding contractors accountable for acquisition outcomes.

The DOD Response (Office of the Under Secretary of Defense Memorandum, 3/29/06)

"Award fee contracts must be structured in ways that will focus the government's and contractor's efforts on meeting or exceeding cost, schedule, and performance requirements. The ability to earn award fees needs to be directly linked to achieving desired program outcomes."

"While award fee contracts are intended to be flexible, this memorandum provides additional guidance on the proper use of award fees."

Link Award Fees to Desired Outcomes (GAO Recommendation I)

"While award fee contracts are used when it is neither feasible nor effective to devise predetermined objective performance targets, it is imperative that award fees be tied to identifiable interim outcomes, discrete events or milestones, as much as possible."

Award Fees Must Be Commensurate with Contractor Performance (GAO Recommendation 2)

"While award fee arrangements should be structured to motivate excellent contractor performance, award fees must be commensurate with contractor performance over a range from satisfactory to excellent performance. Clearly, satisfactory performance should earn considerably less than excellent performance, otherwise the motivation to achieve excellence is negated." "Performance that is less than satisfactory is not entitled to any award fee."

Rollover of Award Fees (GAO Recommendation 4)

"An element of any award fee plans is the ability to 'rollover' unearned award fee money from one period to another." In 2009, the Federal Acquisition Regulation (FAR) Part 16 Types of Contracts was revised to eliminate the use of unearned award fee 'rollover' in all government contracts.

Why Award Fees and Incentive Fees are Important to Government Contractors

All DOD contractors want the opportunity to maximize their profitability based upon their excellent performance. Many companies have extensive experience with the use of Award Fee Contracts. Plus, it is anticipated that many new performance-based contracts may contain task orders done in whole or in part using Award Fees and/or incentive fees. Thus, knowing the importance of this topic and the DOD's latest guidance may prove critical to a DOD contractor's future success.

Time-and-Materials Category

In T&M contracts, the parties negotiate hourly rates for specified types of labor and agree that the seller will be reimbursed for parts and materials at cost. Each hourly wrap rate includes: direct labor costs, overhead costs, general and administrative (G&A) costs, fringe expenses, and profit. The seller performs the work, documenting the types and quantities of labor used and the costs for parts and materials. When the work is finished, the seller bills the buyer for the number of labor hours at the agreed-on hourly rates and for the costs of materials and parts.

Time-and-materials contracts are most often used to procure a wide variety of professional services including: information technology services, acquisition support services, equipment repair and maintenance services, when the cost to provide the certain is uncertain. However, these contracts are also used to procure other support services.

Although T&M contracts appear to be straightforward, they may create some difficulties. This type of contract must be negotiated carefully, because each hourly rate includes a component for overhead costs, which include both *fixed* and *variable costs.* Fixed costs are the costs that will be incurred during a given period of operation, despite the number of work hours performed. To recover its fixed costs, the seller must estimate how many hours will be sold during the contract performance period and allocate a share to each hour. If the parties overestimate how many hours will be sold during the period of performance, the seller will not recover all its fixed costs. If the parties underestimate how many hours will be sold, the seller will enjoy a windfall profit. The U.S. government requires all T&M contracts to include a Not-To-Exceed (NTE) amount and limits the length of the contract to a maximum period of performance of three years (base period plus option periods).

Although the hourly labor rates are fixed, the number of hours delivered and the cost of materials and parts are not. Therefore, the buyer faces the problems of confirming the number of hours delivered and the cost of materials claimed by the seller. These problems are not as great as those under CR contracts, but they are not insignificant.

Figure 8–3 provides a range of contract types keyed to performance measurement and risk. Table 4 compares the advantages, disadvantages, and suitability of fixed-price, cost-reimbursement, and time-and-materials contract categories.

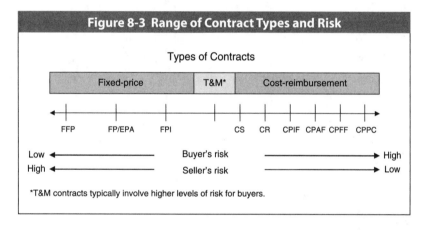

Figure 8-3 Range of Contract Types and Risk

Types of Contracts

| Fixed-price | T&M* | Cost-reimbursement |

FFP   FP/EPA   FPI   CS   CR   CPIF CPAF CPFF CPPC

Low ◄——————————— Buyer's risk ——————————► High
High ◄——————————— Seller's risk ——————————► Low

*T&M contracts typically involve higher levels of risk for buyers.

Table 8-2 Advantages, Disadvantages, and Suitability of Various Contract Types

Type	Fixed-Price Contracts (Greatest Risk for Seller)		
	Essential Elements and Advantages	Disadvantages	Suitability
FFP	Reasonably definite design or performance specifications available. Fair and reasonable price can be established at outset. Conditions for use include the following: ■ Adequate competition. ■ Prior purchase experience of the same, or similar, supplies or services under competitive conditions. ■ Valid cost or pricing data. ■ Realistic estimates of proposed cost. ■ Possible uncertainties in performance can be identified and priced. ■ Sellers willing to accept contract at a level that causes them to take all financial risks. ■ Any other reasonable basis for pricing can be used to establish fair and reasonable price.	Price not subject to adjustment regardless of seller performance costs. Places 100% of financial risk on seller. Places least amount of administrative burden on contract manager. Preferred over all other contract types. Used with advertised or negotiated procurements.	Commercial products and commercial services for which reasonable prices can be established.
FP/ EPA	Unstable market or labor conditions during performance period and contingencies that would otherwise be included in contract price can be identified and made the subject of a separate price adjustment clause. Contingencies must be specifically defined in contract. Provides for upward adjustment (with ceiling) in contract price. May provide for downward adjustment of price if escalated element has potential of falling below contract limits. Three general types of EPAs, based on established prices, actual costs of labor or material, and cost indexes of labor or material.	Price can be adjusted on action of an industry-wide contingency that is beyond seller's control. Reduces seller's fixed-price risk. FP/EPA is preferred over any CR-type contract. If contingency manifests, contract administration burden increases. Used with negotiated procurements and, in limited applications, with formal advertising when determined to be feasible. CM must determine if FP/EPA is necessary either to protect seller and buyer against significant fluctuations in labor or material costs or to provide for contract price adjustment in case of changes in seller's established prices.	Commercial products and services for which reasonable prices can be established at time of award.

Table 8-2 -continued

FPI	Cost uncertainties exist, but there is potential for cost reduction or performance improvement by giving seller a degree of cost responsibility and a positive profit incentive. Profit is earned or lost based on relationship that contract's final negotiated cost bears to total target cost. Contract must contain target cost, target profit, ceiling price, and profit-sharing formula. Two forms of FPI: firm target (FPIF) and successive targets (FPIS). FPIF: Firm target cost, target profit, and profit-sharing formula negotiated into basic contract; profit adjusted at contract completion. FPIS: Initial cost and profit targets negotiated into contract, but final cost target (firm) cannot be negotiated until performance. Contains production point(s) at which either a firm target and final profit formula, or an FFP contract, can be negotiated. Elements that can be incentives: costs, performance, delivery, quality.	Requires adequate seller accounting system. Buyer must determine that FPI is least costly and award of any other type would be impractical. Buyer and seller administrative effort is more extensive than under other fixed-price contract types. Used only with competitive negotiated contracts. Billing prices must be established for interim payment.	Development and production of high-volume, multiyear contracts.
Cost-Reimbursement Contracts (Greatest Risk on Buyer)		
Cost	Appropriate for research and development work, particularly with nonprofit educational institutions or other nonprofit organizations, and for facilities contracts. Allowable costs of contract performance are reimbursed, but no fee is paid.	Application limited due to no fee and by the fact that the buyer is not willing to reimburse seller fully if there is a commercial benefit for the seller. Only nonprofit institutions and organizations are willing (usually) to perform research for which there is no fee (or other tangible benefits).	Research and development; facilities.
CS	Used when buyer and seller agree to share costs in a research or development project having potential mutual benefits. Because of commercial benefits accruing to the seller, no fee is paid. Seller agrees to absorb a portion of the costs of performance in expectation of compensating benefits to seller's firm or organization. Such benefits might include an enhancement of the seller's capability and expertise or an improvement of its competitive position in the commercial market.	Care must be taken in negotiating cost-share rate so that the cost ratio is proportional to the potential benefit (that is, the party receiving the greatest potential benefit bears the greatest share of the costs).	Research and development that has potential benefits to both the buyer and the seller.

Table 8-2 - continued

Type	Essential Elements and Advantages	Disadvantages	Suitability
	Cost-Reimbursement Contracts (Greatest Risk for Buyer)		
CPIF	Development has a high probability that it is feasible and positive profit incentives for seller management can be negotiated. Performance incentives must be clearly spelled out and objectively measurable. Fee range should be negotiated to give the seller an incentive over various ranges of cost performance. Fee is adjusted by a formula negotiated into the contract in accordance with the relationship that total cost bears to target cost. Contract must contain target cost, target fee, minimum and maximum fees, fee adjustment formula. Fee adjustment is made at completion of contract.	Difficult to negotiate range between the maximum and minimum fees so as to provide an incentive over entire range. Performance must be objectively measurable. Costly to administer; seller must have an adequate accounting system. Used only with negotiated contracts. Appropriate buyer surveillance needed during performance to ensure effective methods and efficient cost controls are used.	Major systems development and other development programs in which it is determined that CPIF is desirable and administratively practical.
CPAF	Contract completion is feasible, incentives are desired, but performance is not susceptible to finite measurement. Provides for subjective evaluation of seller performance. Seller is evaluated at stated time(s) during performance period. Contract must contain clear and unambiguous evaluation criteria to determine award fee. Award fee is earned for excellence in performance, quality, timeliness, ingenuity, and cost-effectiveness and can be earned in whole or in part. Two separate fee pools can be established in contract: base fee and award fee. Award fee earned by seller is determined by the buyer and is often based on recommendations of an award fee evaluation board.	Buyer's determination of amount of award fee earned by the seller is not subject to disputes clause. CPAF cannot be used to avoid either CPIF or CPFF if either is feasible. Should not be used if the amount of money, period of performance, or expected benefits are insufficient to warrant additional administrative effort. Very costly to administer. Seller must have an adequate accounting system. Used only with negotiated contracts.	Level-of-effort services that can only be subjectively measured, and contracts for which work would have been accomplished under another contract type if performance objectives could have been expressed as definite milestones, targets, and goals that could have been measured.

Table 8-2 -continued

CPFF	Level of effort is unknown, and seller's performance cannot be subjectively evaluated. Provides for payment of a fixed fee. Seller receives fixed fee regardless of the actual costs incurred during performance. Can be constructed in two ways: Completion form: Clearly defined task with a definite goal and specific end product. Buyer can order more work without an increase in fee if the contract estimated cost is increased. Term form: Scope of work described in general terms. Seller obligated only for a specific level of effort for stated period of time. Completion form is preferred over term form. Fee is expressed as percentage of estimated cost at time contract is awarded.	Seller has minimum incentive to control costs. Costly to administer. Seller must have an adequate accounting system. Seller assumes no financial risk.	Completion form: Advanced development or technical services contracts. Term form: Research and exploratory development. Used when the level of effort required is unknown and there is an inability to measure risk.
Time and Materials			
T&M	Not possible when placing contract to estimate extent or duration of the work, or anticipated cost, with any degree of confidence. Calls for provision of direct labor hours at specified hourly rate and materials at cost (or some other basis specified in contract). The fixed hourly rates include wages, overhead, general and administrative expenses, and profit. Material cost can include, if appropriate, material handling costs. Ceiling price established at time of award.	Used only after determination that no other type will serve purpose. Does not encourage effective cost control. Requires almost constant surveillance by buyer to ensure effective seller management. Ceiling price required in contract.	Engineering and design services in conjunction with the production of supplies, engineering design and manufacture, repair, maintenance, and overhaul work to be performed on an as-needed basis.

Other Pricing Methods

In addition to the variety of pricing arrangements already discussed, buyers and sellers use other kinds of agreements to deal with uncertainty and reduce the administrative costs of contracting. These include *purchase agreements, memorandums of understanding (MOUs),* and *letters of intent (LOIs).*

Purchase Agreements

When two parties expect to deal with one another repeatedly for the purchase and sale of goods and services, they may decide to enter into a long-term purchase agreement. (A universal agreement is an example of such an arrangement.) Rather than negotiating a new contract for every transaction, the parties agree to the terms and conditions that will apply to any transaction between them of a specified type. This arrangement reduces the time required to form a contract and eliminates uncertainty about purchase terms and conditions.

Indefinite Delivery Indefinite Quantity (IDIQ)

The IDIQ agreement itself is not a contract, since neither party undertakes an obligation to the other by signing such an agreement. But it can become an enforceable agreement if it contains a specified minimum quantity of products and/or services that must be ordered within a required period of time. In that situation, if the buyer decides to purchase the products or services, it can issue an order (often called a Task Order (TO)) that, if accepted by the seller, will become a contract. The contract will then include, by previous consent, the terms and conditions of the purchase agreement. In commercial transactions, purchase agreements are usually written by the seller, who reserves the right to modify or terminate the agreement at will. The following sample clause describes this type of arrangement:

Orders and Contract Formation

Each time you [the Buyer] submit an order for Products and ABC Company accepts it or ships the ordered Products to you, a new Contract is formed consisting of this Agreement and the order. If ABC Company accepts an order on your [purchase] order form, this Agreement will prevail and the preprinted language on your order form will not become a part of the Contract unless ABC Company agrees in writing to waive this Section. Your acceptance of or payment for Products (including Equipment Maintenance and other Services) that you do not order creates a Contract comprising this Agreement and ABC Company's applicable published prices. Your request to cancel, reschedule, or modify an order may be subject to a charge under ABC Company's then-current policies. Each Contract is the exclusive agreement between us regarding the Products covered by the Contract. Unless otherwise agreed in writing, the Contract supersedes all oral and written communication between us regarding the ordered Products.

Memorandums of Understanding and Letters of Intent

MOUs and LOIs are precontract agreements that establish the intent of a party to buy products or services from or sell products or services to another party. Buyers commonly provide LOIs to sellers to encourage them to begin work—and incur cost—before awarding a contract.

Although not contracts, MOUs and LOIs are sometimes assumed to be contracts because they are written documents signed by one or more parties. Therefore, MOUs and LOIs should be used with caution. Many companies strongly discourage using MOUs and LOIs because of the problems that have developed as a result of the perception that an MOU or LOI was a contract.

SUMMARY

Contract pricing arrangements are important tools to transfer financial risk between contracting parties. Although most companies use simple firm-fixed-price contracts and, occasionally, time-and-materials contracts, more complex arrangements are available that may be more appropriate and effective. Use of contract incentives by buyers—to motivate sellers to accelerate delivery and improve performance—is increasing worldwide. Business professionals who manage contracts must understand the various contract pricing arrangements to select the most appropriate type for each situation.

CHAPTER **9**

THE
AWARD PHASE

The second phase in the contract management process, the award phase, encompasses critical activities for both buyer and seller. During this phase, the buyer selects a source for needed products or services, and the seller participates in contract negotiation and formation, where both parties negotiate the contract terms and conditions in an attempt to reach an agreement that incorporates their respective goals. This step is a particularly crucial one for the seller, who must make the most of this opportunity to sell its products or services. However, the buyer also has much at stake—a project that depends on those products or services for successful completion. Effective negotiation is an art that requires advanced knowledge, experience, and skill. Through effective negotiation, including using proven tools and techniques, win-win contracts that are in the best interests of both buyer and seller can be achieved. Figure 9-1 depicts the steps in the award phase for both buyer and seller.

Figure 9-1 Contract Management Process: Award Phase

Participating from the Buyer's Perspective

Source selection is a process of comparison and decision. The buyer must—

- Develop source selection evaluation criteria and procedures
- Obtain information about potential sources for the required goods or services
- Evaluate the potential sources
- Select the best source

The nature of the source selection process, the techniques for getting information, the procedures used in evaluation, and the decision-making methods vary from procurement to procurement, buyer to buyer, and industry to industry.

Buyer Step 4: Source Selection

Input	Tools & Techniques	Output
Proposals	Contract negotiation	Contracts
Evaluation criteria	Weighting system	
Evaluation standards	Screening system	
Organizational policies	Independent estimates	

Source selection entails receiving bids or proposals and applying evaluation criteria to select a provider. This process is seldom an uncomplicated one because–

■ Price may be the primary determinant for an off-the-shelf item, but the lowest proposed *price* may not be the lowest *cost* if the seller proves unable to deliver the product in a timely manner
■ Proposals are often separated into technical (approach) and commercial (price) sections, with each evaluated separately
■ Multiple sources may be required for critical products

Proposals may be simple, requiring only one person to evaluate the sources and select the best alternative; they may be complex, requiring a panel of experts. In fact, some proposal evaluations may require a consultant's assistance. But no matter the complexity, the following procedure must be followed:

Input

The input to source selection consists of the following items:

■ *Proposals:* The buyer will ultimately select a seller from among the proposals submitted in response to the solicitation.

■ *Evaluation criteria:* In the selection process, the buyer compares sources of goods and services and decides which one has the greatest potential for successful performance. Accomplishing this task requires applying evaluation criteria to assess the attributes offered by potential sellers. (See "Evaluation Criteria" later in this chapter for detailed information.)

- *Evaluation standards:* An evaluation standard is a gauge to measure a potential source against to determine its value. (See "Evaluation Standards" later in this chapter for detailed information.)

- *Organizational policies:* Determining the value of a product or service attribute requires having an organizational standard of value. Assume, for example, that one attribute in an automobile that a consumer thinks is important is how quickly it can accelerate from a stop to a speed of 100 kilometers per hour. Assume further that the consumer wants fast acceleration. The question is, when comparing different automobile models, what will the consumer consider to be a fast rate of acceleration? In other words, what is the consumer's standard for "fast"?

Tools and Techniques

The following tools and techniques are used for source selection:

- *Contract negotiation:* Contract negotiation involves clarification and mutual agreement on the structure and requirements of the contract before its signing. To the extent possible, final contract language should reflect all agreements reached. Subjects covered generally include, but are not limited to, responsibilities and authorities, applicable terms and law, technical and business management approaches, contract financing, and price. For complex procurement items, contract negotiation may be an independent process with input (such as an issues or open-items list) and output (such as an MOU) of its own.

- *Weighting system:* After selecting the attributes for evaluation and establishing evaluation standards, the next task is to determine the importance of each attribute relative to the others. (See "Weighting System" later in this chapter for specific information.)

Assume that the prospective buyer of a product decides that price and quality are the attributes of interest and that quality is more than twice as important as price. Accordingly, the buyer assigns quality a fixed weight of 0.70 and price a fixed weight of 0.30. However, after receiving the proposals, the buyer discovers that the quality differences among the proposed products are small but that the differences in price are relatively large. Under these circumstances, the assigned fixed weights could result in the buyer's paying a premium for a relatively small quality gain. When comparing the actual ranges of variance, the buyer may decide that price is more important than quality in making the final decision.

■ *Screening system:* A screening system is used to process the information about potential sources. The buyer must read and analyze the information, apply the appropriate standards, and assign scores that express how well or how poorly each proposal measures up. Depending on the amount of information to be analyzed and the technical complexity of the requirement, this work might be performed by a purchasing agent or a panel of experts.

If the procurement is complex enough to warrant establishing a panel of experts, the evaluators on the panel should include someone from the buyer's organization who will ultimately use the product or service and someone from the buyer's purchasing office. Additional advice may be needed from accountants and attorneys. In some cases, the buyer may need to hire consultants to provide technical assistance. All evaluators should be thoroughly familiar with the specification, statement of work, and evaluation criteria.

Before the evaluation begins, the buyer must decide how the evaluators will present their findings, to whom, and what kind of documentation they will prepare. The process should be kept as simple as possible. To ensure the confidentiality of information received from competing sources, many organizations require that the evaluators communicate with the sources under consideration only through the purchasing department.

■ *Independent estimates:* Using consultants or outside experts to help in this process is common and can be of great value.

Output

The output of the source selection step is the contract.

Evaluation Criteria

Developing the evaluation criteria for source selection requires three prerequisites. First, the buyer must understand what goods or services it wants to buy. Second, the buyer must understand the industry that will provide the required goods or services. And third, the buyer must understand the market practices of that industry. Market research provides this information.

During requirements analysis and development of the specification or statement of work, the buyer gains an understanding of the required products or services. Understanding the industry means learning about the attributes of the goods or services in question and the firms that make them: What features do those goods or services have? What processes are used to produce or render them? What kinds and quantities of labor and capital are required? What are the cash requirements? Understanding the market means learning about the behavior of buyers and sellers: What are the pricing practices of the market, and what is the range of prices charged? What are the usual terms and conditions of sale?

After gaining an understanding of these issues, the buyer is ready to develop the evaluation criteria by selecting attributes for evaluation.

Attributes

A consumer shopping for an automobile does not evaluate an automobile, per se, but rather selected attributes of the automobile, such as acceleration, speed, handling, comfort, safety, price, fuel mileage, capacity, appearance, and so forth. The evaluation of the automobile is the sum of the evaluations of its attributes.

An automobile has many attributes, but not all are worthwhile subjects of evaluation. The attributes of interest are those that the consumer thinks are important for satisfaction. The attributes that one consumer thinks are important may be inconsequential to another.

In most procurements, multiple criteria will be required for successful performance, for the following reasons: First, buyers usually have more than one objective; for example, many buyers look for both good quality and low price. Second, attributes essential for one objective may be different from those essential for others; for example, in buying an automobile, the attributes essential for comfort have little to do with those essential for quick acceleration.

To complicate matters further, some criteria will likely be incompatible with others. The attributes essential to high quality may be inconsistent with low price; high performance, for example, may be incompatible with low operating cost. Thus, for any one source to have the maximum desired value of every essential attribute— for example, highest quality combined with lowest price—may be impossible. If so, the buyer must make trade-offs among attributes when deciding which source is best. These are considerations that make source selection a problem in *multiple attribute decision making*, which requires special decision analysis techniques. *

As a rule, source selection attributes fall into three general categories relating to the sources themselves, as entities; the products or services they offer; and the prices they offer. Thus, the buyer must have criteria for each category that reflect the buyer's ideas about what is valuable. The criteria concerning the sources themselves, as entities, are the *management criteria*; the criteria concerning the products or services offered are the *technical criteria*; and the criteria concerning the prices of the products or services are the *price criteria*.

Management Criteria

In the contracting process, the buyer enters a relationship with a seller, and each party exchanges promises about what it will do for the other in the future. Thus, when comparing sources, the buyer must determine which entity would make the best partner. Management criteria relate to this set of attributes.

---

* For more information about multiple attribute decision-making techniques, consult the following references: Ching-Lai Hwang and Kwangsun Yoon, *Multiple Attribute Decision Making Methods and Applications: A State-of-the-Art Survey* (Berlin: Springer-Verlag, 1981); Paul Goodwin and George Wright, *Decision Analysis for Management Judgment* (Chichester, England: John Wiley & Sons Ltd., 1991); and Thomas Saaty, *Decision Making for Leaders: The Analytic Hierarchy Process for Decisions in a Complex World* (Pittsburgh, Pa.: RWS Publications, 1995).

The specific attributes that will make for a good partner and the relative emphasis the buyer should place on them will depend on the buyer's contractual objectives and the practices in the industry and marketplace. Nevertheless, certain categories of attributes should always be considered, such as reputation for good performance, technical capability, qualifications of key managerial personnel, capabilities of facilities and equipment, capacity, financial strength, labor relations, and location.

Technical Criteria

In response to the buyer's solicitation, each potential source will likely offer the buyer something that is somewhat different or offer the same product or service as the others but propose to use different production or performance procedures. If these differences are significant enough to affect the source's prospects for success, the buyer must compare them to determine their relative merits. The buyer must develop criteria to evaluate *what* each source will do or deliver and *how* each source will proceed with the work—in other words, determine product or service quality and procedural effectiveness. These attributes are called technical criteria.

The precise nature of the technical criteria will depend on the specification or statement of work. If the solicitation specifies all aspects of product design or service performance, the buyer will not have to develop further criteria to evaluate what the source will do or deliver. However, the buyer may want to evaluate proposed production plans, policies, procedures, and techniques to decide which source is most likely to do the best job. However, if the buyer specifies only function or performance, it also must evaluate each proposal to determine which proposed product or service will satisfy the requirement and which will do it best. The buyer's criteria should reflect the significant attributes of function or performance.

Price Criteria

Besides evaluating management and technical attributes, the buyer must evaluate the reasonableness of each proposed price, in terms of realism and competitiveness:

- *Realism:* Regarding whether a proposed price is too low, realism is determined by evaluating consistency among a potential source's management, technical, and price proposals. The question is whether a source's proposed price entails too much risk given what the source's qualifications are as a company, what it has promised to do, and what methods it has proposed to use. Risk affects behavior, often in undesirable ways. If a price is too low, entailing too much risk, the seller may fail to achieve project objectives. Therefore, each proposal must be analyzed to determine whether the proposed price allows for sufficient resources to do the job. The technique used to evaluate realism is *cost analysis.*

The prices of commercial goods and services, however, are not necessarily determined entirely by the cost of their manufacture or performance, at least in the short term. Thus, a source may offer something for sale at prices set below cost for various sound business reasons. Still, the buyer must investigate if a price seems too low; otherwise, the risk of poor performance may become a reality.

- *Competitiveness:* Competitiveness refers to whether a proposed price is too high compared with what is available in the marketplace. Competitiveness is evaluated by comparing each proposed price to the others and to other pricing information. The technique used to evaluate competitiveness is *price analysis.*

Qualitative vs. Quantitative Evaluation Criteria

The source selection evaluation criteria describe a level of value that must be met. Some values may be stated *quantitatively*, such as size, weight, speed, mean-time-between-failure, mean-time-to-repair, and price. Other values must be stated *qualitatively*, using words rather than numbers (unless the buyer is willing to go to great effort to develop quantitative expressions of them). Examples include attractiveness, experience, and comfort.

Theorists of decision making sometimes refer to qualitative criteria as "fuzzy" criteria, and they have developed various ways to convert qualitative judgments to quantitative expressions. One example is the scale used to evaluate the taste of food samples. Quantitative criteria are generally easier to use, but qualitative criteria are frequently unavoidable.

Evaluation Standards

Three types of evaluation standards—*absolute*, *minimum*, and *relative*—express values. The main difference between these three types of standards is the amount of information required to establish them and the kind of information they provide to the buyer.

Absolute Standards

Absolute standards include both the maximum and the minimum acceptable values. When a buyer uses an absolute standard during evaluation, the performance of the source being rated is compared to the standard to determine the absolute value of its performance. For example, assume an absolute standard for price that ranges from no cost, the best value, to $5 million, the worst value. A potential source's proposed price of $4.5 million can be compared to the standard to determine its absolute value.

If the buyer's utility for price is a straight-line function, a source whose proposed price is $4.5 million could earn 10 out of 100 value points, a source whose price is $4 million could earn 20 points, and a source whose price is $2 million could earn 60 points. Each point score tells the buyer absolutely how good or bad the price is relative to the buyer's standard of value and relative to the other potential sources.

The problem with an absolute standard is that the buyer needs a great deal of information to develop an absolute range of values. The buyer must know the highest preference level as well as the lowest. The evaluation result may not be worth the effort of developing this information.

Minimum Standards

A minimum, or ratio, standard requires only that the buyer know the minimum acceptable level of performance. Each potential source is compared to that minimum, and the source with the highest level of acceptable performance receives the highest score, 100 on a scale of 0 to 100. Sources that do not meet the minimum standard are eliminated. All other sources are scored in comparison to the best.

Assume that the highest acceptable price for a product or service is $5 million. Assume that of all potential sources, the one with a price of $2 million is considered the best. That source receives a score of 100 points. A source whose price is $4 million could receive a score of 33 points, and one whose price is $4.5 million could receive a score of 17 points.

The advantage of the minimum standard over the absolute standard is that the buyer needs less information. The obvious disadvantage is that the evaluation scores will not tell the buyer absolutely how good or bad each alternative is.

Relative Standards

A relative standard entails direct comparison of each potential source to the others to determine which is best and which is worst. The best source receives the maximum number of points, 100 on a scale of 0 to 100. The worst receives no points. Having established the best and the worst alternatives, the buyer can construct a graph to determine the scores of the sources that fall between them. Those scores also can be determined mathematically.

Using a relative scale to score the same prices described in the example used for minimum standards, the $2 million price would receive 100 points, the $4.5 million price would receive no points, and the $4 million price would receive 20 points.

The relative standard requires the least amount of advance information on the part of the buyer. Scores developed on a relative standard tell the buyer how good or bad each source is relative to the others but not how good or bad it is absolutely. Nevertheless, this information will be sufficient for many source selections.

Weighting System

The evaluation of each source will be the sum of the evaluations of its individual attributes. The scores initially assigned to attributes during the evaluation will not reflect differences in importance among the attributes. The scores will be *raw* (unweighted). The decision to add the raw scores together to determine the value of the source is tantamount to a decision that each attribute is equally important. But such may not be the case. If some attributes are more important than others, the buyer must assign a weight to each.

Assume that a consumer decides that the relevant attributes in an automobile are acceleration, maximum speed, attractiveness, price, and fuel mileage. If any of these is more important than the others, the raw scores must be weighted to take that fact into account before adding the scores. The weights will reflect the consumer's trade-off decisions among the various attributes and will affect the final determination of which automobile is the best.

The buyer may establish either *fixed weights* or *variable weights.* Fixed weights are established before receiving the proposals and do not change. Variable weights are established only after determining the raw scores. Variable weights allow for making trade-offs when comparing the ranges of actual performance among the alternatives.

PARTICIPATING FROM THE SELLER'S PERSPECTIVE

The process involves having your bid or proposal evaluated by the buyer, anticipating and responding to questions the buyer may have, negotiating, and forming a contract between the parties.

Seller Step 4: Contract Negotiation and Formation

Input	Tools & Techniques	Output
Solicitation	Contract negotiation process	Contract or
Bid or proposal	Highly skilled negotiators	Walk away
Buyer's source selection process	Market and industry practices	
Seller's past performances	Legal review	
Previous contracts		
Competitive analysis report		

Contract negotiation is the process by which two or more competent parties reach an agreement to buy or sell products or services. Contract negotiation may be conducted formally or informally and may involve many people or just two—a representative for the buyer and a representative for the seller. Contract negotiation may take a few minutes or may involve many discussions over days, months, or years.

The desired result of the contract negotiation process is a contract. Contract formation is the process of putting together the essential elements of the contract and any special items unique to a particular business agreement.

Input

The input to contract negotiation and formation consists of the following items:

- *Solicitation:* The solicitation is either an oral or written request for an offer (RFP, RFQ, ITB, and so on) prepared by the buyer and provided to one or more potential sellers.

- *Bid or proposal:* The bid or proposal is either an oral or written offer by potential sellers to provide products or services to the buyer, usually in response to a solicitation.

- *Buyer's source selection process:* Source selection is the process by which a buyer selects a seller or source of supply for products or services. Buyers typically apply evaluation criteria to select the best seller to meet their needs. (See "Buyer Step 4: Source Selection" earlier in this chapter.)

- *Seller's past performance:* The past performance of a seller is often a critical aspect of contract negotiation. Has the seller delivered previous products and services on time? Has the seller provided high-quality products and services?

  Past performance can be seen as a separate evaluation factor or as a subfactor under technical excellence or management capability. Using the past performance history also reduces the emphasis on merely being able to write a good proposal.

- *Previous contracts:* Has the seller provided products or services to this buyer in the past? If so, what did the previous contract say? How was it negotiated? Who negotiated it?

- *Competitive analysis report:* The competitive analysis report provides a written summary of the seller's competitors and their respective strengths and weaknesses compared to the seller's.

Tools and Techniques

The following tools and techniques are used for contract negotiation and formation:

■ *Contract negotiation process:* The contract negotiation process is discussed in detail in "The Contract Negotiation Process" later in this chapter.

■ *Highly skilled negotiators:* Conducting contract negotiation is a complex activity that requires a broad range of skills. Providing negotiators with the best available training in contract negotiation is vital. Top negotiators help their companies save money and make significant profits.

■ *Market and industry practices:* Knowing what the competitors are offering (most-favored pricing, warranties, product discounts, volume discounts, and so on) is essential for a successful outcome to negotiation.

■ *Legal review:* A legal review should be conducted, if not as a regular part of the contract negotiation process, then at least for all key contracts.

Output

■ *Contract:* The output from contract negotiation and formation may be the contract, which is both a document and a relationship between parties.

Or it may be best to—

■ *Walk away:* Do not agree to a bad deal. No business is better than bad business.

The Contract Negotiation Process

The contract negotiation process comprises planning, conducting, and documenting the negotiation and forming the contract. Table 9-1 describes an effective, logical approach to plan, conduct, and document contract negotiations based on the proven best practices of world-class organizations.

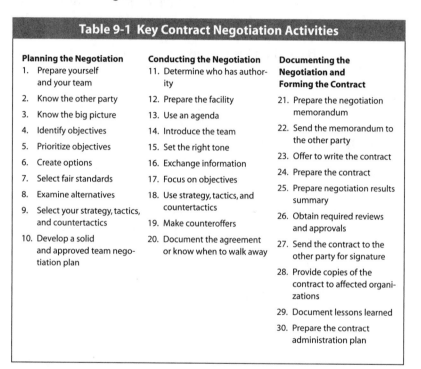

Table 9-1 Key Contract Negotiation Activities		
Planning the Negotiation	**Conducting the Negotiation**	**Documenting the Negotiation and Forming the Contract**
1. Prepare yourself and your team	11. Determine who has authority	21. Prepare the negotiation memorandum
2. Know the other party	12. Prepare the facility	22. Send the memorandum to the other party
3. Know the big picture	13. Use an agenda	23. Offer to write the contract
4. Identify objectives	14. Introduce the team	24. Prepare the contract
5. Prioritize objectives	15. Set the right tone	25. Prepare negotiation results summary
6. Create options	16. Exchange information	26. Obtain required reviews and approvals
7. Select fair standards	17. Focus on objectives	27. Send the contract to the other party for signature
8. Examine alternatives	18. Use strategy, tactics, and countertactics	28. Provide copies of the contract to affected organizations
9. Select your strategy, tactics, and countertactics	19. Make counteroffers	29. Document lessons learned
10. Develop a solid and approved team negotiation plan	20. Document the agreement or know when to walk away	30. Prepare the contract administration plan

Planning the Negotiation

The following activities are performed to plan the negotiation:

1. *Prepare yourself and your team:* Ensure that the lead negotiator knows both his or her personal and professional strengths, weaknesses, and tendencies as well as those of other team members. (Many self-assessment tools are available, including the Myers-Briggs Type Indicator® assessment. It can provide helpful insight on how an individual may react in a situation because of personal or professional tendencies.) Preparing a list of the strengths and weaknesses of team members can be an important first step in negotiation planning. (See Appendix A Form 4.)

2. *Know the other party:* Intelligence gathering is vital to successful negotiation planning. Create a checklist of things to know about the other party to help the team prepare for negotiation. (See Appendix A Form 5.)

3. *Know the big picture:* In the words of Stephen R. Covey, author of *The Seven Habits of Highly Effective People,* "begin with the end in mind." Keep focused on the primary objectives. Be aware that the ability of either party to be flexible on some issues may be limited because of internal policies, budgets, or organizational politics.

   One of the proven best practices to keep the negotiation focused is using interim summaries. The key is not to get caught up in small, unimportant details that take the negotiation off track.

4. *Identify objectives:* Know what both you and the other party want to accomplish. (See Appendix A Form 6.) Successful negotiators know that nearly everything affects price, as illustrated in Figure 9–2: changes in schedule, technology, services, terms and conditions, customer obligations, contract type, products, and other contracting elements affect contract price.

Figure 9-2 Importance of Price

5. *Prioritize objectives:* Although all terms and conditions are important, some are clearly more important than others. Prioritize your objectives to help you remain focused during negotiation. (See Appendix A Form 7.) Figure 9–3 shows that various terms and conditions affect cost, risk, and value.

6. *Create options:* Creative problem solving is a critical skill of successful negotiators. Seek to expand options; do not assume that only one solution exists to every problem. Conducting team brainstorming sessions to develop a list of options to achieve negotiation objectives is a proven best practice of many world-class organizations. (See Appendix A Form 8.)

7. *Select fair standards:* Successful negotiators avoid a contest of wills by turning an argument into a joint search for a fair solution, using fair standards independent of either side's will. Use standards such as the–
   ■ Uniform Commercial Code
   ■ United Nations Convention on Contracts for the International Sale of Goods
   ■ American Arbitration Association standards
   ■ ISO 9000 quality standards
   ■ State, local, and federal laws
   ■ Market or industry standards

8. *Examine alternatives:* Prepare in advance your alternatives to the important negotiation issues or objectives. Successful negotiators know their best-case, most-likely, and worst-case (walk-away) alternatives for all major objectives. (See Appendix A Form 9.)

9. *Select your strategy, tactics, and countertactics:* Negotiation strategies provide the overall framework that will guide how you conduct your negotiation. Negotiation strategies can be divided into two types: win-lose and win-win.

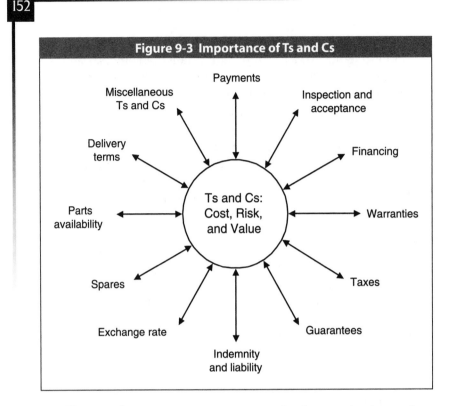

Figure 9-3 Importance of Ts and Cs

Payments

Miscellaneous Ts and Cs

Inspection and acceptance

Delivery terms

Financing

Parts availability

Ts and Cs: Cost, Risk, and Value

Warranties

Spares

Taxes

Exchange rate

Guarantees

Indemnity and liability

The win-lose negotiation strategy is about winning today, despite the potential long-term effect tomorrow and beyond. Common characteristics of the win-lose strategy include concealing one's own position and interests, discovering the other party's position and interests, weakening the other party's resolve, and causing the other party to modify its position or accept your position on all key issues. Although the win-lose negotiation strategy is not a politically correct approach, it is a commonly used negotiation strategy worldwide.

The win-win negotiation strategy is about creative joint problem solving, which develops long-term successful business relationships. The win-win negotiation strategy, however, may sometimes be difficult to accomplish. Among the obstacles to developing the win-win business environment are previous adverse buyer-seller relations, lack of training in joint problem solving and conflict resolution, and complex and highly regulated contracting procedures in some organizations, especially large companies and government agencies.

Winning or losing a contract negotiation is, indeed, a matter of perspective, which is based on your knowledge, experience, and judgment. The only way to know whether you have won or lost a negotiation is to compare the results to your negotiation plan. Did you get what you wanted? Is what you got closer to your best-case, most-likely, or worst-case alternative? Clearly, without a contract negotiation plan, you have no basis against which to evaluate the negotiation outcome.

To achieve your desired contract negotiation results, you need not only a strategy, but also tactics and countertactics, which are a means to a desired end. The key to using tactics successfully is to know what they are, identify the tactic when it is being used, and know how best to counter the tactic.

Table 9–2 presents some common tactics and countertactics used in contract negotiation.

Table 9-2 Negotiation Tactics and Countertactics

Tactics	Countertactics
	■ Disclose the attack
Attacks (personal insults, emotional reactions, professional insults)	■ Strike back ■ Give in ■ Break off ■ Explore alternatives
Tricks (false data, no authority to negotiate)	■ Know the truth (have the right data, establish in writing who has authority) ■ Escalate
Arbitrary deadlines	■ Agree with deadline ■ Counter the offer with compromise schedule
Limited availability	■ Refuse to change schedule ■ Coordinate schedules in advance ■ Counter with your limited availability ■ Be flexible ■ Escalate
Third-party scapegoat (third-party approval required, pretending that such approval is required)	■ Escalate to third party ■ Compromise
Giveaways	■ Disclose them as giveaways ■ Exchange giveaways
Good guy–bad guy	■ Counter with bad guy–good guy ■ Escalate
Prolonging the negotiation	■ Take a break or have a caucus ■ Maintain silence
Delays (submission of data, start of negotiation, return from breaks)	■ Start on time ■ Claim limited availability ■ Leave or create greater delays
Diversions (questions, telephone calls, fax messages, personal breaks)	■ Keep things on track (refocus the team, have no phones in the room, allow no interruptions) ■ Take a break
Stonewall ("take it or leave it," "I shall not move")	■ Give in ■ Say "Yes, and…" ■ Walk away ■ Escalate
End-of-quarter or end-of-year negotiation pressure [management wants to spend money now (buyer) or get the deal now (seller)]	■ Settle next quarter or next year (do not let time pressure you into a bad deal)

Many other negotiation tactics and countertactics are available. Those listed in the table will provide a basis for discussing good and bad tactics and countertactics that may be used by either party while conducting the negotiation.

10. *Develop a solid and approved team negotiation plan:* The conclusion of contract negotiation planning should be the summary and documentation of all planned actions. If necessary, have the negotiation plan reviewed and approved by higher management to ensure that all planned actions are in the best interests of the organization. (See Appendix A Form 10.)

Conducting the Negotiation

The following activities are necessary to conduct the negotiation:

11. *Determine who has authority:* If possible, before the negotiation, determine who has the authority to negotiate for each party. At the start of the negotiation, ensure that you know who has that authority, who the lead negotiator is for the other party, and what limits, if any, are placed on the other party's authority.

12. *Prepare the facility:* Most buyers want to conduct the negotiation at their offices to provide them with a sense of control. Try to conduct the negotiation at a neutral site, such as a hotel or conference center.

Other key facility considerations include the—

- Size of the room
- Use of break-out rooms
- Lighting
- Tables (size, shape, and arrangement)
- Seating arrangements
- Use of audiovisual aids
- Schedule (day and time)
- Access to telephone, fax, restrooms, food, and drink

13. *Use an agenda:* A proven best practice of successful negotiators worldwide is creating and using an agenda for the negotiation. Provide the agenda to the other party before the negotiation begins. (See Appendix A Form 11.) An effective agenda helps a negotiator to—

- Set the right tone
- Control the exchange of information
- Keep the focus on the objectives
- Manage time
- Obtain the desired results

14. *Introduce the team:* Introduce your team members, or have team members make brief self-introductions. Try to establish a common bond with the other party as soon as possible.

15. *Set the right tone:* After introductions, make a brief statement to express your team strategy to the other party. Set the desired climate for contract negotiation from the start.

16. *Exchange information:* Conducting contract negotiation is all about communication. Be aware that information is exchanged both orally and through body language, visual aids (pictures, diagrams, photographs, or videotapes), and active listening.

17. *Focus on objectives:* Never lose sight of the big picture.

18. *Use strategy, tactics, and countertactics:* Do what you said you were going to do, but be flexible to achieve your objectives. Anticipate the other party's tactics, and plan your countertactics. Adjust them as necessary.

19. *Make counteroffers:* A vital part of conducting the negotiation is providing substitute offers, or counteroffers, when the other party does not accept what you are offering. Document all offers and counteroffers to ensure that both parties understand any changes in the terms and conditions. (See Appendix A Form 12.)

20. *Document the agreement or know when to walk away:* Take time throughout the negotiation to take notes on what was agreed to between the parties. If possible, assign one team member to take minutes. To ensure proper documentation, periodi-

cally summarize agreements on all major issues throughout the negotiation. At the end of the negotiation, summarize your agreements both orally and in writing. (See Appendix A Form 13.) If a settlement is not reached, document the areas of agreement and disagreement. If possible, plan a future meeting to resolve differences.

Remember: Do not agree to a bad deal—learn to say, "No thank you," and walk away.

Documenting the Negotiation and Forming the Contract

The following activities are conducted to document the negotiation and form the contract.

21. *Prepare the negotiation memorandum (minutes or notes):* Document what was discussed during the negotiation. After having the memorandum word processed, spell checked, and edited, have it reviewed by someone within your organization who attended the negotiation and someone who did not. Then determine whether they have a similar understanding.

22. *Send the memorandum to the other party:* As promptly as possible, provide a copy of your documented understanding of the contract negotiation to the other party. First, e-mail or fax it to the other party. Then send an original copy by either overnight or 2-day mail. Verify that the other party receives your negotiation memorandum by following up with an e-mail or telephone call.

23. *Offer to write the contract:* As the seller, offer to draft the agreement so that you can put the issues in your own words. Today, most contracts are developed using electronic databases, which facilitate reviews, changes, and new submissions.

24. *Prepare the contract:* Writing a contract should be a team effort with an experienced contract management professional at the lead. Typically, automated standard organizational forms, modified as needed, are used with standard terms and conditions that were tailored during negotiation. At other times, a contract must be written in full. Ensure that no elements of the contract are missing. (See Appendix A Form 14.) After the initial contract draft, obtain all appropriate reviews and approvals, preferably through electronic data.

25. *Prepare negotiation results summary:* Prepare an internal-use-only summary of key negotiation items that have changed since originally proposed. Many organizations have found such a summary to be a valuable tool for explaining changes to senior managers.

26. *Obtain required reviews and approvals:* Depending on your organizational procedures, products, services, and other variables, one or more people may be required to review and approve the proposed contract before signature. Typically, the following departments or staff review a contract: project management, financial, legal, procurement or contract management, and senior management. Increasingly, organizations are using automated systems to draft contracts and transmit them internally for the needed reviews and approvals.

27. *Send the contract to the other party for signature:* Send a copy of the contract to the other party via e-mail or fax, and then follow up with two mailed original copies. With all copies include an appropriate cover letter with a return mail address and time/date suspense for prompt return. Verify receipt of the contract by phone or e-mail. Today, many organizations, as well as the laws of many nations, recognize an electronic signature to be valid.

28. *Provide copies of the contract to affected organizations:* The contract is awarded officially after it is executed, signed by both parties, and delivered to both parties. Ensure that all other affected organizations or parties receive a copy.

29. *Document lessons learned:* Take the time to document everything that went well during the contract negotiation process. Even more important, document what did not go well and why, and what should be done to avoid those problems in the future.

30. *Prepare the contract administration plan:* At the end of the contract negotiation process, follow a proven best practice by having the team that negotiated the contract help the team that is responsible for administering it develop a contract administration plan.

Best Practices: 45 Actions to Improve Results

Buyer (Source Selection)

- Know what you want—lowest price or best value
- State your requirements in performance terms and evaluate accordingly
- Conduct market research about potential sources before selection
- Evaluate potential sources promptly and dispassionately
- Follow the evaluation criteria stated in the solicitation: management, technical, and price
- Use absolute, minimum, or relative evaluation standards to measure performance as stated in your solicitation
- Develop organizational policies to guide and facilitate the source selection process
- Use a weighting system to determine which evaluation criteria are most important
- Use a screening system to prequalify sources
- Obtain independent estimates from consultants or outside experts to assist in source selection
- Use past performance as a key aspect of source selection, and verify data accuracy
- Conduct price realism analysis
- Conduct competitiveness price analysis
- Create a competitive analysis report
- Use oral presentations of proposals by sellers to improve and expedite the source selection process

Buyer and Seller (Contract Negotiation and Formation)

- Understand that contract negotiation is a process, usually involving a team effort
- Select and train highly skilled negotiators to lead the contract negotiation process
- Know market and industry practices
- Prepare yourself and your team
- Know the other party
- Know the big picture
- Identify and prioritize objectives
- Create options—be flexible in your planning
- Examine alternatives
- Select your negotiation strategy, tactics, and countertactics
- Develop a solid and approved team negotiation plan

- Determine who has the authority to negotiate
- Prepare the negotiation facility at your location or at a neutral site
- Use an agenda during contract negotiation
- Set the right tone at the start of the negotiation
- Maintain your focus on your objectives
- Use interim summaries to keep on track
- Do not be too predictable in your tactics
- Document your agreement throughout the process
- Know when to walk away
- Offer to write the contract
- Prepare a negotiation results summary
- Obtain required reviews and approvals
- Provide copies of the contract to all affected parties
- Document negotiation lessons learned and best practices
- Prepare a transition plan for contract administration
- Understand that everything affects price
- Understand that Ts and Cs have cost, risk, and value
- Tailor Ts and Cs to the deal, but understand the financial effects on price and profitability
- Know what is negotiable and what is not

SUMMARY

Source selection is a matter of the buyer's choosing the right seller for the situation. However, the process used to accomplish this varies dramatically depending on the company, the products or services involved, the complexity of the procurement, and many other factors. The current trend is to spend more time planning and conducting source selection to obtain the best source of supply and then to establish a long-term contract. Thus, fewer source selection efforts are needed.

Contract negotiation and formation are keys to the success of sellers worldwide. When skilled contract negotiators follow a proven process approach, successful business agreements are reached. Through effective contract formation practices, win-win contracts are developed and documented, yielding beneficial results for both parties.

CHAPTER 10

THE POSTAWARD PHASE

The final phase in the contract management process, postaward, consists of contract administration and contract closeout or termination for both the buyer and the seller. Contract administration can be straightforward or complex, depending on the nature and size of the project. Administering a contract entails monitoring it throughout the many, varied activities that can occur during project execution. Key contract administration activities are monitoring compliance with contract terms and conditions, practicing effective communication and control, managing contract changes, invoicing and payment, and resolving claims and disputes. Appropriate contract administration procedures are essential to ensure that both parties know what is expected of them at all times; to avoid unpleasant surprises regarding requirements, costs, or schedule; and to solve problems quickly when they occur. Contract closeout entails taking care of all last-minute details and officially bringing the contract to an end. Figure 10-1 illustrates these steps in the postaward phase.

Figure 10-1 Contract Management Process: Postaward Phase

Phase 1: Preaward

Buyer — 1. Procurement planning → 2. Solicitation planning → 3. Solicitation

Seller — 1. Presales activity → 2. Bid/no-bid decision making → 3. Bid or proposal preparation

Phase 2: Award / **Phase 3: Postaward**

Buyer — 4. Source selection → 5. Contract administration → 6. Contract closeout or termination

Seller — 4. Contract negotiation and formation → 5. Contract administration → 6. Contract closeout or termination

DEFINING CONTRACT ADMINISTRATION

Contract administration is the process of ensuring that each party's performance meets contractual requirements. On larger projects with multiple product and service providers, a key aspect of contract administration is managing the interfaces among the various providers. Because of the legal nature of the contractual relationship, the project team must be acutely aware of the legal implications of actions taken when administering the contract.

The principal objective of contract administration is the same for both parties—to ensure the fulfillment of the contractual obligations by all the parties to the contract. If the parties are individuals, this task is a matter of self-discipline. However, when organizations are involved, the problem is more complicated. Organizations must perform as systems, integrating the efforts of many people who compose the components of the organization. Thus, for organizations to function efficiently requires communication and control, which is the primary task of contract administration.

Effective contract administration is critical to effective project management, because an organization's failure to fulfill its contractual obligations could have legal consequences. Thus, someone must observe performance of contractual obligations. That person is the contract manager, who must always be aware of the legal consequences of an action or a failure to act and who must take steps to ensure that required actions are taken and prohibited actions are avoided. In a real sense, a contract manager is a project manager, and the principles of project management apply to his or her work.

Each party to the contract appoints a contract manager, who monitors not only his or her own organization but also the other party to ensure that both parties are keeping their promises. The contract manager must maintain these two perspectives throughout contract performance.

Buyer and Seller Step 5: Contract Administration

Input	Tools & Techniques	Output
Contract	Contract analysis and planning	Documentation
Work results		Contract changes
Change requests	Preperformance conference	Payment
Invoices and payments		Completion of work
Contract administration policies	Performance measuring and reporting	
	Payment system	
	Change control system	
	Dispute management system	

Contract administration includes applying the appropriate project management processes to the contractual relationships and integrating the output from these processes into the general management of the project.

Input

Input to contract administration consists of the following items:

- *Contract:* The contract document is the primary guide for administering the contract.
- *Work results:* The results of performing the requirement will affect the administration of the contract.

- *Change requests:* Change requests are a common element of most contracts. An effective process for managing change must be in place to ensure that all requests are handled smoothly. Changes may be called amendments, modifications, add-ons, up-scopes, or down-scopes. Changes are opportunities either to increase or decrease profitability for the seller. Changes are a necessary aspect of business for buyers, because of changes in their needs.

- *Invoices and payments:* An efficient process must be developed for handling invoices and payments throughout contract administration. Few areas cause more concern to sellers than late payment. Buyers can realize savings by developing an efficient and timely payment process, because sellers are often willing to give discounts for early payment.

- *Contract administration policies:* Although the specific policies that will apply to contract administration depend on the contracting parties, four policies are key: compliance with contract terms and conditions, effective internal and external communication and control, effective control of contract changes, and effective resolution of claims and disputes. * These policies will be discussed further in this chapter in "Contract Administration Policies."

Tools and Techniques

The following tools and techniques are used for contract administration:

■ *Contract analysis and planning:* Before the award of a contract, each party should develop a contract administration plan and assign the responsibility of administering the contract to a contract manager. To whom should the job be assigned? A project manager could do double duty as contract manager. However in most large companies, contract administration is a specialized function, usually performed by someone in the contracting department, because doing the job will require special knowledge and training.

Contract administration is an element of both contract management and project management. If the project is under a contract, then project management and contract administration will overlap considerably, depending on how the company defines those terms. If the project is not under a contract but contracts to obtain goods and services essential to project implementation, contract administration will be a smaller element of project management.

Assume for the moment that a project is under a contract and that the project manager and contract manager are different people. What should their relationship be? Although organizations divide the responsibilities differently (as discussed in Chapter 4, "Teamwork–Roles and Responsibilities"), in general the project manager will have overall responsibility for executing the project, and the contract manager will oversee the contractual aspects of the project. The contract manager's special knowledge and training about contracts will be an asset to the project manager. Whether the contract manager

---

* This book uses the word *claim* to refer to a demand by one party to the contract for something from the other party, usually but not necessarily for more money or more time. Claims are usually based on an argument that the party making the demand is entitled to an adjustment by virtue of the contract terms or some violation of those terms by the other party. The word does not imply any disagreement between the parties, although claims often *lead* to disagreements. This book uses the term *dispute* to refer to disagreements that have become intractable.

reports to the project manager or to someone else will depend on whether the work is organized along project, functional, or matrix lines of authority.

In anticipation of contract award, the project manager and contract manager should analyze the terms and conditions of the prospective contract and develop a work breakdown structure that reflects both the technical and administrative aspects of contract performance. They should then determine which departments of the organization will be affected by those terms and conditions.

Many department managers will be affected by contract terms and conditions. Consider, for example, the following clause from a services contract:

Fitness of Employees

Seller shall employ on or in connection with the Project only persons who are fit and skilled for the Project. Should any objectionable person be employed by Seller, Seller shall, upon request of ABC Company, cause such person to be removed from the Project.

Clauses of this type are not unusual in services contracts, particularly when the work will be performed at the buyer's facility. The clause is not unreasonable, and to many it would even seem innocuous. Not so, however, because this clause has potentially great significance to a company's human resources department and for labor relations in general. The human resources department may have specific procedures for removing an employee from an assignment. Therefore, the project manager and contract manager should contact that department to discuss the contract and the appropriate personnel procedures to be followed.

The project manager and contract manager must meet with the managers of all affected departments to inform them of the contract, the terms and conditions related to their operations, and contract administration policies and procedures. In some companies, the department managers will already know about the contract and will have made preliminary preparations for performance. In others, they will not have been informed and may be completely unprepared for what they must do.

The project manager and contract manager should try to reach agreement on intermediate performance goals with each manager who has performance responsibility. Intermediate goals will enable the contract manager and the functional manager to measure progress, detect significant performance variances, take corrective action, and follow up. Of course, performance goals must reflect contract performance obligations.

The project manager, contract manager, and other business managers also must decide how and when to measure and report actual performance. The techniques, timing, and frequency of measurement and reporting should reflect the nature and criticality of the work. A reasonable balance must be struck between excessive reporting and no measurement or reporting of any kind. Department managers may see these requirements as nuisances that are of little value to themselves.

The realities of contract administration, however, are often quite different from the ideal situation. First, most companies devote more effort to source selection and contract formation than to contract administration. Project commencement often depends on contract award, so more resources are devoted to startup than to oversight. Second, in performing these tasks, the project manager and contract manager will face all the challenges that confront all project managers, but their responsibility may not come with formal authority. In many companies, department managers simply do not appreciate the importance of contracts and contract administration and will resent the imposition of what they see as additional performance burdens. Third, the project manager and contract manager may not have the luxury of working on only one project or contract at a time. Nevertheless, a reasonable effort must be made to ensure that all personnel recognize their responsibilities under the contract and attempt to ensure that those responsibilities are fulfilled.

■ *Preperformance conference:* Before performance begins, the buyer and the seller should meet to discuss their joint administration of the contract. The meeting should be formal; an agenda should be distributed in advance, and minutes should be taken and distributed. Each party should appoint a person who will be its organization's official voice during contract performance. At the meeting, the parties should review the contract terms and conditions and discuss who will do what. They also should establish protocols for written and oral communication and for progress measurement and reporting and discuss procedures for managing change and resolving differences. Buyer and seller department managers who will have performance responsibilities should attend the preperformance conference or, at the least, send a representative. Important subcontractors also should be represented. The meeting should be held at the performance site, if possible. (See Appendix A Form 15 for a checklist of items to do before and after a preperformance conference.)

■ *Performance measuring and reporting:* During contract administration, the project manager, contract manager, and responsible business managers must observe performance, collect information, and measure actual contract achievement. These activities are essential to effective control. The resources devoted to these tasks and the techniques used to perform them will depend on the nature of the contract work, the size and complexity of the contract, and the resources available. Performance measuring and reporting will be discussed further in this chapter in "Performance Measurement and Reporting."

■ *Payment system:* Every contract must establish a clear invoicing and payment system or process. The buyer and seller must agree to whom invoices should be sent and what information is required. Sellers must submit proper invoices in a timely manner. (See Appendix A Form 16.) Buyers should pay all invoices promptly. (See Appendix A Form 17.) Sellers should insist that late payment penalty clauses be included in all contracts.

■ *Change control system:* As a rule, any parties that can make a contract can agree to change it. Changes are usually inevitable in contracts for complex undertakings, such as system design and systems integration. No one has perfect foresight; requirements and circumstances change in unexpected ways, and contract terms and conditions must often be changed as a result. (Details are presented later in this chapter in "Change Management")

■ *Dispute management system:* No one should be surprised when, from time to time, contracting parties find themselves in disagreement about the correct interpretation of contract terms and conditions. Most such disagreements are minor and are resolved without too much difficulty. Occasionally, however, the parties will find themselves entangled in a seemingly intractable controversy. Try as they might, they cannot resolve their differences. If the dispute goes unresolved for too long, one or both of the parties may threaten, or even initiate, litigation.

Litigation is time consuming, costly, and risky. No one can ever be entirely sure of its result. It rarely results in a truly satisfactory resolution of a dispute, and it sours commercial relationships. For these reasons, it should be avoided. One goal of business managers and contract managers should be to resolve disputes without litigation whenever possible.

The keys to effective dispute resolution are as follows:
❑ Recognize that contract documents are not perfect
❑ Keep larger objectives in mind
❑ Focus on the facts
❑ Depersonalize the issues
❑ Be willing to make reasonable compromises

When disputes become intractable, seeking the opinion of an impartial third party can sometimes help. When this approach is formal, and the third party's decision is binding on the parties, it is called *arbitration.* Some companies include a clause in their contracts that makes arbitration the mandatory means of resolving disputes. Such a clause might read as follows:

Disputes

Should any dispute occur between the parties arising from or related to this Agreement, or their rights and responsibilities to each other, the matter shall be settled and determined by arbitration under the then current rules of the American Arbitration Association. The arbitration shall be conducted by a single arbitrator, the decision and award of the arbitrator shall be final and binding, and the award so rendered may be entered in any court having jurisdiction thereof.

The language to be used in the arbitral proceeding shall be English.

In an international contract, the "Disputes" clause may be modified to provide for an international forum. The clause might read–

The arbitral tribunal shall be composed of three (3) arbitrators who shall be appointed by the Chairman of the Royal Arbitration Institute of the Stockholm Chamber of Commerce.

The arbitration process will be more formal than ordinary negotiation between the parties (which may be represented by attorneys), but it will be less formal than court proceedings.

Output

The following output results from contract administration:

■ *Documentation:* Documentation is essential to provide proof of performance, management of changes, justification for claims, and evidence in the unlikely event of litigation.

The most important documentation is the official copy of the contract, contract modifications, and conformed working copies of the contract. Other important forms of documentation include the following items:

❑ *External and internal correspondence:* All contract correspondence should be maintained by the contract manager in a central, chronological reading file, with separate files for external and internal correspondence. Each piece of correspondence should be dated and assigned a file number. The project manager or contract manager should initial and date each piece of correspondence to acknowledge that it was read. Ideally, only one person should be authorized to correspond with the other party to the contract. However, if more than one person on the project team is authorized to correspond with the other contract party, copies of all correspondence must be sent to the contract manager for filing. All mail requiring an answer must be addressed promptly, preferably in writing; this is a fundamental rule of effective contract administration.

❏ *Meeting minutes:* Minutes should be recorded for all meetings between the seller and the buyer. The minutes should state the date, time, and location of the meeting and identify all attendees by name, company or organization, and title. They should describe all issues discussed, decisions made, questions unresolved, and action items assigned. Copies of the minutes should be provided to each attendee and to others interested in the meeting but unable to attend. Minutes of internal meetings must be kept only for purposes of project management, not for contract management.

❏ *Progress reports:* Progress reports should be filed chronologically, by subject. The project manager and contract manager should initial and date each progress report to acknowledge that they have read it and are aware of its contents.

❏ *Project diaries:* On large projects, the project manager and contract manager should keep a daily diary, in which they record significant events of the day. They should update their diaries at the end of each workday. The entries should describe events in terms of who, what, when, where, and how. Preferably, the diary should be kept in a perfect-bound book with prenumbered pages.

A diary supplements memory and aids in recalling events. A diary is also useful as an informal project history when a new project manager or contract manager must take over. It can be of great assistance in preparing, negotiating, and settling claims or in the event of litigation. However, a diary may become evidence in court proceedings, so a diarist should be careful to record only facts, leaving out conclusions, speculations about motives, and personal opinions about people or organizations.

❏ *Telephone logs:* Another useful aid to memory is a telephone log, which is a record of all incoming and outgoing calls. It identifies the date and time of each call, whether it was incoming or outgoing, and if outgoing, the number called.

It lists all parties to the call and includes a brief notation about the discussion.

❑ *Photographs and videotapes:* When physical evidence of conditions at the site of performance is important, a photographic or videotape record can be helpful. This record will greatly facilitate communication and will provide an excellent description of the exact nature of the site conditions. Whenever a contract involves physical labor, the project manager, contract manager, or other on-site representative should have a camera and film available for use.

The purpose of documentation is to record facts and reduce reliance on human memory. Efforts to maintain documentation must be thorough and consistent.

■ *Contract changes:* As a result of changes in the buyers' needs, changes in technologies, and other changes in the marketplace, buyers need flexibility in their contracts. Thus changes are inevitable. Sellers must realize that changes are not bad, that they are in fact good, because changes are often an opportunity to sell more products or services.

■ *Payment:* Cash is important–sellers want their money as quickly as possible. Buyers should seek product or service discounts for early payments. Likewise, sellers should improve their accounts receivable management and enforce late payment penalties.

■ *Completion of work:* This last step is the actual accomplishment by the seller of the buyer's requirement for products, services, systems, or solutions.

Performance Measurement and Reporting

Observing, collecting information, and measuring progress will provide a basis for comparing actual achievement to planned achievement. Generally, observing and collecting information cover three categories of concerns: cost control, schedule control, and compliance with specifications and statements of work. Cost control and schedule control are usually integrated; the latter category is often addressed in quality assurance and control. However, a fourth category–compliance with paperwork requirements, that

TEN

is, the administrative aspects of performance—is recommended. Observation in this area may be direct or indirect.

Direct Observation

Direct observation means personal, physical observation. The project manager, contract manager, or a representative is physically present at the site of the work during its performance to see how it is progressing. This approach is practical when the work is physical in nature and performed at a limited number of sites. Construction projects, for example, are good candidates for direct observation.

Direct observation by the project manager or contract manager is of limited use, however, if the work is largely intellectual in nature or if it is too complex for physical inspection alone to provide enough information to measure progress. In such cases, direct observation must be supplemented with or replaced by indirect observation.

Indirect Observation

Indirect observation includes testing, progress reports from many observers, and technical reviews and audits. Indirect observation is appropriate whenever direct observation would provide insufficient or ambiguous information. For example, determining by personal observation whether, at a given point in time, actual project costs are greater than, equal to, or less than budgeted costs would be difficult. Likewise, for projects involving an intellectual effort, such as system design, personal observations at the offices where the work is performed are unlikely to reveal whether the work is on, ahead of, or behind schedule.

In these circumstances, the project manager and contract manager must devise an indirect way to collect information. For some small, noncritical contracts, a telephone call may be all that is necessary to find out whether everything is proceeding according to plan. For large, complex contracts, however, the project manager or contract manager may require extensive reports, regular progress meetings, formal testing, and technical reviews and audits.

Sometimes a contract will specify such requirements, as in the following excerpt from a clause in a consultant agreement:

Reports

> Consultant shall provide ABC Company with monthly progress reports during the term of this Agreement, describing the status of the work, and shall participate in monthly status review meetings with ABC Company, at such times and locations reasonably specified by ABC Company. Additional meetings will be held if reasonably requested by either party.

Note that the clause does not describe specific information that must be included in the monthly report to describe the status of the work, so the seller may determine the information to be provided and its format. If the project manager or contract manager has specific information requirements, they should be described in the contract.

Reports

Generally, indirect observations are presented in reports that may be written or oral and may include raw data, informational summaries, analyses, conclusions, or a combination thereof. In the "Reports" clause, the monthly report is likely to be a collection of statements describing the seller's conclusions about the work's status. The conclusions may or may not be supported by raw data and an account of the seller's analysis. Often, this kind of report is adequate; other times, it is not.

Progress meetings are simply oral reports of progress. They have some advantages and some disadvantages. Listeners are able to ask questions about the information, analyses, and conclusions reported and have discussions with the reporter. However the listeners may not have time during the meeting to ponder the information provided and make their own analyses before the meeting ends.

Reports rarely provide real-time data. They do not describe how things are now; rather they provide a picture of some past point in time. How old the data are will depend on the nature and frequency of the report and on the reporter's capabilities. A cost and schedule performance report that is submitted on July 1 and de-

TEN

pends on accounting data may actually describe cost and schedule status as of May 30, depending on the capabilities of the seller's accounting system.

Reported conclusions about project status are valid only if the information on which they are based is accurate and the analyst is competent, realistic, and honest. Sellers are renowned for their optimism during the period before a crisis emerges. Facts can be presented in ways that permit almost any conclusion to be drawn from them.

In deciding to rely wholly or in part on reports (including meetings), the project manager or contract manager also must decide what information each report must contain. Following are some issues that should be addressed:

- What aspects of performance should the report address?
- What information should the report include—conclusions about performance, analyses, raw information, or some combination thereof?
- How frequently must the report be submitted and at what points in time?
- What is the cut-off point ("as of" date) for information to be included in the report?
- In what format should the report be submitted?
- To whom should the report be submitted, and to whom should copies be sent?

Identification and Analysis of Performance Variances

Observed and collected information about project performance must be analyzed to determine whether the project is proceeding as planned. The analyst compares actual performance to performance goals to determine whether any variances exist. An analyst who discovers a variance between actual and expected performance must determine several things: Is it significant? What was its cause? Was it a one-time failure, or is it a continuing problem? What type of corrective action would be most effective?

Variance analysis must be timely, particularly when the information is obtained through reports. That information is already old by the time it is received. Delays in analyzing its significance may allow poor performance to deteriorate further, perhaps beyond hope of effective corrective action. Acting promptly is particularly important during the early phases of contract performance, when corrective action is likely to have the greatest effect.

It is not uncommon for project managers and contract managers to collect reams of information that sit in their in-baskets and file cabinets, never put to use. When a project has gone badly, a review of information in the project files frequently shows that there were warning signs—reports, meeting minutes, letters, memos—but that they were unnoticed or ignored. Often, several people, perhaps a variety of business managers, share the responsibility for monitoring performance. In these instances, the project manager and contract manager must take steps to ensure that those people promptly analyze the information, report their findings, and take corrective action.

Corrective Action

When the project manager and contract manager discover a significant variance between actual and expected performance, they must take corrective action if possible. They must identify the cause of the problem and determine a solution that will not only eliminate it as a source of future difficulty, but also correct the effect it has already had, if possible. If the effect cannot be corrected, the parties may need to negotiate a change to the contract, with compensation to the injured party, if appropriate.

Follow-Up

After corrective action has been taken or is under way, the project manager and contract manager must determine whether it has had or is having the desired effect. If not, further action may be needed. Throughout this corrective action and follow-up process, the parties must keep each other informed about what is going on. Effective communication between the parties is essential to avoid misunderstandings and disputes when things are not going according to plan. The party taking corrective action must make every effort to let the other party know that it is aware of the problem and is addressing it seriously. Sometimes this step is more important than the corrective action itself.

TEN

Change Management

With change comes the risk that the parties will disagree on the nature of their obligations to one another. This situation is particularly likely to occur in contracts between organizations in which many people on both sides are in frequent contact with one another. These people may make informal, undocumented arrangements that depart from the contract terms and conditions. Thus, performance may be at variance with expectations, which can lead to misunderstandings and disputes.

Even when the parties formally agree to make changes, they may disagree about who should bear the burden of the effect on cost and schedule. Changes can affect budgets and schedules in unexpected ways, leading to serious disputes. A risk also exists that a proposal for a formal change may provide one party with an opportunity to renegotiate the entire contract based on issues not connected with the change.

Best Practices: Seven Actions to Improve Change Management

These considerations demand careful management of change. Best practices in change control include the following:

- Ensure that only authorized people negotiate or agree to contract changes
- Make an estimate of the effect of a change on cost and schedule, and gain approval for any additional expense and time before proceeding with any change
- Notify project team members that they must promptly report (to the project manager or contract manager) any action or inaction by the other party to the contract that does not conform to the contract terms and conditions
- Notify the other party in writing of any action or inaction by that party that is inconsistent with the established contract terms and conditions
- Instruct team members to document and report in writing all actions taken to comply with authorized changes and the cost and time required to comply
- Promptly seek compensation for increases in cost or time required to perform, and negotiate claims for such compensation from the other party in good faith

■ Document all changes in writing, and ensure that both parties have signed the contract; such written documentation should be completed before work under the change begins, if practical (See Appendix A Form 18.)

Managing change means ensuring that changes are authorized, their effect is estimated and provided for, they are promptly identified, the other party is properly notified, compliance and impact are reported, compensation is provided, and the entire transaction is properly documented. (See Appendix A Form 19.)

Contract Change Clauses

Contracts frequently include a clause that authorizes the buyer to order the seller to conform with certain changes made at the buyer's discretion. Such clauses are called *change clauses.* The following clause is an example:

Changes

ABC Company reserves the right at any time to make changes in the specifications, drawings, samples, or other descriptions to which the products are to conform, in the methods of shipment and packaging, or in the time or place of delivery. In such event, any claim for an adjustment shall be mutually satisfactory to ABC Company and Seller, but any claim by Seller for an adjustment shall be deemed waived unless notice of a claim is made in writing within thirty (30) days following Seller's receipt of such changes. Price increases or extensions of time shall not be binding upon ABC Company unless evidenced by a purchase order change issued by ABC Company. No substitutions of materials or accessories may be made without ABC Company's written consent. No charges for extras will be allowed unless such extras have been ordered in writing by ABC Company and the price agreed upon.

This clause does not expressly tie the amount of the seller's claim to the effect of the change on its cost or time requirements. Moreover, there is no express mention of reductions in price or time. However, the clause does say that any claim must be "mutually satisfactory" to both parties. It is unclear what, if any, legal significance there is in these subtle differences in language.

The clause requires that "notice of a claim" by the seller be made in writing within 30 days of the seller's receipt of the change order.

Documentation of Change

Whenever the parties make a change in the contract, it is important that they maintain the integrity of that document as trustworthy evidence of the terms and conditions of their agreement. Logically, a change will add terms and conditions, delete terms and conditions, or replace some terms and conditions with others. Thus, when modifying the contract, the parties should decide what words, numerals, symbols, or drawings must be added, deleted, or replaced in the contract document.

Parties to a contract will often discuss the change they want to make but fail to describe the change in the context of their contract document. After a few such changes, the document will no longer accurately describe the current status of their agreement, and the parties may dispute what the current terms really are. Such an occurrence should surprise no one, human communication and memory being what they are.

The best way to avoid this problem is to draft the language of the change carefully in the context of the contract document, ensuring that the new language describes the intent of the parties. This action should be taken before making any attempt to estimate the cost and schedule effect of any change or to perform the work. People sometimes argue that expediency demands that the work proceed before reaching agreement on the precise language of the change. However, this practice is likely to create confusion over just what changed and how. If the parties cannot reach agreement on the language of the change in a reasonable time, they probably are not in agreement about the nature of the change and should not proceed.

Modification of the Contract Document

One party will have the original copy of the contract. The other party will usually have a duplicate original. These originals should remain with the contract manager, or in the contracts department or legal office.

When parties agree to change the contract, they should never alter the original documents. Instead, they should prepare modification documents that describe the contract changes. These changes can generally be described in two ways: First, the modification document can include substitute pages in which deleted original language is stricken out and new or replacement language is inserted in italics. Second, minor changes can be described in "pen and ink" instructions that strike out certain words and add others.

Copies of each modification should be distributed promptly to all project team members who have a copy of the original document. The project manager, contract manager, and other key team members should maintain a personal conformed working copy of the contract. This copy should be kept in a loose-leaf binder or electronic database so that pages can be replaced easily. The conformed working copy should be altered as necessary to reflect the current status of the agreement between the parties. Changes should be incorporated promptly. Each team member should always keep the conformed working copy readily available and bring it to meetings. The contract manager should periodically check to ensure that each team member's conformed working copy is up-to-date.

Effect of the Change on Price and Schedule

After the parties are in precise agreement as to how the contract was modified, they should try to estimate the cost and schedule impact of the change. They can do this independently, but the most effective approach is to develop the estimate together, as a team, working out the details and their differences in the process. If the parties are open and honest with one another, this approach can save time and give them greater insight into the real effect of the change on cost and schedule. A well-developed work breakdown structure and project schedule graphic can be of enormous value to this process. Work may proceed based either on an estimate of the cost and schedule impact, with a limit on the parties' obligations, or on a firm-fixed adjustment.

If the parties work out their estimates independently (the traditional approach), an agreement will entail a certain amount of bargaining. This approach can lead to time-consuming haggling and even to deadlock, and such delays can be costly when a change is needed during performance.

Another approach is for the parties to agree that the seller can proceed with the work as changed and submit a claim later. This method can spell trouble for both parties, however, particularly if the adjustments are unexpectedly high. For the buyer, it can mean unpleasant surprises about the effect on prices and schedules for changed work. For the seller, it can mean a dismayed buyer and delays in settling claims. For both, it can mean a damaged relationship. Working out the cost and schedule impact before committing to the change is better for both parties.

If the seller must proceed with the work before the change can be fully negotiated, the parties should agree to limits on their mutual obligations in relation to the change. It is common practice for parties to agree on cost and schedule ceilings when work must begin before agreement is complete. Obviously, such limits should be documented in writing.

Authorization of Performance Under the Change

After the parties have agreed to the change and to either an estimate of the impact on cost and schedule or a final price adjustment, the buyer should provide the seller with written authorization to proceed with the work as changed. The easiest way to accomplish this objective is to prepare, sign, and distribute a modification document. If this approach will take too long, a letter or other form of written documentation will suffice. The authorization should include a description of the change, its effective date, and a description of any limits on the obligations of the parties.

Submission, Negotiation, and Resolution of Claims

If price and schedule adjustments are not negotiated before authorizing performance under the change, the parties must negotiate such matters after performance. As a rule, the buyer should try to limit any price adjustments to the cost increases caused by the change, plus reasonable allowances for overhead and profit, and any additional time required to perform the work as changed. However, if the change reduces the cost or time of performance, the buyer should seek a reduction in price or schedule.

The project manager and contract manager should keep detailed records of all costs incurred in complying with changes. They must document the effect of changes on the time required to perform.

The party submitting the claim should be able to make a reasonable demonstration of a cause-and-effect relationship between the change and the increased or decreased cost and time requirements. Ideally, the parties will have reached an advance agreement about the nature and extent of claim documentation. The objective of negotiation should be to seek a reasonable settlement that will fairly compensate the seller for performing additional work or fairly reduce the buyer's price when work is deleted.

Contract Administration Policies

Four contract administration policies are key to every contract. They are compliance with contract terms and conditions, effective communication and control, effective control of contract changes, and effective resolution of claims and disputes.

Compliance with Contract Terms and Conditions

The policy of compliance with contract terms and conditions is the policy of keeping one's promises. Contracting parties should know and understand the contract terms and keep their promises to comply in good faith. Such a policy is essential to effective risk management for both parties. No one should enter into a contract intending not to comply with its terms and conditions, because doing so would risk legal and commercial consequences.

However, these principles can become problematic, particularly when contracting parties are organizations. Often the people who plan, select the seller, and negotiate and sign the contract are different from those who must perform the contract work, and each group may have different goals and objectives. The negotiators may agree to terms and conditions that conflict with the objectives, policies, practices, and customs of the functional departments that do the work.

In such circumstances, because of failures of internal communication and control, department managers may inadvertently or even willfully violate contract terms. Common explanations include "I thought the contract was wrong, so we did it the right way"; "I didn't interpret it that way"; "I wasn't sure what it meant, so I did it the way we always do it"; "I never saw the contract, we just handled it in a routine manner"; and "What contract?" Thus, one of the greatest problems in contract administration is communicating contract obligations to all affected people and maintaining control over their contract performance.

Effective Communication and Control

The policy of compliance with contract terms and conditions requires that organizations maintain effective communication about, and control over, contract performance. Each party to the contract must establish both communication procedures to ensure that people within its organization know what they must do and the necessary controls to ensure that they do it. Good intentions about contract performance will not be enough to avoid legal consequences in the absence of effective communication and control. Contracts must specify who is the designated point of contact and who has the authority to modify the contract.

Ensuring that the parties to the contract communicate with each other is equally important. A contract is a relationship. Because virtually every contract entails some degree of interaction between the contracting parties, each party must keep the other informed of its progress, problems, and proposed solutions, so that the other can respond appropriately.

Like all human relationships, contracts are dynamic. As performance proceeds and events unfold, the parties will find that they must modify their original expectations and plans to adjust to real events. As they do so, they must modify the contract terms and conditions to reflect the current status of their agreement. Changes are an inevitable part of contracting, because no one can predict the future with perfect accuracy. However, the parties should make changes consciously and openly, so that they remain in agreement about what they should be doing. Lack of communication can result in dispute over what their obligations really are.

Effective Control of Contract Changes

Part of communication and control is the effective management of changes, which are inevitable. Effectively controlling changes includes establishing formal procedures for changing the contract and limiting the number of people entitled to make changes. It also entails establishing recognition and notification procedures in response to unauthorized changes. Finally, it requires establishing procedures for identifying, estimating, and measuring the potential and actual effect of changes on all aspects of contract performance.

It is natural for the functional managers of one party to work directly with their counterparts in the other party's organization—people who will speak their language and understand their policies and customs. These colleagues will often bypass formal channels of communication. Such relationships frequently lead to informal, undocumented agreements that depart from contract terms and conditions. These informal agreements can lead to trouble. Policy must be backed by procedures to ensure that the changes brought about through these relationships are controlled.

Effective Resolution of Claims and Disputes

The inherent shortcomings of language as a medium of communication, the organizational nature of the contracting process, and the dynamic nature of contract relationships all contribute to the potential for disagreements between the parties. In fact, like changes, disagreements are virtually inevitable. They should be expected as a normal part of contract management. The larger and more complex the project, the greater the potential for misunderstanding and disagreement.

However, the parties must not allow disagreements and disputes to prevent the execution of the contract. They must commit themselves to resolving disputes that will arise between them in an amicable way. Although claims and disputes cannot be avoided, they can be resolved effectively, fairly, and without rancor and litigation. Experienced parties to a contract will anticipate claims and disputes and recognize that they do not necessarily indicate incompetence or ill will but, rather, reflect the fact that human foresight, planning, and performance are imperfect.

Professional contract managers understand that contract disputes must be resolved dispassionately. They also recognize that personalities may affect disputes. But they know that the objective is final disposition in an inexpensive, expeditious, and less formal manner, before disputes fester and infect the contractual relationship.

TEN

Each party to the contract has the power to litigate if it believes it has been wronged. Ultimately a losing proposition for all involved, litigation is costly and time consuming, and its results are uncertain. Negotiation and arbitration are preferable to litigation, and the parties to the contract should strive to use those techniques to the fullest extent practical.

DEFINING CONTRACT CLOSEOUT AND TERMINATION

A contract can end in one of three ways: successful performance, mutual agreement, or breach of contract. Most contracts end by successful performance. However, under some circumstances, the parties may agree to end their contract even though the original objectives were not met. They may reach this agreement through negotiation or arbitration. In a breach of contract, one or both of the parties fail to keep their promises; this could result in arbitration or litigation. Contract closure by mutual agreement or breach of contract is called *contract termination.*

Contract closeout refers to verifying that all administrative matters are concluded on a contract that is otherwise physically complete. In other words, the seller has delivered the required supplies or performed the required services, and the buyer has inspected and accepted the supplies or services.

Many sellers have a policy that their contract manager sign a contract completion statement confirming that all administrative actions were performed. Standard times for closing out a contract vary depending on many factors.

Occasionally, contracts take on lives of their own. For instance, "administrative convenience," "extensions of time" or "additional goods and services" are often added to an existing agreement that may have been completely executed by the seller. Closing out the completed contract and opening a new one may be more appropriate in such cases, especially when new or different terms and conditions might lead to confusion.

Buyer and Seller Step 6: Contract Closeout or Termination

Input	Tools & Techniques	Output
Completion of work Contract documentation or Termination notice	Compliance verification Contract documentation Contract closeout checklist or Termination	Product or service completion Acceptance and final payment Contract closeout or termination document Documented lessons learned

Input

Input to contract closeout includes the following items:

- *Completion of work:* A contract is physically complete when one of two events has occurred:
  - ❑ All required supplies or services are delivered or performed, inspected, and accepted, and all existing options were exercised or have expired
  - ❑ A contract completion notice was issued by one party to the other

- *Contract documentation:* The purpose of closeout is to ensure that no further administrative action is necessary on the contract. Part of this task is to check that all paperwork was submitted. The following forms, reports, and payments may be outstanding after a contract is physically complete:

  For the buyer—
  - ❑ Closeout report
  - ❑ Certificate of completion or conformance
  - ❑ Seller's release of claims

  For the seller—
  - ❑ Closeout report
  - ❑ Proof of buyer's final payment
  - ❑ Release of performance bonds and letter of credit

- *Termination notice* (for termination only): A written or oral notification to cancel the contract due to cause or default of contract, or for convenience, is issued in the event of contract termination.

TEN

Tools and Techniques

The following tools and techniques are used in contract closeout or termination.

■ *Compliance verification:* Administrative tasks, incidental to contract performance, may have to be accomplished before closing out the file. Final payment cannot be authorized until the seller has accomplished all administrative tasks, such as—

❏ Return, or other disposition, of buyer-furnished property
❏ Proper disposition of intellectual property
❏ Settlement of subcontracts
❏ Fulfillment of procedural requirements of termination proceedings (for termination only)

■ *Contract documentation:* Several types of documentation must be dealt with at this time:

❏ *Outstanding claims or disputes:* Some issues related to basic contract performance may not be resolved, and the buyer may not have raised some issues. All outstanding issues must be addressed at this time. To avoid reopening a closed file, some sellers make a standard practice of requesting a signed statement from the buyer that all contract terms and conditions were met. Some unscrupulous buyers have attempted to coerce sellers into abandoning outstanding claims in return for getting paid amounts that are not in dispute. Such actions are bad faith on the part of the buyer.

❏ *Payments:* Final payments or outstanding underpayment should be collected by the seller. The buyer's payment office should make payment based on the seller's invoice and its receipt of a receiving report. On more complex requirements, contract managers generally have a more active role in these tasks. Underpayment can be the result of many factors, including liquidated damages, adjustments after an audit, and retroactive price reductions.

❏ *Files:* The project manager or contract manager must keep a log of closed-out files containing information, such as the date the file was closed out, date the file was transferred physically to a storage center, location of the storage center, and filing location provided by the storage facility. Some information in contract files must be kept for a certain number of years. Such information should be specified in the contract.

❑ *Contract completion statement:* The contract manager should prepare a contract completion statement.

■ *Contract closeout checklist:* A checklist can be a useful tool during contract closeout. (See Appendix A Form 20.)

■ *Termination* (for termination only): Termination is the administrative process exercising a party's contractual right to discontinue performance completely or partially under a contract. The three types of terminations are termination for cause or default, termination by mutual agreement (for convenience), and no-cost settlement. (See "Termination Types" later in this chapter for further discussion.)

Output

The following output results from contract closeout:

■ *Product or service completion:* The seller provides the required products or services to the buyer.

■ *Acceptance and final payment:* The buyer accepts the products or services and pays the seller.

■ *Contract closeout or termination documents:* Both the buyer and seller document all contract closeout actions and summarize project performance. (See Appendix A Form 21.)

■ *Documented lessons learned:* At the completion of each contract, the project manager, contract manager, and project team should jointly develop a lessons-learned summary, which should describe the major positive and negative aspects of the contract. The lessons-learned summary focuses on sharing best practices with other company project teams, warning others of potential problems, and suggesting methods to mitigate the risks effectively to ensure success. (See Appendix A Form 22.)

Termination Types

Termination with respect to a contract refers to an ending before the closure of the anticipated term of the contract. The termination may be by mutual agreement or may be by one party's exercising its remedies due to the other party's omission or failure to perform a contractual or contract law duty (default).

Termination by Mutual Agreement

Both parties may agree at any time that they do not wish to be bound by the contract and terminate their respective rights and obligations stemming from the contract.

Termination for Cause or Default

The right to terminate a contract may originate from either the general principles of contract law or the express terms of the contract. Contracts may be terminated for default for the following reasons:

- *Failure to tender conforming supplies or services:* If the seller fails, or is unable, to cure a nonconforming tender, the seller is in default and the contract can be terminated or other remedial action can be taken.

- *Failure to complete performance substantially within the time specified in the contract:* Usually, the buyer does not consider or have the legal right of termination for default actions when only minor corrective work remains on the contract.

- *Repudiation of the contract by the seller:* A repudiation, or anticipatory breach, occurs when a seller or buyer clearly indicates to the other party that it cannot or will not perform on the contract. Examples indicating that an anticipatory repudiation may exist include a letter stating an intention of nonperformance or job abandonment.

- *Failure to perform any other terms of the contract:* A failure to comply with bonding requirements, progress-schedule submission requirements, or fraud statutes would constitute a failure to perform other contract terms.

Although authority to terminate may be expressly provided to both parties, contract managers must exercise this authority in good faith based on conditions of the termination clause or a material breach of contract terms. The decision is highly discretionary, based on the business judgment of the contract manager and business advisors.

Factors to be considered before terminating a contract for default include—

- Contract terms and conditions and applicable laws and regulations
- Specific failure of the buyer or seller and the excuses made by the breaching party for such failure
- Availability from other sources
- Urgency of the need and time that would be required by other sources as compared with the time in which completion could be obtained from the current contract
- Degree of essentially of the seller, such as unique seller capabilities
- Buyer's availability of funds to finance repurchase costs that may prove to be uncollectible from the defaulted seller, and the availability of funds to finance termination costs if the default is determined to be excusable
- Any other pertinent facts and circumstances

Termination for Convenience

It is the right of the parties, usually the buyer, to terminate a contract unilaterally when completing the contract is no longer in the buyer's best interest. This has long been recognized in U.S. government contracts, and the consequences are defined by law. This type of termination of government contracts has been the subject of many U.S. court and legal decisions. In U.S. government contracts, the buyer has the right to terminate without cause and limit the seller's recovery to the—

- Price of work delivered and accepted
- Costs incurred on work done but not delivered
- Profit on work done but not delivered if the contract incurred no loss
- Costs of preparing the termination settlement proposal

In commercial contracts, the concept of buyer's best interest is not used. Termination occurs only as a result of default due to breach of contract or due to mutual agreement. Recovery of anticipated profit is generally precluded.

No-Cost Settlement

Used without normal termination procedures, no-cost settlement can be considered when—

- The seller has indicated it will accept it
- No buyer property was furnished under the contract
- No outstanding payments or debts are due the seller, and no other obligations are outstanding
- The product or service can be readily obtained elsewhere

Note that termination for convenience is not a commercial contracting concept. Thus, if a contract contains a statement allowing parties to terminate the contract unilaterally, the parties should exercise extreme caution in defining specific remedies and consequences of such action.

Best Practices: 30 Actions to Improve Results

Buyer and Seller

- Read and analyze the contract
- Develop a contract administration plan
- Appoint a contract manager to ensure that your organization does what it proposed to do
- Develop and implement contract administration policies or guidelines for your organization
- Comply with contract terms and conditions
- Maintain effective communication and control
- Control contract changes with a proactive change management process
- Resolve claims and disputes promptly and dispassionately
- Use negotiation or arbitration, not litigation, to resolve disputes
- Develop a work breakdown structure to assist in planning and assigning work
- Conduct preperformance conferences
- Measure, monitor, and track performance
- Manage the invoice and payment process
- Report on progress internally and externally

- Identify variances between planned versus actual performance
- Be sure to follow up on all corrective actions
- Appoint authorized people to negotiate contract changes and document the authorized representatives in the contract
- Enforce contract terms and conditions
- Provide copies of the contract to all affected organizations
- Maintain conformed copies of the contract
- Understand the effects of change on cost, schedule, and quality
- Document all communication—use telephone and correspondence logs
- Prepare internal and external meeting minutes
- Prepare contract closeout checklists
- Ensure completion of work
- Document lessons learned and share them throughout your organization
- Communicate, communicate, communicate!
- Clarify team member roles and responsibilities
- Provide leadership support to the team throughout the contract management process
- Ensure that leadership understands the contract management process and how it can improve business relationships from beginning to end.

SUMMARY

The postaward phase of the contract management process is simply a matter of both parties doing what they promised to do. The ongoing challenge is maintaining open and effective communication, timely delivery of quality products and services, responsive corrective actions to problems, and compliance with all other agreed-on terms and conditions. After the project has been successfully completed, proper procedures are put into place to close out the contract officially. In these instances where the contract is terminated due to cause of default, action is taken to legally cancel the contract.

Remember the power of precedent. Your organization is always evaluated based on your past performance and the precedents it sets. Your contract management actions taken years ago affect your organization's reputation today. Likewise, the contract management actions that you take today form your organization's reputation for tomorrow. Clearly, the actions taken in the preaward and award phases significantly affect your results in the postaward phase.

CHAPTER **11**

GLOBAL CONTRACT MANAGEMENT– MISCONCEPTIONS AND BEST PRACTICES

In a highly competitive global marketplace, most companies must try to hold down the cost of getting goods and services to market while still ensuring quality, on-time delivery, and customer satisfaction. World-class companies continually benchmark, internally and externally, to discover innovative and proven practices that can offer better results. Prominent among those practices are effective means of contract management.

Similarly, governments worldwide are seeking ways to provide more to their constituents with less. Like the United States, many countries are recognizing the fiscal and quality benefits to be obtained through the judicious transfer of certain government-employee-performed functions to the private sector. In conjunction, governments are re-examining their own, often highly regulated, processes for buying and selling. Seeking to free those processes from unnecessary constraints, they are looking to the private sector for streamlined contract management models.

To help organizations in pursuing these goals, this chapter explains some common misconceptions about global contract management and provides a summary of 15 of the most important best practices.

Correcting Misconceptions

■ *Misconception:* Commercial contracting differs radically from government contracting—so much so that parallels cannot be drawn.

Reality: The commercial and government contracting processes share many phases, functions, procedures, and challenges. Many differences are rapidly diminishing, so even greater similarities will emerge in the coming years.

■ *Misconception:* The Uniform Commercial Code is a clear, precise document that uniformly and specifically governs all commercial transactions throughout the United States.

Reality: On most points, the UCC's guidance is anything but clear and precise. It does not attempt to provide the type of detailed, step-by-step guidance provided by the Federal Acquisition Regulation system, nor does it prescribe contract clauses. Numerous UCC articles are vague and subject to interpretation.

Furthermore, the UCC's articles come into play only when a contractual dispute arises and the matter must be arbitrated or settled in the courts.

Developed and adopted in the 1950s and 1960s, the UCC was intended only to provide broad guidance on conducting commerce within the United States. Moreover, as a product of its times, the UCC primarily addresses the commercial transactions that were most prevalent when it was introduced—transactions for the sale of manufactured goods—as opposed to the more complex procurements of services and systems that prevail today. Many individual states have adopted their own modifications to the UCC, which complicates the situation, because the rules applied in a legal proceeding in one state may differ from those applied in another.

- *Misconception:* There is no international source of guidance on buying and selling.

Reality: The United Nations Convention on Contracts for the International Sale of Goods (CISG) sets forth rules intended to govern sales and purchases between companies from different nations. Its scope of influence is limited, however. First, not all nations have agreed to the CISG; currently 48 nations are signatories (see Table 11-1) Second, although the nation in which a company is incorporated has signed the CISG, that company need not select the CISG as the source of law that will govern its contracts. The CISG represents a compromise between the UCC and other sources that have arisen out of English common law and the different civil laws prevailing in many other countries. The CISG may be excluded in favor of another source of law if both parties agree and expressly so state in the contract. Finally, the CISG, like the UCC, addresses primarily the buying and selling of goods, which limits its guidance in a time when most transactions involve the provision of services or complex systems.

Table 11-1 Countries Accepting CISG (as of November 1, 1996)			
Australia	Denmark	Lesotho	Slovakia
Austria	Ecuador	Lithuania	Slovenia
Belarus	Egypt	Mexico	Spain
Belgium	Estonia	Netherlands	Sweden
Bosnia and	Finland	New Zealand	Switzerland
Herzegovina	France	Norway	Syrian Arab
Bulgaria	Georgia	Poland	Republic
Canada	Germany	Republic of Moldova	Uganda
Chile	Ghana	Romania	Ukraine
China	Guinea	Russian	United States
Cuba	Hungary	Federation	Venezuela
Czech Republic	Iraq	Singapore	Yugoslavia
	Italy		Zambia

■ *Misconception:* All private-sector companies use the same, or similar, standard terms and conditions in their contracts for goods and services.

Reality: No global set of standard terms and conditions exists for commercial contracts. Each company develops its own standard terms and conditions and then tailors them to meet the requirements of specific contracts.

■ *Misconception:* Commercial contracts do not require any contract documentation.

Reality: Per UCC Article 2, commercial contracts in the United States for the sale of goods valued at more than US $500 must be in writing. However, many countries throughout the world do not require contracts between companies within their boundaries to be written. Thus, oral contracts are binding and, indeed, quite common in many countries, including Mexico, Brazil, Argentina, France, South Korea, Ukraine, and Chile. As more multinational contracts are formed, however, the criticality of ongoing contract documentation—modifications, invoices, meeting notes, payments, and correspondence—is increasingly apparent and the maintenance of such documentation increasingly practiced.

- *Misconception:* Contract managers tend to be highly trained, highly experienced, and professionally certified.

  Reality: It depends! Although many contract managers fit this description, most have little experience, have received little or no professional training or continuing education in contract management, and are not certified by a recognized professional association or accredited university. Although thousands are certified in either purchasing management or contract management, millions are not. Many companies hire only well-trained, experienced, certified contract managers, often because they do not want to invest in training a person in the basics. Other companies have internal training programs for contract management personnel, but those programs are frequently taught by company managers who are not experienced instructors and who teach primarily the company's own practices. Some companies use the training programs of organizations such as the National Contract Management Association, the Institute of Supply Management, the American Management Association, or various institutions of higher learning. Yet most of those programs are limited, because they focus on the buyer's, as opposed to the seller's, side of the contracting equation. Increasingly, however, companies are recognizing the value of well-trained, professionally certified managers in contracting and in accounting, engineering, project management, and numerous other related professions.

USING BEST PRACTICES

- *Use a contract management methodology:* Every company should have a logical, organized, yet flexible process by which it buys and sells goods and services. An effective contract management methodology thoroughly addresses the entire buying and selling process. It sets forth all steps required and clearly defines the roles and responsibilities of everyone involved. Some companies have such a process in place to detail the roles and responsibilities of employees in all stages of an acquisition, from sales through contract formation through project management and contract administration; to set forth all the steps required; and to clearly define the roles and responsibilities of everyone involved.

■ *Commit to a contract management professional development program:* As business transactions become increasingly customized and complex, more organizations are recognizing that successful contract management requires trained, experienced, professional personnel, not simply clerks. ESI International has worked with Lucent Technologies Inc., for example, to establish a professional development program composed of continuing education training leading to a master's certificate in global contract management from The George Washington University School of Business and Public Management. Lucent also provides on-the-job training, time-phased work assignments, and cross-functional work experience.

■ *Establish a list of prequalified suppliers:* Many private-sector companies are taking this proactive approach, widely practiced among government agencies. Potential suppliers are screened in advance to determine which are qualified for subsequent contract opportunities. Buying lead time is thus reduced.

■ *Take advantage of electronic commerce or electronic data interchange:* Many private-sector entities, like many agencies in the U.S. government, use electronic means of issuing solicitations, submitting bids and proposals, awarding contracts, exchanging contract correspondence, submitting invoices, and receiving payments. Many large manufacturers and retailers, in fact, are requiring that their suppliers institute an electronic data interchange program. The electronic exchange of data reduces cycle time, cuts costs, increases productivity, and improves customer service.

■ *Use corporate credit cards:* More companies are using credit cards to simplify relatively small-scale or routine purchases. Most establish clear controls, including dollar thresholds, limited access, and specific purchasing guidelines. Cycle times, internal documentation, and overhead costs are all being lowered through this practice.

■ *Adopt value-based pricing where sensible:* Value-based pricing, sometimes called customer-based pricing, is top down rather than cost based. Instead of pricing products and services by estimating the cost to manufacture or provide them and then adding a desired margin, value-based pricing focuses on the customer's needs and the benefits the customer expects to reap. In other words, it offers a sound business rationale for charging more for the same products or services, thereby increasing profitability.

■ *Use universal sales agreements:* Such agreements—in the form of distributor agreements, supply agreements, master agreements, framework agreements, basic ordering agreements, and more— are widely used in commercial contracting. They greatly reduce administrative time, effort, and paperwork by establishing a mutually agreed-on set of terms and conditions that will apply to all business transactions made pursuant to the agreement.

■ *Conduct risk versus opportunity assessments:* Nothing is more profitable than a good bid/no-bid decision. The ability to make informed bid/no-bid decisions, intelligently weighing risk against opportunity, is critical in today's highly competitive marketplace. Many companies have developed sophisticated tools that help their managers identify and quantify both risk and opportunity.

■ *Simplify standard contract terms and conditions:* Too many companies use standard terms and conditions that are needlessly wordy, overly legalistic, and difficult to understand. More companies are realizing that such terms and conditions are viewed negatively by the other party and constitute obstacles to successful business deals. Some are attacking the problem head-on by rewriting their standard terms and conditions in language that is clear, concise, and easy for all parties involved to understand.

■ *Permit oral presentation of proposals:* This time-saving practice is used increasingly by purchasing organizations worldwide. Most establish a few presentation guidelines and state them expressly in their solicitations to ensure that all competing sellers use the same rules.

■ *Employ highly skilled contract negotiators:* For many years, companies have realized the value of developing and maintaining a team of extremely skilled contract negotiators to negotiate the megadeals for their companies.

■ *Hold preperformance conferences:* Many headaches can be avoided and a lot of money saved through conferences that bring together the contracting parties before work under the contract begins. The primary purpose of such a conference is to ensure that the parties are fully aware of and clearly understand all contract requirements. Conferences may be face-to-face meetings or they may be videoconferences, teleconferences, or e-mail exchanges.

■ *Adopt a uniform solicitation, proposal, and contract format:* This logical, organized approach—issuing all solicitations in a common format, requiring that proposals follow the same format, and awarding contracts that use the format—has been used by the U.S. government for many years. Although only a few private-sector entities use this practice, it greatly simplifies the source selection and proposal evaluation process, as well as facilitating contract management for both parties.

■ *Use alternative dispute resolution (ADR) methods to resolve disputes:* Most commercial firms use binding arbitration to resolve disputes, typically using arbitration rules approved by the American Arbitration Association or, if outside the United States, an international arbitration association. In addition to arbitration, many companies use mediation, facilitation, minitrials, early neutral evaluation, and dispute resolution panels. ADR methods such as these save time and money. NCR Corporation, for example, has used ADR methods with some outstanding results during the past decade. The company has reduced in-house legal costs and outside legal fees, slashed the time it takes to resolve disputes, and preserved sound customer relations in the face of problems that were not easily resolved.

■ *Develop and maintain a best-practices and lessons-learned database:* Corporations are increasingly realizing the value of maintaining a database containing comprehensive information—both current and historical—about customers, suppliers, products, and services. The database, ideally in electronic form, must be user friendly and accessible to all appropriate personnel. Few companies pursue this practice and even fewer pursue it well, primarily because of the initial and continuing investment involved in cost, time, and effort. Yet that investment can pale in comparison with the benefits of significant cost avoidance, increased customer satisfaction, and more successful long-term business relationships.

Sharing Information

Despite widespread perceptions to the contrary, the worlds of government and commercial contracting are not alien to one another. The most significant difference is the absence in commercial contracting of prescriptive guidance addressing each stage and each element of the contracting process.

The learning process is a two-way street. As illustrated by several items in the discussion of best practices, those responsible for contract management in the commercial realm are benefiting by adopting practices long used by government, just as government contract managers are benefiting from adapting commercial practices.

What Matters Most

What matters most is that the senior leadership of an organization realizes the value of contract management as a critical aspect of integrated business management.

For sellers, it is not enough to have good sales managers and quality products and services—an organization must have professional business managers to successfully manage the entire process from sales to implementation.

For buyers, it is not enough to know what they need to purchase—organizations must have a process to ensure that they effectively communicate their needs, select the right source, negotiate a successful contracts, and obtain quality products and services.

Finally, the contract management process and the more than 100 best practices contained in this book will only contribute to more effective business management when adopted with foresight and implemented with commitment by everyone.

Teamwork is the essential element of success. In today's highly complex world of integrated products (hardware and software), services, and business solutions, it takes a highly talented, focused, and multi-functional team to deliver results, with buyers and sellers working together as business partners.

CHAPTER 12

CREATING VALUE AND GETTING RESULTS

The Big Picture of e-business is simply sellers creating value for buyers. Value may come from sellers providing leading-edge technology products, just-in-time quality services, and/or integrated business solutions—including large-scale outsourcing. Actual Value to a buyer varies, but it is usually related to financial results. The following diagram depicts how many winning companies are trying to enhance the value that they provide for their customers by moving up the Value Pyramid.

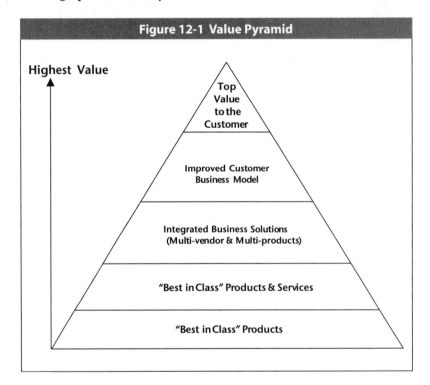

Figure 12-1 Value Pyramid

Highest Value

Top Value to the Customer

Improved Customer Business Model

Integrated Business Solutions (Multi-vendor & Multi-products)

"Best in Class" Products & Services

"Best in Class" Products

How Improving PM = Better Business Results

With increased competition and rapid changes in all aspects of business, every organization, in both the public and private sectors, needs effective and efficient solutions for completing business on time, on budget, and with the highest quality. More and more companies are using the project management discipline, internally and externally, to provide a highly focused, integrated, multifunctional solution that meets or exceeds their customers' expectations.

In most companies today, project managers or program managers (PM) serve as multifunctional team leaders on one or more

TWELVE

projects, shouldering the responsibility for achieving the desired results for these projects. The PMs–whether they are buying or selling products, services, and solutions–often must work closely with contract managers (CM) to achieve the desired business results. Every CM should understand the role, responsibilities, and challenges that PMs face in order to help them achieve the team/ organization goals and objectives.

LUCENT TECHNOLOGIES: PM BEST PRACTICES

Lucent Technologies has aggressively worked to create a world-class program management capability during the past five years. Its story during tough times serves as a case study for any large company or organization this is going through a similar process of institutionalizing program management to achieve success.

To get to the stage they are at today, Lucent's program management organization rapidly went through four distinct phases: awakening, implementing, professionalizing, and enterprising (see figure 12–2).

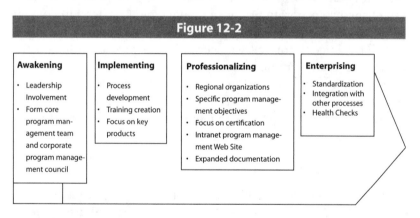

Figure 12-2

Awakening	Implementing	Professionalizing	Enterprising
• Leadership Involvement • Form core program management team and corporate program management council	• Process development • Training creation • Focus on key products	• Regional organizations • Specific program management objectives • Focus on certification • Intranet program management Web Site • Expanded documentation	• Standardization • Integration with other processes • Health Checks

The Awakening Phase

The first phase that an organization creating an institutionalized program management culture will experience is the *awakening phase.* During this stage of development, the leadership's involvement and support is critical because it is during this stage that program management's effect on the business is evaluated. Lucent's leadership was convinced that program management had the potential to improve business performance. To Lucent–a manufacturer, planner, and implementer of communication networks for the world's largest service providers–improved business performance translated to reduced cycle times, reduced cost, improved on-time delivery, and greater customer satisfaction. Moving rapidly to take advantage of its promise, Lucent's leadership team initiated the implementation of program management as a discipline within the services organization. It formed a headquarters core program management team charged with establishing a constant but flexible program management discipline that could be quickly applied to all Lucent projects around the world.

Additionally, in a non-project-based organization, such as Lucent, functional organizations such as engineering, manufacturing, installation, and sales have traditionally operated independently from their peer organizations. For program management to be successfully implemented, it was clear to the leadership team that Lucent needed to change from a functionally operated structure to a project-oriented one. The team led the way.

To ensure that all of Lucent Technologies would benefit from the implementation of program management, the executives also established a corporate program management leadership council consisting of program management directors from every business unit. This Lucent council was chartered to provide a forum for the project management community in order to foster the growth and development of a world-class corporate project management resource. The council helps foster program management's attributes by sharing program management lessons learned and best practices throughout the company.

The Implementing Phase

The second phase that an organization will experience is the *implementing phase,* the most expensive and labor-intensive phase in creating a disciplined program management organization. At Lucent, the core program management team was critical to making the implementing phase work. Staffed with a small group of experienced PMs from both internal and external sources, this core program management team focused on developing processes and training, and supporting selected large projects. To help jump-start the effort, they supplemented their knowledge by bringing in experienced external program management consultants. Initially, Lucent's core program management team established a highly customized three-course program management training curriculum. The training, essential in the implementing phase, focused on program management principles and on customer and Lucent requirements management. The intent of this program management curriculum was to provide managers with sufficient knowledge to start applying the program management discipline in their work environments. Upon completion of the three courses, students receive a company training certificate in program management.

During the implementation phase, the main function of the core program management team was to provide experienced PMs to augment, sometimes temporarily, newly formed project teams. In this phase, program management implementation was concentrated on selected large projects. The driver behind placing experienced PMs on selected programs was the belief that concentrating talent on the largest projects would lead to the highest return. On the international front, Lucent initially focused on a number of high-profile, global, multiyear, and multimillion to billion-dollar programs, such as those in Saudi Arabia, Mexico, and Russia. In the United States, it concentrated on AT&T programs, where it achieved its first significant successes. Choosing highly visible projects to internally showcase program management and document successes and lessons learned is vital in this phase. Internal support can only be obtained by successfully performing on these showcase programs.

The Professionalizing Phase

The third phase an organization will undergo is the *professionalizing phase,* in which the program management discipline is strengthened and program management tools are improved. During the professionalizing phase, Lucent established program management organizations led by vice presidents in all regions of the world. The establishment of these vice presidents is an important step in the implementation of program management. It signals the importance the company has put on institutionalizing program management. It also establishes champions of program management that are highly visible both internally and externally. To ensure that the business regions were aligned, specific program management objectives were established to proactively manage scope, schedule, cost, and customer relations. Clear objective setting is essential in the first steps toward globalization of program management.

During the professionalizing phase, Lucent undertook several actions to improve its level of program management professionalism. Today, more than 150 Lucent PMs have obtained the Project Management Institute (PMI) Project Management Professional certification, which is one of the internal measurements of success.

To further support communication and professionalism within Lucent, a yearly program management conference was established. In 2000, more than 850 PMs attended this annual conference, which is an important medium for communicating and applying lessons learned worldwide. Lucent also improved professionalism by creating an Intranet program management Web site to facilitate the dialog within the Lucent global program management community. In addition, the introduction of project control specialists helped to improve the efficiency of PMs by allowing them to focus on the customer and management issues instead of data collection.

In the professionalizing phase, Lucent also continued to develop its internal program management process documentation to facilitate rapid and consistent implementation. Today, the documentation includes a program management professional development guide (it provides career path information, training programs, and job descriptions), a program management handbook (it focuses on essential program management tasks and provides checklists for program management activities), and a project controls handbook, and other practical guides. Another important tool that was created is a program management sales brochure. It is used by Lucent sales teams to educate existing and potential customers on the project management capabilities of Lucent and the value it can add for the customer.

Building an internal reputation as a value-added benefit that boosts sales is another important success factor for program management during the professionalizing phase. Currently, Lucent PMs are proactively engaged with the sales teams during the preaward phase and have been vital in obtaining many new sales opportunities. As a result, Lucent is building an excellent worldwide reputation as a premier project management company. One of the tangible results of this excellent program management reputation has been the sale of stand-alone project management services to a number of major communication companies worldwide.

The Enterprising Phase

The *enterprising phase* is the fourth and final phase in the process of creating a world-class program management organization. Connecting the various projects and programs together is pivotal in taking companywide advantage of program management. Effective use of company resources across multiple projects can be obtained if processes and tools are compatible between these projects. Within Lucent, the standardization of progress reports, and the tools that generate these reports, is the first step in this phase. Initiated by the program management vice presidents of Europe, the Middle East, and Africa, a tool was created to support communication between individual project offices and regional program management offices. This tool, called Wall Chart, uses the power of the Internet to create and communicate project reports. Providing project offices with an effective way to create and distribute reports will increase their willingness to communicate real-time project status both internally and with customers. The Wall Chart has proven to be a successful tool in facilitating resource management and escalation processes.

Another important step in establishing enterprise-wide project management is standardizing resource codes and names used in the planning tools. In organizations that manage projects that consume hundreds of resources, the tracking of these resources is often done by using resource categories (e.g., engineers) instead of specific individual resources. It is essential to have a cross-project agreement on how to use and code these resources before enterprise-wide project management can become a success.

Finally, integrating the project management processes with other processes within the company, like engineering, manufacturing, installation, customer service, logistics, asset management, and contract management is essential within the enterprising phase. Lucent has developed an integrated project implementation process description. In this process, all interfaces, such as those between program management and contract management, for example, were agreed to and documented. This integrated process description also includes an analysis of current information systems and outlines the target system architecture for the business.

The integrated process description is used in "health checks" or team assessments. During a health check, members of the headquarters organizations visit program teams and evaluate the performance of the program team against the integrated process and systems architecture description. An outcome of these health checks is a roadmap for migrating the program to standard processes and systems and documented best practices. An important difference between a financial audit and this health check is that the health checks are done by request and are conducted in a team building environment. This collaboration between the programs and the core headquarters organizations uses the strengths of both and is a sign of a world-class program management organization.

Beyond the enterprising phase, a project management organization should view every internal and external business activity as a project. A true world-class company uses the power of the program management discipline to reduce cycle times, reduce costs, improve on-time delivery, and ensure customer satisfaction. Nearly any organization can evolve through the four phases (awakening, implementing, professionalizing, and enterprising) of the program management organizational life cycle, given executive support and resources. The real key to successful program management introduction is the ability to do it well, do it fast, and do it within budget, and exceed customer expectations.

SUMMARY

The big picture of e-business is simply sellers creating value for buyers. Value to a buyer varies, but, is typically directly or indirectly financial in nature. Winning Companies are constantly finding new ways to both acquire and provide value for their customers. True World-Class companies are expert in using the buying and selling process to create value for customers.

THE CONTRACT MANAGEMENT MATURITY MODEL

INTRODUCTION

Maturity, according to the Random House Dictionary, means "full development or a perfected condition." Maturity also implies knowledge and understanding as to what it takes to prevent problems and achieve success. In terms of Contract Management (CM), this relates to organizational capabilities that can consistently produce successful business results for buyers and sellers of products, services, and integrated solutions.

The Contract Management Maturity Model (CMMM©) creates a vision of excellence to help buying and selling organizations focus on the key areas of process improvement. CMMM© provides its users with a framework or a guide for improving their respective levels of performance. It is envisioned that the model and survey assessment tool will serve as the foundation for ongoing discussion and further development within the contract management profession. The CMMM© provides a visual tool to help an organization assess the six major steps which it must accomplish when either buying or selling products, services, and integrated solutions, in either the public or private business sectors. The maturity levels reflected in the model allow an organization to assess its level of capability for each of the six major steps, in its respective buying or selling process.

This chapter describes the development of the CMMM© as a systematic approach for assessing and improving the capability maturity level of an organization's contract management process for buying and selling, thus, the creation of the Contract Management Maturity Model (CMMM©). The CMMM© was developed by Dr. Rene Rendon. A more complete discussion can be found in the book *Contract Management Organizational Assessment Tools* by Gregory A. Garrett and Dr. Rene Rendon, NCMA 2005.

For the purpose of this discussion, the following terms and definitions will be used:

Capability Maturity Model: An evolutionary roadmap for implementing the vital practices for one or more domains of organizational processes. It contains the essential elements of effective processes for one or more disciplines. It describes an evolutionary improvement path from an ad hoc, immature process, to a disciplined mature process with improved quality and effectiveness (Curtis, Hefley & Miller, 2001).

Competency: An underlying characteristic that is causally related to effective or superior performance, as determined by measurable, objective criteria, in a job or in a situation (Curtis, Hefley & Miller, 2001).

Contract Management: The art and science of managing a contractual agreement(s) throughout the contracting process (Garrett, 2003).

Maturity: A measure of effectiveness in any specific process (Dinsmore, 1998).

Maturity Level: A level of organizational capability created by the transformation of one or more domains of an organization's processes. It is an evolutionary plateau on an organization's improvement path from ad hoc practices to a state of continuous improvement (Curtis, Hefley & Miller, 2001).

Process Capability: The inherent ability of a process to produce planned results (Ahern, Clouse & Turner, 2001).

DEVELOPING AN ORGANIZATIONAL CONTRACT MANAGEMENT PROCESS CAPABILITY MATURITY MODEL FOR BUYERS AND SELLERS

In conducting this research, existing process capability maturity models were reviewed to determine which features and characteristics should be adopted for the contract management maturity model. The maturity models reviewed included the Software Engineering Institute's Capability Maturity Model (SEI-CMM) (Ahern, Clouse, & Turner, 2001; Persse, 2001); Kerzner's Project Management Maturity Model (PMMM) (Kerzner, 2001); Project Management Solutions, Inc.'s Project Management Maturity Model (Crawford, 2001); People Capability Maturity Model (Curtis, Hefley & Miller, 2001); and the Berkley Project Management Process Maturity (PM2) Model (Ibbs & Kwak, 2000). Thus, the majority of maturity models reviewed were project management maturity models. These were appropriate models to review since the project management process is closely related to the procurement and contracting process.

The majority of these models consisted of a five-level maturity model, with each level of maturity building upon the previous maturity level. In almost all of the models, the first level of maturity reflected processes considered ad hoc, chaotic, inconsistent, and ill defined. These models labeled the first maturity level as "Initial" or "Ad Hoc." However, Kerzner's model described the first level of maturity by focusing on the use of a common language of project management and less on the sporadic use of a project management methodology. Kerzner labeled the first maturity level in his model as "Common Processes" (Carr, 2001; Dinsmore, 1998; Foti, 2002; Kerzner, 2001).

The maturity models were generally in agreement in describing the second maturity level. This level described the processes as structured, basic, planned, consistent, common, or managed (Carr, 2001; Dinsmore, 1998; Foti, 2002; Kerzner, 2001).

The maturity models differed slightly in describing the third maturity level. Some of the models described this level as processes that were standardized and institutionalized throughout the organization, and thus using a singular process methodology. However, the Berkley Model described the third maturity level as "Managed at the Project Level," while the other models described this level as processes having an organizational focus (Carr, 2001; Dinsmore, 1998; Foti, 2002; Kerzner, 2001).

For the most part, all of the maturity models were consistent in describing the fourth maturity level. The models described this level as organizations having integrated corporate processes, focusing on evaluation of practices and gauging process performance in terms of effectiveness and reduced variation. The labels used for this maturity level included "Managed," "Benchmarking," "Comprehensive," and "Quantitatively Managed" (Carr, 2001; Dinsmore, 1998; Foti, 2002; Kerzner, 2001).

There was also strong consistency in the fifth maturity level. The models reviewed characterized this level of maturity as processes focused on continuous improvement, establishing lessons learned and best practice databases. The transferring of knowledge between organizations, making adjustments to processes, eliminating common failures, and a continual effort to improve and innovate process capability were also characteristics of this maturity level. The reviewed maturity models labeled the fifth maturity level as "Optimizing," "Continuous Improvement," or "Learning" (Carr, 2001; Dinsmore, 1998; Foti, 2002; Kerzner, 2001).

Thus, in total, the maturity models reviewed reflect an evolutionary increase in maturity from an ad hoc level (Level 1), to a basic, disciplined process capability level, (Level 2), to an institutionalized and repeatable processes level, (Level 3), to a level characterized by processes integrated with other corporate processes resulting in synergistic corporate benefits (Level 4), and finally, to a level in which processes focused on continuous improvement and adoption of lessons learned and best practices (Carr, 2001; Dinsmore, 1998; Foti, 2002; Kerzner, 2001).

Another important characteristic of these maturity models was that most project management maturity models centered on the project management methods and processes outlined in *A Guide to the Project Management Body of Knowledge* (PMBOK) published by the Project Management Institute (2000). The models used the PMBOK processes as a basis for identifying key processes and practices within the project management area.

It should be noted that some of the project management maturity models did include the procurement process as a focus area within its maturity model. For example, the Project Management Solutions model did include the procurement process; however, this model did not break down the procurement process into a level of detail that would provide adequate insight and visibility to organizational contract management key processes and practice activities. The Kerzner model also included the procurement process in its project management focus; however, neither the model nor its related assessment tool provided sufficient detail or visibility in the contracts management processes and activities (Crawford, 2001; Kerzner, 2001).

This research also identified the lack of granularity and specificity as a common criticism of current maturity models (Jugdev & Thomas, 2002). The criticism refers to the lack of detailed information in the focus area of the maturity model. In order to combat this criticism in the development of the contract management maturity model, a strong focus was applied to breaking down the contract management process into its specific sub-processes, thus allowing visibility into the more detailed contract management processes and practices. The purpose of this research was to develop a contract management maturity model specifically designed to focus on the detailed contract management processes and activities, thus giving organizations sufficient insight into its contract management processes.

Develop the basic structure of the contract management maturity model. This research entailed reviewing current contract management, procurement, and purchasing textbooks, journals, and other body of knowledge documents to identify generally accepted key contract management processes and activities.

Based on the results of the Phase One research, a five-level maturity model was developed using the levels of "Ad Hoc," "Basic," "Structured," "Integrated," and "Optimized." The contract management maturity model with the descriptions of each maturity level is fully described in Table 13-1.

Table 13-1 Contract Management Maturity Model (CMMM©) - Narrative

Level 1 — Ad Hoc
- Organization acknowledges that contract management processes exist; that there are accepted contract management processes, and understands the value of contract management processes.
- Contract management processes and standards are used only on an ad hoc and inconsistent basis.
- Documentation of any contract management processes is ad hoc and inconsistent throughout the organization.
- Managers and contract management personnel are not held to any specific accountability for complying with any contract management process standards.

Level 2 — Basic
- Basic contract management processes are used only on selected procurements, typically large, highly visible projects.
- Some documentation exists on these basic contract management processes.
- Basic contract management processes are not considered an organizational standard.
- There is no organizational mandate to use these basic contract management processes.

Level 3 — Structured
- Basic contract management processes are standardized, institutionalized, and mandated throughout the organization.
- Formal documentation has been developed for these standardized contract management processes, and some processes are even automated.
- Procurement processes are tailorable for each specific procurement, allowing consideration for the unique aspects of each procurement.
- Senior management is involved in providing input and approval of key procurement decisions and documents.

Level 4 — Integrated
- The procurement project's end-user customer is an integral member of the procurement team.
- Basic contract management processes are integrated with other organizational core processes such as cost control, schedule management, performance management, and systems engineering.
- Management uses efficiency and effectiveness metrics to make procurement-related decisions.
- Management understands its role in the procurement management process and executes the process well.

Level 5— Optimized
- Contract management processes are evaluated periodically using efficiency and effectiveness metrics.
- Continuous process improvement efforts are implemented to improve the contract management process.
- Lessons learned and best practice programs are implemented to improve contract management processes, standards, and documentation.
- Procurement process streamlining initiatives are implemented as part of the process improvement program.

As previously stated, an important characteristic of the project management maturity models was that most models centered on the project management methods and processes that were universally established and accepted by the project management profession. For most project management maturity models, the project management methods and processes adopted were those from *A Guide to the Project Management Body of Knowledge* (PMBOK) published by the Project Management Institute (2000).

These maturity models used the PMBOK processes as a basis for identifying key processes and practices within the project management area. One problem in developing the contract management maturity model was the lack of an established, universally accepted contract management key processes and practices. Thus, one of the first steps in developing the contract management maturity model was selecting an appropriate model to reflect the contract management process. Several current models were reviewed resulting in the selection of a representative contract management process. The following summarizes this review and selection process.

In 1972, the Commission on Government Procurement (COGP) published its model of the procurement process, which has been widely accepted as representative of the federal procurement process. The COGP procurement model consists of six phases: (1) Needs and Funding, (2) Planning, (3) Solicitation, (4) Selection, (5) Award, and (6) Contract Administration (Sherman, 1985). This model was developed to reflect the various federal procurement statutes and regulations as well as focus on the procurement workforce. Although this model was developed for the federal procurement process, it is also somewhat reflective of procurement processes used by commercial organizations. One limitation of this model is the lack of granularity into the contract termination and closeout phase of the procurement process. The COGP model combines the termination and closeout phase with the contract administration phase. This aspect of the COGP model reflects a model not providing adequate visibility and insight into these two aspects of the procurement process.

Raedels (2000) describes the procurement/purchasing process as a nine-step process that is focused on acquiring materials and services of the right quality, in the right quantity, at the right price, at the right time, and from the right source. This purchasing process includes the following steps: (1) User Identifies Needs, (2) Requisition Process, (3) Identify Potential Sources, (4) Develop Solicitation Proposal, (5) Evaluate Proposals, (6) Evaluate Suppliers, (7) Develop Contract, (8) Manage Contract, and (9) Close Contract (Raedels, 2000). The model seems to be all-inclusive and provides sufficient visibility and focus into the various phases of procurement. This model is unique in that it separates the proposal evaluation from the supplier evaluation. Although both evaluations are separate and have different objectives, most models combine these phases into one phase usually called "source selection." Raedels' model is similar to the process described by Leenders and Fearon (1997). Both models consist of nine separate steps, but the Leenders and Fearon model focuses more on the procurement of small-dollar value, commodity-type supplies, using mechanical steps such as "Follow Up and /or Expedite the Order," "Receipt of Inspection of Goods," and "Maintain Records."

With the transformation of the procurement function towards a "supply management" perspective, Burt, Dobler and Starling (2003) developed a model describing the four phases of supply management. This supply management model consists of the following phases: (1) Generation of Requirements, (2) Sourcing, (3) Pricing, and (4) Post-Award Activities. Although a much simpler model than the previous models discussed, the supply management model focuses more on the development of supply alliances, the total cost of ownership, supplier development, and supplier relationship management. As can be seen, this model does not delve too much into the processes of establishing procurement strategy, structuring and awarding a contract, and administering and closing out a contract.

An excellent depiction of the federal acquisition process is provided by Engelbeck (2002) who uses an eight-step Acquisition Process Model, illustrating the major events associated with the procurement of goods and services. These steps include Requirements Determination, Acquisition Planning, The Solicitation, Source Selection, Negotiation, Contract Award, Contract Performance, and Contract Closeout. This model is primarily based on the Department of Defense system for managing major defense programs.

In 1997 Gregory A. Garrett developed a contract management model using a six-phase process covering the totality of contract management activities for both the buyer and the seller. This model captures all of the contract management activities beginning with the procurement strategy planning processes and concluding with the contract termination or contract completion process. A unique aspect of Garrett's model (1997) is that it reflects not only the "buyer's process" side of contract management, but also the "seller's process." Garrett's contract management model, reflecting the buyer's activities consists of the following phases: (1) Procurement Planning, (2) Solicitation Planning, (3) Solicitation, (4) Source Selection, (5) Contract Administration, and (6) Contract Closeout. The contract management model reflecting the seller's activities consist of the following phases: (1) Pre-sales Activity, (2) Bid/No-Bid Decision Making, (3) Bid or Proposal Preparation, (4) Contract Negotiation and Formation, (5) Contract Administration, and (6) Contract Closeout (Garrett, 1997). Each of the phases in the seller's model coincides with the related phase in the buyer's process. Of all of the models reviewed, Garrett's model was the only one that focused on both the buyer and seller's contract management activities. This is reflective of the perspective that contract management is about developing and maintaining professional business relationships between the buyer and the seller (Garrett, 1997). Garrett's model is based on the project procurement management process established by the Project Management Institute in its Guide to the Project Management Body of Knowledge, referred to as the PMBOK (Project Management Institute, 2000). The Project Management Institute has developed standards for the project management profession that have been accepted and adopted world-wide. The PMBOK is considered by some to be the world's de facto standard for project management knowledge and practices in today's global marketplace. The PMBOK has established a standard process for each area of the project management discipline. These areas include integration management, scope management, time management, cost management, quality management, human resource management, communications management, risk management, and procurement management. Garrett has expanded on the PMBOK project procurement management process by adding visibility to the buyer's as well as seller's side of the contract management process.

Based on the review of these current contract management models, as well as other current procurement and contract management textbooks, to include the National Contract Management Association's Contract Management Body of Knowledge (Bruce, Norby & Ramos, 2002), and the Institute for Supply Management's (formerly the National Association of Purchasing Management) Purchasing Handbook, (Cavinato & Kaufman, 1999), a decision was made as to which contract management process to adopt in the development of the maturity model. The review of these contract management bodies of knowledge also identified key practice activities for the selected contract management process (Burt, Dobler & Starling, 2003; Garrett, 2001; Huston, 1996; Leenders & Fearon, 1997).

For the purpose of developing the contract management maturity model, it was decided to adopt Garrett's six-phase contract management process, based on the PMI PMBOK (Garrett, 1997). Adopting an existing industry-accepted contract management model, which provided the level of detail needed in establishing the process capability maturity model proved beneficial in accomplishing this research objective.

The Garrett model provided an established baseline of the contract management process for both buyers and sellers that could be expanded upon in developing the contract management maturity model. The contract management maturity model reflecting the buyer's activities consists of the following six *key process areas* -- Procurement Planning, Solicitation Planning, Solicitation, Source Selection, Contract Administration, and Contract Closeout. The contract maturity model reflecting the seller's activities consists of the following six *key process areas* -- Pre-sales Activity, Bid/No-Bid Decision Making, Bid or Proposal Preparation, Contract Negotiation and Formation, Contract Administration, and Contract Closeout. It should be noted that the contract management key process areas of Contract Administration and Contract Closeout are identical for *both* the buyer and seller—that is, both the buyer and seller perform identical contract administration and contract closeout functions during the management of a contractual relationship. These contract management *key process areas* and *key practice activities* were instrumental in developing assessment tools for buyers and sellers for measuring an organization's contract management process capability.

Table 13-2 illustrates the CMMM© reflecting the five levels of maturity and the six contract management key process areas for both buyers and sellers. These key process areas provide detailed insight and visibility into an organization's contract management process capability. Tables 13-3 and 13-4 illustrate the contract management key process areas and key practice activities for the buyer, respectively. Tables 13-5 and 13-6 illustrate the contract management key process areas and key practice activities for the seller, respectively. The next section discusses the development of an appropriate assessment tool for buyers and sellers for measuring organizational contract management maturity.

Table 13-2 Contract Management Muturity Model

Maturity Levels	Buyer	Contract Management Process Areas						
		Procurement Planning	Solicitation Planning	Solicitation	Source Selection	Contract Admin	Contract Closeout
	Seller	Presales Activity	Bid/No-Bid Decision	Bid/Proposal Preparation	Negotiation Formation		
5 Optimized								
4 Integrated								
3 Structured								
2 Basic								
1 Ad Hoc								

Table 13-3 Contract Management Key Process Areas (Buyer's Perspective)

1. Procurement Planning: Determining what to procure and when.

2. Solicitation Planning: Documenting program requirements and identifying potential sources.

3. Solicitation: Obtaining quotations, bids, offers, or proposals, as appropriate.

4. Source Selection: Choosing from among potential offerors.

5. Contract Administration: Managing the relationship with the contractor.

6. Contract Closeout: Completion and settlement of the contract, including resolution of any open items.

Table13-4 Contract Management Key Practice Activities (Buyer's Perspective)

Procurement Planning

The organization has an established process for effectively determining the scope of work or description of the product to be procured.

The process for determining the scope of work or description of the product to be procured includes representatives from procurement, program management, technical, and other affected functional areas.

Adequate resources to conduct procurement planning are obtained by the organization, either internally or externally.

Effective market research is conducted as part of the procurement planning process.

The procurement planning process considers other program team areas such as funds availability, preliminary cost and schedule estimates, quality management plans, cash flow projections, work breakdown structures, risk management, and manpower resources.

The procurement planning process provides an integrated assessment of contract type selection, risk management, and contract terms and conditions.

The result of the procurement planning process is a documented acquisition management plan that effectively provides a roadmap for the upcoming procurement.

The statement of work adequately describes the buyer's requirement in sufficient detail to allow the prospective sellers to submit a bid or proposal.

Table 13-4 Contract Management Key Practice Activities (Buyer's Perspective) Cont'd.

Solicitation Planning

The solicitation planning process includes the use of standard procurement forms and documents such as solicitations, model contracts, item descriptions, terms and conditions, statements of work, work breakdown structures, and data item descriptions.

Solicitation planning processes have incorporated automated and paperless processes as much as possible within the organization, as well as with customers and contractors.

Adequate resources to conduct solicitation planning are obtained by the organization, either internally or externally.

Solicitations are structured to facilitate accurate and complete responses from prospective contractors.

Solicitations are rigorous enough to ensure consistent, comparable responses but flexible enough to allow consideration of contractor suggestions for better ways to satisfy the requirements.

Solicitation documents include appropriate evaluation criteria consistent with the acquisition strategy of the project.

The solicitation planning process allows for amendments to solicitation documents prior to issuing the solicitation.

Solicitation

The organization maintains a qualified bidders list providing information on prospective sellers such as relevant experience, areas of expertise, and other information.

The organization conducts market research and advertising to identify new sources of supplies and services as part of the solicitation process.

Depending on the nature of the procurement, a pre-solicitation conference, or a pre-bid conference may be conducted to ensure all prospective contractors have a clear common understanding of the technical and contractual requirements of the procurement.

The organization solicits inputs from industry to be used in developing solicitations for certain types of procurements.

The organization uses a paperless process to the greatest extent possible in issuing solicitations and receiving proposals

Source Selection

The organization uses evaluation criteria, evaluation standards, and a weighting system to evaluate proposals.

Proposal evaluation focuses on management criteria, technical criteria, and price criteria.

The evaluation criteria for selecting contractors, either lowest cost/technically acceptable, or best value, are tailored to meet the objectives of the procurement plan.

The price proposals are compared against the organization's independent cost estimate during the proposal evaluation process.

Price evaluation includes a determination of price reasonableness, in terms of realism and competitiveness.

The organization takes into consideration a contractor's past performance on previously awarded contracts in evaluating proposals.

The organization uses a team approach to conducting negotiations with potential contractors.

If needed, the organization may conduct a pre-award survey on the potential contractor to verify the contractor's technical, managerial, and financial capability.

The organization provides debriefings to the successful as well as unsuccessful contractors.

Table 13-4 Contract Management Key Practice Activities (Buyer's Perspective) Cont'd.

Contract Administration

The organization has an established method for assigning contracts to individuals or teams for managing the post-award phase of the contract.

For applicable contracts, a pre-performance meeting is conducted to discuss buyer and seller contract administration responsibilities, as well as protocols for communication, performance management, and contract change management.

The organization uses a team approach for monitoring the contractor's performance to ensure the fulfillment of contractual obligations by all parties of the contract.

The organization has an established process for managing and controlling contract changes to cost, schedule, and performance requirements, ensuring that only authorized individuals negotiate or agree to contract changes.

The organization has an established process for managing contractor invoices and payments.

An established process for administering contract incentive fee and award fee provisions is used on applicable contracts.

An established process for conducting periodic and integrated cost, schedule, and performance evaluations, such as Earned Value Management, on the contractor is used as part of the contract administration process.

The organization encourages contract disputes to be resolved using alternate disputes resolution methods.

An established process for maintaining a conformed copy of the contract is used to document all changes to contract requirements.

Contract Closeout

The organization has an established process for closing out contracts, ensuring completion of work, complete documentation, and financial resolution of issues.

The contract closeout process involves checklists, templates, and forms for ensuring proper documentation of closed-out contracts.

The closeout process requires obtaining the seller's release of claims as well as verifying final payment from the buyer.

The contract termination process requires a written or oral notification to terminate a contract due to cause or default.

The organization maintains a lessons-learned and best practices database for use in future projects and contracts.

Table 13-5 Contract Management Key Process Areas (Seller's Perspective)

1. Presales Activity: Identifying prospective and current customers, determining customer's needs and plans, and evaluating the competitive environment.

2. Bid/No-Bid Decision Making: Evaluating the buyer's solicitation, assessing the competitive environment and the risks against the opportunities of a potential business deal, and then deciding whether to proceed.

3. Bid or Proposal Preparation: Developing offers in response to a buyer's solicitation or based on perceived buyer needs, for the purpose of persuading the buyer to enter into a contract.

4. Contract Negotiation and Formation: Reaching a common understanding of the nature of the project and negotiating the contract terms and conditions for the purpose of developing a set of shared expectations and understandings.

5. Contract Administration: Managing the relationship with the buyer.

6. Contract Closeout: Completion and settlement of the contract, including resolution of any open items.

Table 13-6 Contract Management Key Practice Activities (Seller's Perspective)

Presales Activity

The organization has an established process for effectively identifying prospective and current customers, determining customer's needs and plans, and evaluating the competitive environment.

The process for identifying prospective and current customers involves an integrated and proactive sales management effort between the organizations' marketing, sales, and other functional personnel, and involves the customer's process needs, desires, budgets, and key decision makers.

The process for determining and influencing customer needs and plans includes conducting market research and benchmarking to determine who buys the types of products the organization sells, and to stay up to date on the technologies relevant to its products and services, the needs of its buyers, the strategies and activities of its competitors, and the dynamics of the market. The result of the market research and benchmarking is a prioritized list of potential and existing customers.

The process for evaluating the competitive environment involves an objective analysis of the buyer, seller, and the seller's competitors. This includes a competitive analysis report of the strengths, weaknesses, opportunities and threats (SWOT analysis) of all players in the competitive environment, as well as a complete financial Business Case analysis assessing the expected costs, revenue, cost of money, desired margin, rate of return, and realized revenue of any potential sales opportunity.

The results of presales activity consist of a formal documented sales management plan that effectively provides a roadmap for obtaining and retaining customers. This sales management plan includes the prioritized list of potential and existing customers, competitive analysis report, and the complete Business Case analysis.

Table 13-6 Contract Management Key Practice Activities (Seller's Perspective) Cont'd

Bid/No-Bid Decision Making

The organization has an established process for effectively evaluating the buyer's solicitation, assessing the competitive environment and the risks against the opportunities of a potential business deal, and then deciding whether to proceed.

The process for effectively evaluating the buyer's solicitation involves an integrated team effort between the organization's contracts, cost, program management, and other functional personnel.

The process for effectively assessing risks involves identifying, analyzing, and mitigating the risks associated with a potential project, using practical risk management tools—surveys, checklists, models and reports--containing both quantitative and qualitative information. Software programs are often used in performing this risk assessment.

The process for effectively assessing opportunities involves identifying and analyzing the opportunities that are potentially viable from the project, using standard forms, surveys, checklists or models.

The processes used for analyzing the risk versus opportunities reflect a solid understanding of risk management and a designated risk management team process to identify, analyze, and mitigate risks.

The results of the Bid/No-Bid Decision Making consist of the final decision on whether to bid on the project, and a formal document justifying the seller's reason for its decision.

Bid or Proposal Preparation

The organization has an established process for effectively developing offers in response to a buyer's solicitation or based on perceived buyer needs, for the purpose of persuading the buyer to enter into a contract.

The process of developing proposals involves an integrated, coordinated, planned, and controlled team effort between the organization's contracts, cost, program management, and other functional personnel.

The organization conducts an in-depth analysis of the buyer's solicitation and develops a compliance matrix showing where it meets, exceeds, or fails to meet the buyer's stated requirements.

The organization uses a competitive analysis report to compare the seller's strengths and weaknesses to those of its competitors.

The organization has an established process for reviewing standard contract terms and conditions as a basis for developing terms and conditions tailored to a particular solicitation.

The organization reviews past proposals as a tool to share lessons learned and maintains a lessons-learned database for documenting and sharing proposal preparation best practices.

Proposals are either supplemented or replaced with oral presentations to reduce cycle time, increase the quality of the products or services offered, and provide more information for better decision-making.

The organization uses an external review team to objectively evaluate the proposal prior to submission of the proposal to the potential buyer.

The results of the Bid or Proposal Preparation process consist of the proposal and/or oral presentation with executive summary and supporting documentation.

Table 13-6 Contract Management Key Practice Activities (Seller's Perspective) Cont'd

Contract Negotiation and Formation

The organization has an established process for reaching a common understanding of the nature of the project and negotiating the contract terms and conditions for the purpose of developing a set of shared expectations and understandings.

An integrated team approach consisting of highly skilled negotiators knowledgeable of market and industry practices is used for planning, conducting, and documenting the negotiation process.

The negotiation team develops a solid and approved team negotiation plan and uses negotiation agendas, interim summaries, final negotiation summary, and negotiation reviews and approval as part of the organizational negotiation process.

A documented transition plan and contract administration plan is used for transitioning to the contract administration phase of the project.

The organization maintains a database of documented lessons learned and best practices for use in planning future negotiations.

The results of the Contract Negotiation and Formation phase is either a contract agreement acceptable to the seller's organization with supporting documentation (negotiation memorandum) or a documented decision to "walk away" from a bad business deal.

Contract Administration

The organization has an established method for assigning contracts to individuals or teams for managing the post-award phase of the contract.

For applicable contracts, a pre-performance meeting is conducted to discuss buyer and seller contract administration responsibilities, as well as protocols for communication, performance management, and contract change management.

The organization uses a team approach for monitoring the contractor's performance to ensure the fulfillment of contractual obligations by all parties of the contract.

The organization has an established process for managing and controlling contract changes to cost, schedule, and performance requirements, ensuring that only authorized individuals negotiate or agree to contract changes.

The organization has an established process for managing contractor invoices and payments.

An established process for administering contract incentive fee and award fee provisions is used on applicable contracts.

An established process for conducting periodic and integrated cost, schedule, and performance evaluations, such as Earned Value Management, on the contractor is used as part of the contract administration process.

The organization encourages contract disputes to be resolved using alternate disputes resolution methods.

An established process for maintaining a conformed copy of the contract is used to document all changes to contract requirements.

Contract Closeout

The organization has an established process for closing out contracts, ensuring completion of work, complete documentation, and financial resolution of issues.

The contract closeout process involves checklists, templates, and forms for ensuring proper documentation of closed-out contracts.

The closeout process requires obtaining the seller's release of claims as well as verifying final payment from the buyer.

The contract termination process requires a written or oral notification to terminate a contract due to cause or default.

The organization maintains a lessons-learned and best practices database for use in future projects and contracts.

DEVELOPING AN APPROPRIATE ASSESSMENT TOOL FOR BUYERS AND SELLERS FOR MEASURING CONTRACT MANAGEMENT MATURITY

This discussion applies the information obtained in developing the CMMM© to developing a tool for assessing an organization's contract management process capability maturity–the Contract Management Maturity Assessment Tool (CMMAT©).

The literature review on the software management, workforce management, and project management maturity models indicates that the self-administered survey was an effective and timely assessment method for obtaining information on these business processes (Persse, 2001; Curtis, et al., 2001; Carr, 2001; Dinsmore, 1998; Foti, 2002; Kerzner, 2001). Thus, the survey was selected as the assessment method for the contract management maturity model. This contract management survey will be used to obtain information on the organization's key contract management processes and practices. This information will, in turn, be used to assess the maturity level of the organization's contract management process capability. The following discussion is presented on how the survey statements were developed and response options were structured.

Developing survey statements. The Contract Management Maturity Assessment Tool (CMMAT©) consists of two self-administered surveys, one for Buyers and one for Sellers, containing specifically developed statements related to each of the contract management buying and selling key process areas and related key practice activities identified in the first research objective. The contract management key process areas for the buyer (procurement planning, solicitation planning, solicitation, source selection, contract administration, and contract closeout) and the contract management key process areas for the seller (Pre-sales Activity, Bid/No-Bid Decision Making, Bid or Proposal Preparation, Contract Negotiation and Formation, Contract Administration, and Contract Closeout) were used as the basis for the development of the maturity assessment tool. A separate set of survey statements was developed for each key process area. Furthermore, for each key process area, survey statements were developed to address the contract management key practice activities, related to each key process area. The survey statements were constructed to obtain information on the extent to which the organization executed or implemented the various key practice activities. Additionally, the survey statements were structured such that the extent of the implementation of each key practice activity by the organization indicated the maturity level for that specific contract management process area. Thus, the respondent's answers to specific survey statements would determine if the organization was at the "Ad Hoc," "Basic," "Structured," "Integrated," or "Optimized" level of maturity for that specific process.

Structuring survey responses. The maturity assessment tools were designed using a Likert scale response protocol. With this type of response structure, the respondent is asked to agree or disagree with each statement. The respondent has six choices ranging from "Never" to "Always," or "Don't Know (DK)," depending on the respondent's opinion on each statement. Each response is given a numerical score to reflect its degree of attitude favorableness, for example, a response of "Never" equates to a score of 1, while a response of "Always" equates to a score of 5. The response option of "Don't Know" was given a numerical value of 0. The rationale for assigning a numerical value of 0 to the "Don't Know" response option is that in order for an organizational process to be capable and effective, it must be well known and accepted throughout the organization. A response of "Don't Know" indicates that key process area and activity is not well established, nor understood throughout this program office. The Likert scale allows the optional responses to be correlated with the different levels of the maturity model, for that specific contract management key process area. Thus, the response options chosen by the respondents for each survey item will be used to determine the level of process capability maturity for that specific aspect of the contract management process. The scores for all of the survey statements for that key process area are then totaled. The total score is then converted to the maturity level for that specific contract management key process area. A conversion table was developed to convert the total scores for each contract management key process area to a specific maturity level. Once the surveys for each of the six contract management key process areas are completed, a maturity level assessment could be made for each key process area. Upon development of the completed assessment tool, a "test run" of the survey was performed to ensure understanding, clarity, and effectiveness of the survey statements, optional responses, and overall mechanics of the assessment tool.

CHAPTER 14

CONTRACT MANAGEMENT RISK AND OPPORTUNITY ASSESSMENT TOOL

INTRODUCTION

The Contract Management Risk and Opportunity Assessment Tool (CMROAT©) is designed to help organizations, both buyers and sellers, assess the risk and opportunities associated with a pending/potential or actual contract. CMROAT© was developed in 1992 by Garrett Consulting Services, a Virginia, USA based international consulting practice. CMROAT© has evolved over the past 15 years as a tool designed to provide contract and project, preaward or postaward, risk and opportunity assessment. The tool was originally designed for use by buyers and has evolved to provide a similar assessment capability for sellers in both the U.S. Government and commercial markets worldwide. The tool provides a high-level, first pass evaluation of the risks and opportunities associated with a contract. The tool is intended to be completed by the Contract Manager, Project Manager, and other functional team members. The best time to use CMROAT© is prior to contract award.

The process for performing the risk and opportunity assessment involves four basic steps.

1. *There are two versions of CMROAT©*, one for buyers (CMROAT-BP©), and on for sellers (CMROAT-SP©). Select the appropriate version and complete the survey.

2. *Evaluating the risk.* A series of ten questions on Risk Analysis are to be answered, with a score for each to be calculated. The questions have been weighted on a scale of 1 (low) to 5 (high) in terms of their relative importance to each other. The score is calculated by multiplying the raw score (Risk Factor (R)) by the pre-established weight value (W). The total risk score for each question is then calculated and entered into the space provided, for the Total Risk Score on each page. Plus, transfer the total risk score for each question to the Summary Scorecard. After completing all of the ten questions on Risk Analysis, add up the Grand Total Risk on the Summary Scorecard.

3. *Evaluating the opportunity.* A series of ten questions on Opportunity Analysis are to be answered, with a score for each to be calculated. The questions have been weighted on a score of 1 (low) to 5 (high) in terms of their relative importance to each other. This score is calculated by multiplying the raw score

(Opportunity Factor (O) by a pre-established Weight Value (W). After each question has been scored, then transfer the Total Opportunity Score to the Summary Scorecard. After completing all of the ten questions on Opportunity Analysis, add up the Grand Total Opportunity on the Summary Scorecard.

4. *Mapping the risk and opportunity to the matrix.* The Grand total scores for risk and opportunity are plotted on the matrix. The location of this score on the matrix helps determine the extent of opportunity and the level of risk that will need to be managed to ensure on-time delivery of quality products, services, or solutions at a fair and reasonable price.

Interpreting the Results

Once the grand total scores have been mapped on the matrix, the Contract Manager, Project Manager, and other team members can determine the next appropriate step. Normally, a meeting with management is held to review the contract. This meeting should include management representation from each of the functional organizations that would be responsible for performing the work, developing a Project Plan, and administering the contract. These same organizations will ultimately be responsible for contract and project execution.

If the contract risk and opportunity assessment is unfavorable, the Contract Manager in conjunction with the Project Manager may search for ways to improve the opportunity and/or reduce the risk prior to contract award. Alternatively, the Contract Manager with concurrence from the Project Manager and organization executives may conclude the proposed contract should not be awarded or accepted.

Contract Management
Risk and Opportunity Assessment Tool

Seller's Perspective
(CMROAT-SP©)

RISK ANALYSIS

The Seller's Perspective

Weight Factor (W)	x	Risk Factor (R)	=	Total Score (W x R)

1. Buyer Commitment

Buyer commitment is a vital factor in the success of a contract. A committed Buyer will place a high degree of importance on the contract and will make it part of its business plan. A committed Buyer will apply resources, such as a Project Manager and staff, as well as a budget to implement the contract. A committed Buyer is less likely to change or cancel the contract, and therefore represents a lower risk.

Risk Factor (R)

1 2 3 4

__5__ x ⬜⬜⬜⬜ = _____

How committed is the Buyer to the contract?

1. The Buyer has assigned personnel and a budget.
2. The Buyer has assigned a budget, but no personnel.
3. The Buyer has assigned personnel, but no budget.
4. The Buyer has not assigned personnel or a budget.

RISK ANALYSIS

The Seller's Perspective

	Weight Factor (W)	x	Risk Factor (R)	=	Total Score (W x R)

2. Contract Timetable

Each contract has a set start and completion date. The Buyer will normally require that the contract be completed within a specific time. Typically, this is driven by the Buyer's business cycle, selling season, and other factors. The ability to meet the contract timetable requirements is highly dependent on the magnitude of the contract and the availability and coordination of the correct skills and resources. A contract timetable that is flexible and can be established by the Supplier, with no penalty clauses, represents the least risk.

Risk Factor (R)

$$\underline{\quad 4 \quad} \times \boxed{\begin{array}{cccc} 1 & 2 & 3 & 4 \\ & & & \end{array}} = \underline{\qquad}$$

How has the contract timetable been established?

1. Contract start and end dates are flexible and will be established by the Seller.

2. Contract start and end dates will be mutually established by the Buyer and the Seller.

3. Contract start and end dates have been set by the Buyer. There is no penalty clauses, but changing the schedule and milestones is difficult and must be negotiated with the Buyer.

4. Contract start and end dates have been set by the Buyer and are not changeable. Penalty clauses may exist for not meeting milestones.

RISK ANALYSIS

The Seller's Perspective

	Weight Factor (W)	x	Risk Factor (R)	=	Total Score (W x R)

3. Contract Duration

The duration of the contract has a bearing on the level of risk associated with it. The longer the contract, the greater the chance of significant changes. Personnel, customer environment, and the business climate are a few examples of areas subject to significant change as time passes. These changes can pose substantial risk to the contract.

Risk Factor (R)

$$\underline{\quad 3 \quad} \quad x \quad \boxed{\begin{array}{|c|c|c|c|} 1 & 2 & 3 & 4 \\ \end{array}} \quad = \quad \underline{\qquad}$$

What is the projected duration of the contract from the time it is awarded to the time it is expected to be completed?

1. Three months to six months
2. Between six months and one year
3. One year
4. More than one year

RISK ANALYSIS

The Seller's Perspective

Weight Factor (W)	x	Risk Factor (R)	=	Total Score (W x R)

4. Previous Seller's Experience

Experience with a previous contract that was similar to this one can reduce risk. Determine how many of the contract requirements can be met using products, technologies, and/or skills that have been used by the Seller on other contracts. Consider:

_ The skills available at the local level to manage and carry out this contract

_ How much of the system solution needs to be developed as opposed to having been done before somewhere within the Seller.

_ The Seller's experience with the non-Seller's products needed for the solution

_ The Seller's experience with the external suppliers and subcontractors required.

Risk Factor (R)

$$\underline{\quad 4 \quad} \quad x \quad \boxed{\begin{array}{c|c|c|c} 1 & 2 & 3 & 4 \end{array}} \quad = \quad \underline{\qquad}$$

What is the Seller's experience with similar solutions?

1. The contract is a replication of a previous contract managed locally.

2. A majority (50% or greater) of the contract requirements replicate a previous contract done by the Seller.

3. A minority (less than 50%) of the contract requirements replicate a previous contract done by the Seller.

4. None of the contract requirements can be satisfied using previous experience, either local or worldwide.

RISK ANALYSIS

The Seller's Perspective

Weight Factor (W)	x	Risk Factor (R)	=	Total Score (W x R)

5. The Seller's Participation in Contract Definition

Many Buyers develop contract requirements without the participation of those who will bid on the contracts. In this type of situation, those who bid will have had little or no input regarding schedules, technology, product selection, and so on. The less the Seller is involved in the development of the requirements, the higher the risk presented by the contract.

Risk Factor (R)

1 2 3 4

  3   x ☐☐☐☐ = _____

Did the Seller have any involvement in the development of the requirements?

1. The Seller developed requirements for the Buyer.
2. The Seller guided the Buyer in developing requirements.
3. The Seller was asked for comments after requirements were developed.
4. The Seller had no involvement in developing the requirements.

RISK ANALYSIS

The Seller's Perspective

	Weight Factor (W)	x	Risk Factor (R)	=	Total Score (W x R)

6. External Resource Coordination

Most contracts that provide a customized solution use the resources of one or more organizations external to the Seller. At a minimum, coordination with the Buyer is required. External organizations can also include non-Seller hardware and software manufacturers and/or distributors, application software developers, professional Service Providers, and consultants. The number of external organizations involved directly relates to the amount of risk in the contract; the more external resource coordination needed, the higher the risk.

Risk Factor (R)

<u> 3 </u> x 1 2 3 4 [ ] [ ] [ ] [ ] = _____

Not including the Buyer, how many suppliers and/or subcontractors will need to be coordinated for this Contract?

1. None
2. One or two
3. Three to five
4. Six or more

FOURTEEN

RISK ANALYSIS

The Seller's Perspective

	Weight Factor (W)	x	Risk Factor (R)	=	Total Score (W x R)

7. Requirements Evaluation Timeframe

Bid requests usually specify a date when a response must be returned to the requester. This time requirement presents an element of risk. A request requiring a quick response may not give the Seller the necessary time to do a thorough evaluation of the request. A complex contract requiring a bid response (proposal) in 30 days or less could be considered aggressive. Conversely, a simple contract allowing more than 30 days for a response could be considered conservative. The shorter the time allowed to develop a response, the higher the risk.

Risk Factor (R)

1 2 3 4

___3___ x ☐☐☐☐ = _____

Which of the following best describes the time frame allotted for assessing Buyer requirements and generating a proposal?

1. Not a significant factor
2. Moderate
3. Aggressive
4. Very Aggressive

RISK ANALYSIS

The Seller's Perspective

	Weight Factor (W)	x	Risk Factor (R)	=	Total Score (W x R)

8. Technology and Product Maturity

Consider the maturity of the technologies and products to be used in this solution. Many products available today are so widely used that they have been accepted as industry standards. Products that have a substantial field population and have been in use for a year or more are considered mature. These types of products are typically very reliable and pose little risk. However, prereleased and newly released products, or products using leading-edge technology, pose greater risks.

Risk Factor (R)

$$\underline{\quad 2 \quad} \quad x \quad \boxed{\begin{array}{|c|c|c|c|} \hline 1 & 2 & 3 & 4 \\ \hline \end{array}} \quad = \quad \underline{\qquad}$$

What percentage of the products needed to satisfy the requirements are mature?

1. All requirements can be satisfied with mature, released products.

2. Less than 30% of the products will be prereleased or new products, or products using leading-edge technology.

3. Between 30% to 70% of the products will be prereleased or new products, or products using leading-edge technology.

4. 70% or more of the products will be prereleased or new products, or products using leading-edge technology.

RISK ANALYSIS

The Seller's Perspective

	Weight Factor (W)	x	Risk Factor (R)	=	Total Score (W x R)

9. Geographic Distribution

The geographic distribution of the contract adds complexity and risk. The greater the geographic distribution, the greater the risk due to factors such as distance, time zone differential, and language barriers.

Risk Factor (R)

$$\underline{\quad 2 \quad} \quad x \quad \begin{array}{|c|c|c|c|} \hline 1 & 2 & 3 & 4 \\ \hline & & & \\ \hline \end{array} \quad = \quad \underline{\qquad}$$

What is the geographic distribution of the contract as it relates to the Seller's locations?

1. Confined to one location
2. Confined to one region, with multiple locations
3. Confined to one country
4. Distributed across multiple countries

RISK ANALYSIS

The Seller's Perspective

	Weight Factor (W)	x	Risk Factor (R)	=	Total Score (W x R)

10. Contract Manager Assessment of the Deal

The Contract Manager or equivalent should provide an overall assessment of the feasibility of the contract. This is the point at which the Contract Manager can express an opinion on the likelihood that the Seller could effectively manage the risk and satisfy the customer project requirements to deliver within the scope and terms of the contract. The Contract Manager may be aware of other risk factors (such as economic or political instability) not yet considered.

Risk Factor (R)

<u> 3 </u>   x   [1 2 3 4]   =   _____

On a scale of 1 (low risk) to 10 (high risk), what is the Contract Manager's overall risk assessment of the Seller's ability to successfully manage this contract? (Briefly describe those reasons in the space provided below.)

1. 5 or less - Manageable risk
2. 6 or 7 - Risk mitigation likely
3. 8 or 9 - Very high risk
4. 10 - Extremely high risk

OPPORTUNITY ANALYSIS

The Seller's Perspective

	Weight Factor (W)	x	Oppt Factor (O)	=	Total Score (W x O)

1. Promotes Seller's Strategic Direction

Any contract and related project, if properly executed, will promote the reputation and image of the Seller. However, the more valuable opportunities are those that are consistent with the Seller's core business and strategic direction. These contracts:

_ Support our strategic market direction

_ Support our focus on key accounts

_ Utilize our knowledge of specific industries

_ Represent an excellent example of the type of business Seller seeks and will serve as a reference for future sales efforts with other accounts

The more of these attributes a contract has, the better the opportunity. If properly executed, a contract has all of the above attributes promotes Seller as a industry leader.

Opportunity Factor (O)

1 2 3 4

   5   x ☐☐☐☐ = _____

How many of the Seller's major strategies as outlined above are matched by this contract?

1. One
2. Two
3. Three
4. Four

OPPORTUNITY ANALYSIS

The Seller's Perspective

	Weight Factor (W)	x	Oppt Factor (O)	=	Total Score (W x O)

2. Revenue Generated within 12 Months of Award

At this point in the contract assessment, exact pricing has not yet been performed. However, an estimate of the amount of revenue expected as a result of the contract should be developed. The estimate should include only revenue that will be generated within the scope of the contract as defined by the contract. The revenues should include all hardware, software, and service revenues (Do not include future revenue potential beyond the scope of this contract).

Opportunity Factor (O)

$$\underline{\quad 4 \quad} \quad x \quad \boxed{\begin{array}{c} 1\ 2\ 3\ 4 \\ \Box\Box\Box\Box \end{array}} = \underline{\qquad}$$

What is the estimated value of the contract in U.S. dollars, including all hardware, software, and services?

1. $500,000 or less
2. Greater than $500,000, but less than $2,500,000
3. At least $2,500,000, but less than $5,000,000
4. $5,000,000 or greater

FOURTEEN

OPPORTUNITY ANALYSIS

The Seller's Perspective

	Weight Factor (W)	x	Oppt Factor (O)	=	Total Score (W x O)

3. Margin Strategy for First 12 Months After Award

Estimate the percentage gross margin that is likely to be realized on the revenue generated by this contract. This gross margin (GM) should be the aggregate for the contract combining hardware, software, and service margins. Ideally, the margin should be consistent with the margin plan for the organization bidding on the contract. However, competitive pressures and the need to win may cause Seller to consider break-even or a loss on the contract. Such might be the case when the contract will lead to a high volume of profitable business in the future. (When generating the profit estimate, do not include the margins generated by future revenues beyond the scope of this contract).

Opportunity Factor (O)

$$\underline{\quad 4 \quad} \quad x \quad \boxed{1\ 2\ 3\ 4} \quad = \quad \underline{\qquad}$$

How does the gross margin in this contract compare to the percentage margin goals stated in the annual plan for the organization bidding on the contract?

1. Negative margins, or break-even
2. Margins up to 50% of annual plan
3. Margins greater than 50%, but less than 100% of annual plan
4. Margins equal to or in excess of annual plan

Example: An organization's annual plan states a 32% GM goal for a given year. For a contract that is contracted to generate up to 16% margin, you should select the second answer.

OPPORTUNITY ANALYSIS

The Seller's Perspective

Weight Factor (W)	x	Oppt Factor (O)	=	Total Score (W x O)

4. Future Business Potential

A contract may represent a good opportunity because of the future business potential. The contract may provide the means to enter a new account, or may be required to protect an existing account. Participation in the contract (either in whole or in part) may be required for the Seller to be considered for future business. Consider the need to do this contract relative to its effect on the relationship between Seller and this Buyer, and the potential for future Seller hardware, software, and services opportunities within this Buyer.

Opportunity Factor (O)

1 2 3 4

 3   x ☐☐☐☐ = _____

What impact will successful conclusion of the contract have on future Seller opportunities with this Buyer?

1. The contract has little or no bearing on future business

2. Future business is possible as a result of this contract.

3. Future business is likely as a result of this contract.

4. Future business is assured as a result of this contract, or participation is mandatory to remain a viable supplier.

OPPORTUNITY ANALYSIS

The Seller's Perspective

	Weight Factor (W)	x	Oppt Factor (O)	=	Total Score (W x O)

5. Provides Added Experience and/or New Skills

Occasionally, a contract is desirable for the education and/or experience to be gained by the Seller. While learning and experience occur on any contract, those that will significantly improve the skills of the Seller Team, and/or develop previously nonexistent critical skills, are the more favored contracts. Skills such as managing the contract, delivering new products and technologies, and supporting the Buyer are just a few examples.

Opportunity Factor (O)

$$\underline{3} \quad x \quad \boxed{} \quad = \quad \underline{}$$

What is the value of the experience and skills to be gained from the contract?

1. Little improvement in existing skills is expected because the Seller's Team is very experienced.
2. Significant improvement in existing skills will be gained by the Seller's Team members.
3. Little improvement in existing skills is expected, but some new skills and expertise will be developed.
4. Significant improvement in existing skills is expected, and new skills and expertise also will be developed by the Seller's Team members.

FOURTEEN

OPPORTUNITY ANALYSIS

The Seller's Perspective

	Weight Factor (W)	x	Oppt Factor (O)	=	Total Score (W x O)

6. Resource Utilization

A contract may be highly desirable if it makes good use of the Seller's resources and assets that are either currently or projected to be underutilized. Even a contract that might otherwise be declined may be desirable for its positive impact on the Seller's resource and asset utilization. The impact on the sales, project management, and support personnel and the use of Technical facilities and equipment should be considered. Evaluate current resource utilization and the number and type of contracts currently underway. Consider how senior management would react to requests for additional resources.

Opportunity Factor (O)

1 2 3 4

___3___ x ☐☐☐☐ = _____

What impact will this contract have on the Seller's resource and asset utilization?

1. The contract will drain significant resources allocated to other projects.

2. The contract will drain some resources allocated to other projects.

3. The contract will have a normal impact on resources.

4. The contract will make use of currently underutilized resources.

OPPORTUNITY ANALYSIS

The Seller's Perspective

Weight Factor (W)	x	Oppt Factor (O)	=	Total Score (W x O)

7. Buyer Favors the Seller

An opportunity involving a Buyer who favors the Seller before the contract has been awarded (for reasons other than price) is highly desirable. Buyer's may prefer the Seller for any number of reasons, including our technology, reputation, past performance, industry commitment, and so on. Of course, they may favor the competition for the same reasons. Consider the number of competitors vying for the project, as well as the Buyer's past experience with the Seller and/or the competition.

Opportunity Factor (O)

$$\underline{\quad 2 \quad} \quad x \quad \boxed{\begin{array}{cccc} 1 & 2 & 3 & 4 \\ \quad & \quad & \quad & \quad \end{array}} \quad = \quad \underline{\qquad}$$

How does the Buyer consider the Seller in comparison to the competition for this contract?

1. The Buyer favors the competition and is negative towards the Seller for this contract.
2. The Buyer favors the competition and is neutral towards the Seller for this contract.
3. The Buyer is neutral towards all potential suppliers for this contract.
4. The Buyer prefers the Seller for this contract.

OPPORTUNITY ANALYSIS

The Seller's Perspective

Weight Factor (W)	x	Oppt Factor (O)	=	Total Score (W x O)

8. Products and Services Content is all the Sellers

Most contracts will require some products and/or services by other suppliers as subcontractors to the Seller. An ideal contract will have all the products and services provided by the Seller and there are no subcontractors to manage, and no third party products to provide.

Opportunity Factor (O)

$$\underline{\quad 2 \quad} \quad \times \quad \overset{\text{1 2 3 4}}{\boxed{\quad\quad\quad}} \quad = \quad \underline{\quad\quad\quad}$$

What percentage of the revenue will be generated by the Seller's products and services?

1. Less than 50% of the contract revenue will come from the Seller's products and services.
2. 50% to 70% of the contract revenue will come from the Seller's products and services.
3. Between 70% and 90% of the contract revenue will come from the Seller's products and services.
4. 90% or more of the contract revenue will come from the Seller's products and services.

OPPORTUNITY ANALYSIS

The Seller's Perspective

	Weight Factor (W)	x	Oppt Factor (O)	=	Total Score (W x O)

9. Presale Expense

Every contract has presale expense associated with it. The amount of presale expense varies greatly from bid to bid. Some contracts are largely a replication of an existing contract with this account or another account. In other contracts, a significant amount of planning and even a demonstration of the system (including a benchmark) are required before the bid is considered by the account. Contracts with little presale expense are more desirable. Examples of items that increase the level of presale expense include:

_ Additional local resources beyond those normally assigned to this account

_ A benchmark system to be constructed

_ Non-Seller's product(s) to be acquired for evaluation before the proposal is generated

_ Resources from other organizations, such as country or group home office

_ Professional services from outside the Seller's sources

Opportunity Factor (O)

1 2 3 4

__1__ x ☐☐☐☐ = _____

What is the estimated level of presale expense for this Contract?

(Use the items listed above as a guide).

1. High (All of the above apply).

2. Moderate (Three or four of the above apply).

3. Low (One or two of the above apply).

4. Minimal presale expense is expected (None of the above).

OPPORTUNITY ANALYSIS

The Seller's Perspective

		Weight Factor (W)	x	Oppt Factor (O)	=	Total Score (W x O)

10. Contract Manager's Assessment of Opportunity

The Contract Manager, should provide an overall assessment of the need to win the opportunity. This is the point at which the Contract Manager can express an opinion on the need to win based on the more tangible aspects of the opportunity. Perhaps they are aware of other opportunity factors not yet considered.

Opportunity Factor (O)

$$\underline{\quad 3 \quad} \quad x \quad \boxed{\begin{array}{c} 1\ 2\ 3\ 4 \\ \square\square\square\square \end{array}} = \underline{\quad\quad}$$

On a scale of 1 (low need) to 10 (high need), which is the Contract Manager's overall assessment of the need to win this business? (Briefly describe those reasons in the space provided below)

1. 5 or less
2. 6 or 7
3. 8 or 9
4. 10

Reasons for overall assessment:

_____

_____

_____

_____

_____

_____

CONTRACT MANAGEMENT
RISK AND OPPORTUNITY ASSESSMENT TOOL
CMROAT©
SELLER'S PERSPECTIVE

SUMMARY SCORECARD

RISK ANALYSIS

	Weight Factor (W)	x	Risk Factor (R)	=	Total Score (W x R)
1.	__5__	x	_____	=	_____
2.	__4__	x	_____	=	_____
3.	__3__	x	_____	=	_____
4.	__4__	x	_____	=	_____
5.	__3__	x	_____	=	_____
6.	__3__	x	_____	=	_____
7.	__3__	x	_____	=	_____
8.	__2__	x	_____	=	_____
9.	__2__	x	_____	=	_____
10.	__3__	x	_____	=	_____

Grand Total Risk = _____

OPPORTUNITY ANALYSIS

	Weight Factor (W)	x	Oppt. Factor (O)	=	Total Score (W x O)
1.	__5__	x	_____	=	_____
2.	__4__	x	_____	=	_____
3.	__4__	x	_____	=	_____
4.	__3__	x	_____	=	_____
5.	__3__	x	_____	=	_____
6.	__3__	x	_____	=	_____
7.	__2__	x	_____	=	_____
8.	__2__	x	_____	=	_____
9.	__1__	x	_____	=	_____
10.	__3__	x	_____	=	_____

Grand Total Opportunity = _____

Action: Plot Grand Total Scores on the CMROAT© Matrix!

Risk and Opportunity Matrix

120

Good Opportunity/Low Risk | Good Opportunity/High Risk

Opportunity Assessment

60

Marginal Opportunity Low Risk | Marginal Opportunity High Risk

30

32   64   128

◄— Risk Assessment —►

Total scores for capture capability and performance that fall on or below the diagonal line require the greatest need for management support, improvement actions, contingency planning, and so on.

Total scores for opportunity and risk that fall on or below the diagonal line require the greatest need for management support, risk containment, contingency planning, and so on.

Contract Management
Risk and Opportunity Assessment Tool

Buyer's Perspective
(CMROAT-BP©)

RISK ANALYSIS

The Buyer's Perspective

Weight Factor (W)	x	Risk Factor (R)	=	Total Score (W x R)

1. Buyer's Executive Commitment to Resources and Budget

Buyer's executive commitment is a vital factor in the success of a contract. Committed executive support is important to Ensure sufficient resources and budget are provided to achieve success. Committed executive support is less likely to cancel A contract and therefore represents a lower risk.

Risk Factor (R)

   5   x   1 2 3 4   =

How committed are the Buyer's Executives to the contract and related project?

1. The Executive's have assigned personnel and a budget.
2. The Executive's have assigned a budget, but no personnel.
3. The Executive's have assigned personnel, but no budget.
4. The Executive's have not assigned personnel or a budget.

RISK ANALYSIS

The Buyer's Perspective

	Weight Factor (W)	x	Risk Factor (R)	=	Total Score (W x R)

2. Contract Delivery Schedule

Each contract has a set start and completion date. The Buyer will normally require that the contract be completed within a specific time. Typically, this is driven by the Buyer's business cycle, and end-customer demands. The ability to meet the contract schedule requirements is highly dependent on the magnitude of the contract and the availability and coordination of the right talent at the right time. A contract schedule that is reasonable and can be established by the Buyer, with penalty clauses for late delivery, represents the least risk to the buyer.

Risk Factor (R)

1 2 3 4

   4   x ☐☐☐☐ = _____

How has the contract delivery schedule been established?

1. Contract start and end dates have been set by the Buyer and are not changeable. Penalty clauses may exist for not meeting milestones.

2. Contract start and end dates have been set by the Buyer. There are no penalty clauses, but changing the schedule and milestone is difficult and must be negotiated with the Buyer.

3. Contract start and end dates will be mutually established by the Buyer and the Seller.

4. Contract start and end dates are flexible and will be established by the Seller.

RISK ANALYSIS

The Supplier's Perspective

Weight Factor (W)	x	Risk Factor (R)	=	Total Score (W x R)

3. Contract Performance Period

The performance period of the contract has a bearing on the level of risk associated with the contract. The longer the contract, the greater the chance of significant changes. Personnel, customer environment, and the business climate are a few examples of areas subject to significant change as time passes. These changes can pose substantial risk to the contract.

Risk Factor (R)

1 2 3 4

$$\underline{\quad 3 \quad} \times \boxed{\ \ \ \ } = \underline{\qquad}$$

What is the estimated performance period of the contract from the time a contract is awarded to the time it is expected to be completed?

1. Three months to six months
2. Between six months and one year
3. One year
4. More than one year

RISK ANALYSIS

The Buyer's Perspective

	Weight Factor (W)	x	Risk Factor (R)	=	Total Score (W x R)

4. Supplier's Past Performance

Experience with a previous contract that was similar to this one can reduce risk. Determine how many of the contract requirements can be met using products, technologies, and/or skills that have been used by the Seller on other contracts. Consider:

— The skills available at the local level to manage and carry out this contract.

— How much of the system solution needs to be developed as opposed to having been done before by the seller.

— The Seller's experience with the third-party products or services needed for the solution.

— The Seller's experience with their supply-chain partners and other Buyer selected 3rd parties.

Risk Factor (R)

$$\underline{\quad 4 \quad} \quad x \quad \boxed{\begin{array}{|c|c|c|c|} 1 & 2 & 3 & 4 \\ \hline & & & \\ \hline \end{array}} = \underline{\qquad}$$

What is the Seller's experience with similar solutions?

1. The contract is a replication of a previous contract managed locally.

2. A majority (50% or greater) of the contract requirements replicate a previous contract done by the Seller.

3. A minority (less than 50%) of the contract requirements replicate a previous project done by the Seller.

4. None of the contract requirements can be satisfied using previous experience, either local or worldwide.

RISK ANALYSIS

The Buyer's Perspective

	Weight Factor (W)	x	Risk Factor (R)	=	Total Score (W x R)

5. Changing Contract Requirements

The more frequent the Buyer's end customer's/ users needs or requirements change - the greater the Risk of contract/project late deliveries and cost overruns.

Risk Factor (R)

<u> 3 </u>   x   [1 2 3 4] = _____

The more frequently the end customers/users needs or requirements change the greater the risk?

1. No contract changes
2. Few contract changes
3. Moderate number of contract changes
4. High number of contract changes

FOURTEEN

RISK ANALYSIS

The Buyer's Perspective

	Weight Factor (W)	x	Risk Factor (R)	=	Total Score (W x R)

6. Level/Extent of Outsourcing

Most contracts that provide a customized solution outsource the resources of one or more vendors or subcontractors. External organizations can also include non-Seller hardware and software manufacturers and/or distributors, application software developers, professional Service Providers, and consultants. The number of external organizations involved with a contract directly relates to the amount of risk in the contract; the more external resource coordination needed, the higher the risk.

Risk Factor (R)

1 2 3 4

____3____   x   ☐☐☐☐   =   _____

How many sellers and/or subcontractors will need to be coordinated for this contract?

5. None
6. One or two
7. Three to five
8. Six or more

RISK ANALYSIS

The Buyer's Perspective

	Weight Factor (W)	x	Risk Factor (R)	=	Total Score (W x R)

7. Procurement Acquisition Lead Time (PALT)

Procurement Acquisition Lead Time (PALT) is the time it takes from when a requirement is determined, a solicitation is issued, bids/proposals are received, bids/proposal are evaluated, a contract is awarded, and quality products, services and/or solutions are provided to the buyer. The longer the Procurement Acquisition Lead Time the higher the risk to the buyer that they will not be able to support their end users and that requirements will change.

Risk Factor (R)

1 2 3 4

_2_ x ☐☐☐☐ = _____

Which of the following best describes the Procurement Acquisition Lead Time?

1. Rapid delivery
2. Slightly accelerated delivery
3. Standard lead time
4. Extended lead time

RISK ANALYSIS

The Buyer's Perspective

	Weight Factor (W)	x	Risk Factor (R)	=	Total Score (W x R)

8. Technology and Product Maturity

Consider the maturity of the technologies and products to be used in this solution. Many products available today are so widely used that they have been accepted as industry standards. Products that have a substantial field population and have been in use for a year or more are considered mature. These types of products are typically very reliable and pose little risk. However, prereleased and newly released products, or products using leading- edge technology, pose greater risks.

Risk Factor (R)

1 2 3 4

_____2_____ x ☐☐☐☐ = _____

What percentage of the products needed to satisfy the requirements are mature?

1. All requirements can be satisfied with mature, released products.

2. Less than 30% of the products will be prereleased or new products, or products using leading-edge technology.

3. Between 30% to 70% of the products will be prereleased or new products, or products using leading-edge technology.

4. 70% or more of the products will be prereleased or new products, or products using leading-edge technology.

RISK ANALYSIS

The Buyer's Perspective

	Weight Factor (W)	x	Risk Factor (R)	=	Total Score (W x R)

9. Geographic Distribution

The geographic distribution for the manufacturing, assembly, and/or delivery of products and services required by the contract adds complexity and risk. The greater the geographic distribution, the greater the risk due to factors such as shipping, time zone differential, language barriers, export/import requirements, taxes, etc.

Risk Factor (R)

$$\underline{2} \quad \times \quad \boxed{\begin{array}{c} 1\ 2\ 3\ 4 \\ \end{array}} \quad = \quad \underline{}$$

What is the geographic distribution of the project as it relates to the Supplier's locations?

1. Confined to one location
2. Confined to one region, with multiple locations
3. Confined to one country
4. Distributed across multiple countries

RISK ANALYSIS

The Buyer's Perspective

	Weight Factor (W)	x	Risk Factor (R)	=	Total Score (W x R)

10. Contract Manager's Assessment of the Deal

The Contract Manager should provide and overall assessment of the contract. This is the point at which the Contract Manager can express an opinion on the likelihood that the Buyer and Seller can effectively manage the risk and satisfy the end customer requirements to deliver within the scope and terms of the contract. The Contract Manager may be aware of other risk factors (such as poor past performance, financial concerns, etc.) not yet considered.

Risk Factor (R)

1 2 3 4

___3___   x   ⬜⬜⬜⬜   =   _____

On a scale of 1 (low risk) to 10 (high risk), what is the Contract Manager's overall risk assessment of the Buyer's and Seller's ability to successfully manage this contract?

1. Low risk
2. Moderate risk
3. High risk
4. Extremely high risk

OPPORTUNITY ANALYSIS

The Buyer's Perspective

	Weight Factor (W)	x	Oppt. Factor (O)	=	Total Score (W x O)

1. The Contract Promotes the Buyer's Strategic Direction

Any contract, if properly executed, will promote the reputation and image of the Buyer. However, the more valuable opportunities are those that are consistent with the Buyer's core business and strategic direction.

Opportunity Factor (O)

1 2 3 4

__5__   x   ⊓⊓⊓⊐ = _____

How much does the contract support the major strategies and goals of the Buyer?

1. Not at all
2. Little
3. Moderate
4. High

OPPORTUNITY ANALYSIS

The Buyer's Perspective

	Weight Factor (W)	x	Oppt. Factor (O)	=	Total Score (W x O)

2. Seller Offers the Lowest Price Technically Acceptable

Obtaining quality products, services, and/or solutions at the lowest possible price is usually a key source selection factor for most buyers.

Opportunity Factor (O)

$$\underline{\quad 4 \quad} \quad x \quad \begin{array}{cccc} 1 & 2 & 3 & 4 \\ \hline \quad & \quad & \quad & \quad \\ \hline \end{array} = \underline{\qquad}$$

Buyer's value obtaining quality products, services, and solutions at the lowest possible price.

1. Offer is not within the competitive price range.
2. Offer is within 10% of the Lowest Price Technically Acceptable.
3. Offer is within 5% of the Lowest Price Technically Acceptable.
4. Offer is the Lowest Price Technically Acceptable.

OPPORTUNITY ANALYSIS

The Buyer's Perspective

	Weight Factor (W)	x	Oppt. Factor (O)	=	Total Score (W x O)

3. Seller Offers Rapid Delivery

Buyer's typically want to obtain quality products, services, and solutions as quickly as possible.

Opportunity Factor (O)

1 2 3 4

___4___ x ☐☐☐☐ = _____

How quickly can the seller provide delivery of quality products, services, and solutions?

1. Seller cannot achieve the delivery schedule required by the buyer.
2. Seller may be able to achieve buyer's delivery schedule - low probability.
3. Seller will most likely be able to deliver on the schedule required by the buyer.
4. Seller and Buyer are highly confident the seller will deliver on or ahead of schedule.

FOURTEEN

OPPORTUNITY ANALYSIS

The Buyer's Perspective

	Weight Factor (W)	x	Oppt. Factor (O)	=	Total Score (W x O)

4. Use of Breakthrough Technology

The Seller's offer includes the use/application of a new breakthrough technology, which is not available from any other source. None of your competitors have this new breakthrough technology. This new breakthrough technology will provide your organization with a significant competitive advantage.

Opportunity Factor (O)

$$\underline{\quad 3 \quad} \quad x \quad \boxed{\begin{array}{|c|c|c|c|} 1 & 2 & 3 & 4 \\ \end{array}} \quad = \quad \underline{\qquad}$$

To what extent does the Seller's offer provide breakthrough technology?

1. The Seller's offer provides no breakthrough technology.
2. The Seller's offer provides little advance technology.
3. The Seller's offer provides some advanced technology.
4. The Seller's offer provides significant breakthrough technology, which is highly valued by the buyer.

OPPORTUNITY ANALYSIS

The Buyer's Perspective

	Weight Factor (W)	x	Oppt. Factor (O)	=	Total Score (W x O)

5. Provides Value Added Experience and/or New Skills

Occasionally, a contract is desirable for the education and/or experience to be gained by the Buyer. While learning and experience occur on any contract, those that will significantly improve the skills of the Buyer and/or develop previously nonexistent critical skills, are the more favored contract. Skills such as managing the contract, delivering new products and technologies, and supporting the end customer/user are just a few examples.

Opportunity Factor (O)

1 2 3 4

__3__ x ☐☐☐☐ = _____

What is the value of the experience and skills to be gained from the contract?

1. Little improvement in existing skills is expected because the Buyer's Team is very experienced.
2. Some improvement in existing skills will be gained by the Buyer's Team members.
3. Some improvement in existing skills is expected, but some new skills and expertise will be developed.
4. Significant improvement in existing skills is expected, and new skills and expertise also will be developed by the Buyer's Team members.

OPPORTUNITY ANALYSIS

The Buyer's Perspective

	Weight Factor (W)	x	Oppt. Factor (O)	=	Total Score (W x O)

6. Ease of Procurement

The Buyer has substantial past experience working with the Seller and finds the Seller easy to work with, including: well established relationship, well defined sales process, user-friendly information systems and outstanding sales support - making the procurement easy for the Buyer.

Opportunity Factor (O)

$\underline{\quad 2 \quad}$ x   [1 2 3 4]   =   _____

How would you describe the Seller in terms of ease of procurement?

1. The Seller is considered by the Buyer to usually be difficult to work with and purchase from.

2. The Seller is considered by the Buyer to be inconsistent, sometimes good to work with and at other times difficult to purchase from.

3. The Seller is considered by the Buyer to usually be good to work with and purchase from.

4. The Seller is considered by the Buyer to be the best supplier to work with for ease of procurement. The most desired Seller.

OPPORTUNITY ANALYSIS

The Buyer's Perspective

FOURTEEN

	Weight Factor (W)	x	Oppt. Factor (O)	=	Total Score (W x O)

7. Doing Business with a High Quality - Small Business Supplier

Most Buyer's value doing business with High Quality Small Business suppliers, especially, Women-Owned Small Businesses, Minority-Owned Small Businesses, and other diverse suppliers.

Opportunity Factor (O)

$$\underline{\quad 3 \quad} \quad x \quad \boxed{\begin{array}{|c|c|c|c|} 1 & 2 & 3 & 4 \\ \hline & & & \\ \end{array}} \quad = \quad \underline{\qquad}$$

Is the Seller a high quality small business supplier?

1. No. The Seller is a large business.
2. The Seller is a small business, but, with inconsistent performance.
3. The Seller is a high quality small business, with an excellent past performance record.
4. The Seller is a high quality, Minority or Woman-Owned Small Business, with an excellent past performance record.

OPPORTUNITY ANALYSIS

The Buyer's Perspective

	Weight Factor (W)	x	Oppt. Factor (O)	=	Total Score (W x O)

8. Seller Offers Lowest Life-Cycle Cost to Buyer

The Seller's offer provides substantial savings to the Buyer in operations and maintenance costs, verses current supplier or other proposed suppliers.

Opportunity Factor (O)

   1 2 3 4

__2__ x ☐☐☐☐ = _____

How much Life-Cycle Cost reduction/savings does the Buyer expect to receive as a result of the new contract?

1. No real Life-cycle cost reduction.
2. Some real Life-cycle cost reduction, less than 10 percent.
3. Real Life-cycle reduction, more than 10 percent less than 20 percent.
4. Significant Life-cycle cost reduction, more than 20 percent.

OPPORTUNITY ANALYSIS

The Buyer's Perspective

	Weight Factor (W)	x	Oppt. Factor (O)	=	Total Score (W x O)

9. Reduced Procurement Expense

Every contract has a procurement expense associated with it. The amount of procurement expense varies greatly from contract to contract. Some contracts are largely a replication of an existing contract with this Seller or another Seller. In other contracts, a significant amount of procurement planning and source selection work is required before the contract can be awarded. Contracts with little procurement expense are more desirable.

Opportunity Factor (O)

$$\underline{\quad 1 \quad} \quad x \quad \boxed{\begin{array}{|c|c|c|c|} 1 & 2 & 3 & 4 \end{array}} \quad = \quad \underline{\qquad}$$

What is the estimated level of procurement expense for this contract?

1. High
2. Moderate
3. Low
4. Minimal procurement expense is expected

OPPORTUNITY ANALYSIS

The Supplier's Perspective

	Weight Factor (W)	x	Oppt. Factor (O)	=	Total Score (W x O)

10. Contract Manager's Assessment of the deal

The Contract Manager should provide an overall assessment of the deal. This is the point at which the Contract Manager can express an opinion on the overall value of the contract, considering the requirements, terms and conditions, delivery schedule, performance metrics, and pricing.

Opportunity Factor (O)

1 2 3 4

  3   x ⬚⬚⬚⬚ = _____

On a scale of 1 (low need) to 10 (high need), which is the Contract Manager's overall assessment of the deal?

1. Low opportunity
2. Moderate opportunity
3. Good opportunity
4. Excellent opportunity

CONTRACT MANAGEMENT
RISK AND OPPORTUNITY ASSESSMENT TOOL
CMROAT©
BUYER'S PERSPECTIVE

SUMMARY SCORECARD

RISK ANALYSIS

	Weight Factor (W)	x	Risk Factor (R)	=	Total Score (W x R)
1.	_5_	x	___	=	___
2.	_4_	x	___	=	___
3.	_3_	x	___	=	___
4.	_4_	x	___	=	___
5.	_3_	x	___	=	___
6.	_3_	x	___	=	___
7.	_3_	x	___	=	___
8.	_2_	x	___	=	___
9.	_2_	x	___	=	___
10.	_3_	x	___	=	___

OPPORTUNITY ANALYSIS

	Weight Factor (W)	x	Oppt. Factor (O)	=	Total Score (W x O)
1.	_5_	x	___	=	___
2.	_4_	x	___	=	___
3.	_4_	x	___	=	___
4.	_3_	x	___	=	___
5.	_3_	x	___	=	___
6.	_3_	x	___	=	___
7.	_2_	x	___	=	___
8.	_2_	x	___	=	___
9.	_1_	x	___	=	___
10.	_3_	x	___	=	___

Grand Total Risk = _____

Grand Total Opportunity = _____

Action: Plot Grand Total Scores on the CMROAT© Matrix!

Risk and Opportunity Matrix

Good Opportunity/ Low Risk — Good Opportunity/ High Risk

Opportunity Assessment

Marginal Opportunity Low Risk — Marginal Opportunity High Risk

120 — 60 — 30

28 — 56 — 112

← Risk Assessment →

Total scores for capture capability and performance that fall on or below the diagonal line require the greatest need for management support, improvement actions, contingency planning, and so on.

Total scores for opportunity and risk that fall on or below the diagonal line require the greatest need for management support, risk containment, contingency planning, and so on.

CMROAT© Results

During the past 12 years, more than 10,000 business professionals from over 500 companies or government organizations (contract managers, project managers, sales managers, purchasing managers, financial/business managers, bid/proposal managers, and others) in both the public and private business sectors, have used the Contract Management Risk and Opportunity Assessment Tool (CMROAT©) or some modified version. According to our CMROAT© user surveys and interviews, most people find CMROAT© simple to use and very effective in providing a quick high level risk and opportunity assessment.

Typically, we find organizations receive the best value from their use of CMROAT© when they have 5 or more representatives/team members from different functional departments or organizations complete the survey tool and compare results.

CMROAT© Conclusion

In the case of CMROAT©, as in any assessment tool, the real value to the organization using the tool is in analyzing the results, then discussing and implementing appropriate actions that should be taken to further improve business performance. Numerous organizations in the aerospace, defense, engineering, electronics, telecommunications and other industries have used CMROAT©, or other modified versions, as an effective tool to conduct a quick multi-functional assessment of risk versus opportunity on a proposed or actual contract.

---

* This chapter is a modified extract from the book "Contract Management Organizational Assessment Tools" by Gregory A. Garrett and Dr. Rene Rendon, NCMA 2005.

CHAPTER 15

ENTERPRISE CONTRACT MANAGEMENT: SYSTEMS & TOOLS TO IMPROVE PERFORMANCE

INTRODUCTION

So what is enterprise contract management? Well, said simply it is integration of business functional areas (including: sales, purchasing, finance, contracts, operations, legal, etc.) throughout the contract management life-cycle focused on optimizing performance results. Unfortunately, many organizations in both the public and private business sectors operate via functional silos, which result in critical handoffs and communications flows that often get mishandled or just not done. As a result, key opportunities, such as contract enhancements, performance incentives, and the on-time-delivery of quality products, services, and integrated solutions may be lost or fall far short of expectations.

For sellers, the linkage between contracts and accounting/finance is extremely important, primarily because revenue recognition is closely tied to the contract's terms and conditions. Without a well integrated or enterprise contract management process, billing, payment, revenue recognition, revenue reporting, and forecasting are difficult, time consuming, and far less accurate. At many companies today, ad hoc interventions are required to collect and reconcile data from sales, purchasing, accounting, and pricing. Thus, many companies have inefficient business practices resulting in lost business opportunities, higher operating costs, and increased risks in their key financial reporting practices. Realizing that we live in a world of increased outsourcing, with highly demanding buyers, and increasing complexity of contracts and related projects, the need for efficient and cost-effective enterprise contract management is both real and significant for both buyers and sellers.

INCREASING CONTRACT MANAGEMENT COMPLEXITY

In both the public and private business sectors contracts are becoming increasingly complex, via: multiple pricing arrangements, use of performance incentives, performance metrics, bundling of products, services, and solutions each with different accounting rules, often involving hundreds or thousands of contract line items or deliverables, with multiple-parties involved. Of course the contracting challenges grow dramatically if you are engaged in multi-national or global contracting, involving complex pricing schedules, most favored nation pricing, multiple currencies, percent complex revenue recognition, value-added taxes, export/import requirements, limitation of liability, etc.

Clearly, the growth of contracting complexity and the aging of the baby-boomer workforce is resulting in a tidal wave effect on contracts and accounting organizations throughout the United States and in many other countries worldwide. To add further pressure in the U.S., the Sarbanes-Oxley Act of 2002 (SOX), Section 404 mandates that public companies comply with a wide range of financial management and reporting requirements. Specifically, SOX requires internal controls over all financial transactions throughout the enterprise be in place, operational, and continually monitored. Contracts are a key piece of the domain that must be effectively controlled and reported on under the Sarbanes-Oxley Act.

BENEFITS OF ENTERPRISE CONTRACT MANAGEMENT

According to Robert O'Connor, President and CEO of Softrax Corporation, in his article entitled "Contract Management: An Enterprise Process Perspective," Contract Management Magazine, (November 2004), "Additional benefits of an integrated approach to contract and accounting processes include the ability to:

- Capture 100 percent of ongoing revenue as negotiated in multi-year agreements;
- Simplify the administration and accounting for multi-element contracts;
- Optimize and automate revenue processes to ensure proper controls are implemented;
- Provide visibility and alerts for all revenue events to ensure that corrective intervention is possible;
- Improve the integrity of revenue data;
- Increase productivity by eliminating unnecessary manual processes;
- Enhance process-monitoring, separation of duties, and use authentication;
- Access detailed revenue histories;
- Report on revenue by embedded components, salesperson, partner, product line, etc.;
- Forecast deferred revenues by product, customer, and general ledger account; and
- Forecast future revenue by customer, product, and byproduct against billing schedules."

Clearly, contract management is a critical and strategic element of the business of buying and selling of products, services, and solutions worldwide. In order for your business enterprise to achieve high performance in buying and/or selling you need to create an enterprise contract management process. The enterprise contract management process should be designed for a seamless flow of information/data to drive all downstream accounting and financial reporting requirements, while supporting cost-effective and efficient contract administration and business operations. The enterprise contract management process must also enable the buying and selling of quality products and services, on-time-delivery, within budget, which meet or exceed the customers requirements.

ENTERPRISE CONTRACT MANAGEMENT: SYSTEMS AND TOOLS TO IMPROVE PERFORMANCE

In an effort to provide you a fair, balanced, and independent assessment of a wide variety of enterprise contract management software applications (products and related services) I have obtained the permission of the National Contract Management Association (NCMA) to provide you a brief summary of six different software applications/systems/tools. Each of the following summaries was written by a different individual and previously published during the period of 2004 - 2006 in the Contract Management Magazine. I hope you will find the following software summaries enlightening, they are not intended to be product/services endorsements. The reviews are each by-lined and express the opinion of the respective author.

SELECTED REVIEW

Written by: *Kathlyn H. Loudin*

Software Applications/Systems/Tools Reviewed:
diCarta: A Proven Contract Management Solution

Situation: Too often, companies "file and forget" what terms and conditions were negotiated into their contracts. This results in suboptimal deals for both parties. For example, a contractor may not realize that interim payments of award fee are allowable under the contract, so the firm misses and opportunity to enhance cash flow. Conversely, the procuring organization may not understand the contractor's obligations well enough to enforce compliance. In both cases, failure to adhere to contractual terms will tend to dilute their effectiveness.

Actions (or lack thereof) often invalidate words - the contract language so diligently crafted by you, the contracts professional. Not only is this demoralizing, it's also bad business. Researchers are the Aberdeen Group (2003) have pinpointed millions of dollars of losses attributable to "maverick buying," pricing errors, and lax monitoring of "evergreen" renewal clauses in service contracts.

"Effective contract management doesn't have to be hard," says Ammiel Kamon, vice president for product management at diCarta, Inc. diCarta is a California-based pioneer of next-generation contract management solutions - this company now offers Contracts Version 5, a sophisticated application for optimizing the total contract life cycle from creation to execution ongoing administration, and large-scale analysis of supplier and customer contracts.

Key Players: Emphasizing diCarta's utility from "quote to cash" in the sales contract arena and from "procure to pay" in the procurement world, Kamon stated that it had been successfully deployed at a diverse range of companies including ADP, Kraft foods, United Healthcare, Walgreens, Kohler, Conoco Phillips, and NBC-Universal. DiCarta's success emanates from its core: an active, intelligent contract repository that integrates directly with existing business transaction systems, such as enterprise resource planning (ERP), customer relationship management (CRM), and supply chain management (SCM) systems.

Processes, Level of Complexity: This Contracts solution sets forth systematic, efficient processes for creating, negotiating, approving, activating/ensuring compliance, and analyzing contracts. This minimizes the efforts often driven by fragmented systems, piecemeal contract administration strategies, and after-the-fact compliance audits.

Kamon demonstrated diCarta's ease of use by unleashing its "contract creation wizard," which develops a contract by asking the user a series of questions. The solution invokes common productivity tools (e.g., Microsoft Word), and features a customizable database of approved terms and clauses, usage guidelines, and policies. It seamlessly exports relevant data (and subsequent changes) to corporate transaction systems. A contract modification that changes unit pricing, for instance, would not only update the conformed master contract but also would be automatically reflected on the next invoice linked to the contract.

Another feature of the diCarta Contracts creation process is "contract negotiator," which fosters intra- and inter-enterprise collaboration, offering a full slate of security and configuration controls, as well as a forum for capturing comments between negotiators. DiCarta Contracts also automatically routes non-standard language or terms to the appropriate reviewer to ensure all the proper approvals are received.

During the activation and compliance phases, diCarta optimizes contract execution, compliance, and renewal. "Obligations manager" alerts stakeholders when milestones are met, volume-based discount thresholds are achieved, rebates are available, or questionable actions are taken. "Renewal manager" notifies decision makers when contracts are coming to term. "Auditor's workbench," my personal favorite, streamlines reporting requirements by producing standard and ad hoc reports and audit trails. No more digging through drawers full of files to support an audit request!

The analysis model enhances visibility not just within any particular contract - it extends across contracts throughout the firm. "Executive dashboard" shows process and performance trends, enabling workload planning and scheduling. "Professional's dashboard" gives contract managers insight into contract status and details. It offers more than 25 pre-built reports such as revenue and spending under contract, operational performance, and period of performance data.

An Overall Look: All in all, diCarta's solution is a robust one, particularly well-suited for the B2B arena. During my virtual desktop demonstration, most of Ammiel Kamon's illustrations and case studies involved supplies and commercial services. However, companies depend on diCarta Contracts to manage all kinds of agreements, from talent agreements at NBC-Universal to provider and payer contracts at United Healthcare and software sales agreements at Network Appliance. These companies' contracts typically have hundreds of different business terms and pricing line items, with dozens of amendments - all managed through the diCarta Contracts Solution.

It will be interesting to witness diCarta's continued evolution in concert with market needs. The new capabilities in the current release of the product, diCarta Contracts Version 6, add:

- A self-service contract creation wizard;
- New capabilities for handling contracts written with the "outside paper" of suppliers and customers;
- Inbound and outbound fax management capabilities;
- Seamless integration with Microsoft Word 2000 XP and 2003;Proposal management features, and
- Multi-dimensional contract "data cubes" for complex analysis.

It looks like diCarta will stay on top of new market needs. I'll bet my bottled water on it.

SELECTED REVIEW

Written by: Joseph Morice

Software Applications/Systems/Tools Reviewed:
Upside Software: Making Your Job Easier

Application: Canadian-based Upside Software Inc. offers excellent applications.

There is no lack of objectivity in that statement. Each of Upside Software's applications was designed with the user in mind. On some scales, Upside may rank below competitors - they don't have the flowing bubble graphical ease of high-end contract applications - but seen as a whole, the company's product is a step ahead of the competition.

Fortunately, there is no universal standard for the evaluation of contract products, so individual buyers can hone in on the one feature most important to them. I confess, I have rated programs on less than the sum of their parts when one of those parts blows me away.

Upside Contract's greatest strength is its "only-limited-by-imagination" customization. The architects understand that no two corporate infrastructures are the same, and their product allow users to pare down the product to what is needed. Most impressive are the customizable summary screens, which present your contract staff with a "greatest-hits" snapshot of pertinent information, as selected by the user. There is no dense configuration; by simply using the program wizard, users can quickly and easily set up the screens. Even better, Upside's wizard has so many options that the products have not required any organizational changes in their broad range of client installations. Simply put, what you get in the Upside install is what you need.

The product is designed like many databases. There are tabs and editable fields - all the usual suspects. Where Upside separates itself from competitors is the ease with which it allows users to customize within windows. You do not need training in SQL or Oracle, Upside's back-end frameworks, to make the application your own.

There are, of course, varying product levels to better serve the needs of your business. For the small shop, Upside offers ContractBuddy, a completely Web-based application (which does not sacrifice customization) available at $65 per month on a month-to-month basis. As your business grows, your company can move to UpsideContract Office, which allows your database information to be integrated directly with Microsoft Word. If your customer is the federal government, Upside offers the option of tracking your GSA Schedules. And, since users are buying directly from and being serviced by Upside, there is no tedious middle person to consume valuable time.

Speaking of saving time, not only does Upside allow the user to customize fields to meet their needs, but the user can also hide, not delete, unused tabs, thereby eliminating the distracting clutter on your database desktop. Users can, as needs dictate, always restore portions to their screen as new business and new requirements arise. In this way, Upside has created a product that your growing venture will not leave behind.

Tabs cover everything related to the contract on one screen. The activities tabs allow users and their supervisors to track all the work performed on each contract, providing a full audit trail of changes and monitoring adherence to corporate policy and procedure. If you are the seller on your contract, you can also track your performance metrics to ensure contract adherence. And, if you are working off delivery orders, your accounting team can match invoices in the billing fields.

As the contract offeror, Upside's prebuilt templates streamline the preparation process while allowing for editing of negotiated points. The security profiles set up by users are particularly useful if they wish to limit access to specific individuals, as opposed to an entire team. If your deals require teaming with multiple vendors, you can color-code their tasking for quick corner-of-your-eye recognition of responsibilities.

Desktop installations, including training can be completed in less than two weeks. An enterprise install, which includes a meeting to determine your organization's wants and needs, is routinely completed within two months. Tier 1 phone support is available with the product, while Tier 2 support is provided for a nominal fee.

Although there are many contract management applications on the market, this one is truly worth your time!

SELECTED REVIEW

Written by: Kunjan Dayal

Software Applications/Systems/Tools Reviewed:
Contracting with the Hummingbird: Fast, Powerful, Versatile

Inside the Product: Hummingbird Enterprise™ for Contract Management provides a key link between sales or user department and contract manager. The product enables organizations to better access, share, and leverage collective knowledge across the enterprise and is designed to provide full life cycle support for all contract management requirements. It offers

- Rapid creation of new contracts;
- On-line secure contract negotiations;
- Integration with back-office financial systems;
- On-line contracts access;
- Contract analysis for terms, disbursements, and content;
- Automated notification of contract renewal;
- Contract archival;
- Clause tracking;
- Contract performance management; and
- Full record management capabilities.

My review session involved envisioning a sales person trying to forge a contract with a client. The example is easily applied to other business or government contracting opportunities. The review session was exciting as the ease and speed with which the sales person executed a contract with the client.

By using approved, readily accessible contract templates, the sales person was able to document the sale into a formal agreement. By use of electronic communications tools, such as PDA, cell phone text messaging, and e-mail, the draft contract was transmitted to the contract manager for review and comment. The sales person provided the client pertinent Internet access to the contract, promoting a partnership approach to assure smoother contract execution. The contract manager played front line in the sales effort, teaming with the sales person to provide the client a sound and equitable contract for execution.

For company management, a dashboard view of the activity is at their fingertips. Such a view provides trend analysis, fiscal and risk reviews, and general health of the organization. And, once again, this information is readily available on PDAs and other electronic tools.

Summary

Hummingbird Enterprise™ for Contract Management is modular. It can be integrated to organizational contracting, finance, sales, or other management activities in numerous ways. Governments and private organizations of all sizes are able to streamline contract creation and approval process, improve contractual performance from suppliers and customers, and maximize financial performance, by managing compliance and ultimately decreasing operational costs - all while maximizing returns.

The experience of fast-paced contracting using the Hummingbird Contract Management product was exhilarating. It was quite like watching a hummingbird: versatile, flexible, powerful, agile, colorful, fast, and steady all at the same time. I recommend the Hummingbird Enterprise™ for Contract Management product to all readers. Details at www.hummingbird.com.

SELECTED REVIEW

Written by: *Edward A. Callaway*

Software Applications/Systems/Tools Reviewed:
Accudraft's DocsEngine Portal:
"Writing the Contract Correctly and Quickly through Automation"

Accudraft's DocsEngine Portal solution expedites your contract generation process through automation, yielding standards-based contracts on a timely basis. Your contracts are based on automated standards (called templates), which allow any organization member (e.g., sales representatives, contracts people, or attorneys) to generate an organizationally approved document quickly.

What It Means to You: As a contracts leader, you know that contract generation presents a series of challenges. You need to (1) handle significant sales volume, while simultaneously tailoring documents to unique case situations; (2) integrate the results into your back-office systems; (3) know with whom and for what you are contracting; and (4) use your organization's support people (e.g., counsel and information technology) appropriately. Through Accudraft's software solution, you retain control of your business process, collaborate on your sales contract documents, and focus your legal and information technology (IT) people on things that require their particular expertise.

Solution Benefits: *DocsEngine* - The DocsEngine uses contract templates you and your team (requirements, legal, financial, contracting) develop and maintain collaboratively to support your business process. It has many benefits.

You are not required to change your process to meet another's or the software's mandates. It can be used for commercial sales contracts, which can vary in size, complexity, and volume. Your contracts can be issued more quickly, with greater accuracy, and with appropriate internal resource use. It allows you to know to whom you are selling what items, and lastly, your contracts can be integrated into your front-end and back-office systems.

The DocEngine's centerpiece is your business process, however you define it. Through collaboration with your people (e.g., sales, counsel, contracts), you define a template (or series of templates) that outlines your business process. This template can support sales activities in many situations (varying contract provisions by state, transaction dollar size, company, or other parameters). When the template is appropriately followed, a contract is generated - which may or may not need internal approvals - because they have already been accomplished in the template creation process. Since you have already coordinate with all your team members in this process, the output can be provided automatically to your back-office systems.

Portal - The Portal's database keeps records, allowing you to do customer relationship data mining. Your key concern is data access, not data maintenance - through the use of its application service provider (ASP) model, Accudraft can hold and maintain your data. Your internal IT resources, therefore, are used more effectively.

The Portal can work well if you have an e-business strategy into which it fits. It will execute as much of your contract transaction dollar and action volume as you desire. Its reporting capability, likewise, is as robust as you want it to be. It allows you to connect both internally and externally for proper contract reporting and customer liaison. Finally, you can assure proper security through your implementation of its ASP model.

Overall: The most impressive aspect of Accudraft's software solution is that your contracts are generated through a collaborative, standards-based, and timely automated process that optimizes use of your organizational assets. For more information, see *www.accudraft.com.*

Selected Review

Written by: Ryan D. Dickover

Software Applications/Systems/Tools Reviewed:
Reviewing CobbleStone Systems: Contract Web

Contract Web is CobbleStone System's flagship product, designed for an enterprise-level implementation to help large companies upkeep, track, and manage their contract awards and proposals. A simpler version of the system is available for smaller businesses in the desktop edition, too - however, this review focuses on the product's use at the corporate level.

Users: The heart of Contract Web is the idea that those who manage contracts in the private sector have a few key concerns. They want to:

- Stay on top of impending deadlines for contract renewals and expirations,
- Monitor actual contract performance versus definitized numbers from the initial agreement, and
- Know who is responsible for particular contracts.

To solve these and other issues, Contract Web uses a database tied into a Web server that can be deployed either by the firm or in the user's own environment. The system is Microsoft-based, using SQL Server 2000 - or users can to host it themselves, using Microsoft Internet Information Services (IIS). An FAQ on the product is available at *http://cobblestonesystems.com/faqs.htm.*

Functions: The Internet product demo I took went smoothly, and the ease of the system's use is clear. The product helps accomplish main contract management goals (mentioned above) very well, without a lot of flash. The user has significant amounts of "idiot-proof" control over configuring system details to best match the particular organization.

There are three significant modules to analyze.

1) *Contract Web Calendar.* This calendar uses embedded links to show users what contracts are expiring. Clicking a link brings up

a customizable details screen, which reveals everything related to the award: tasks, dollar amounts, people, start/end dates, and user-defined text boxes. You also can generate automatic e-mail alerts, triggered by user-defined events in the system. The ability to upload attachments also is impressive: With a scanner (preferably one that can output .tif file format), the user can create a paperless repository for the organization.

2) *Report Generator.* This tool is where Contract Web houses most of its added value. It lets users run canned reports and - with simple "click and fill" templates - make their own reports for whatever purpose desired. Reports can be exported in any data format and automatically e-mailed. The module allows users to find out what contracts are behind in payments or soon to expire, and also can be tailored to assist in getting contracts (via a list of outstanding RFPs, assigned by category). This system can track subcontracts - and once, CobbleStone configured it to support multiple companies, too.

3) *Company Information.* This module permits the user to establish a user base of employees, locations, departments, and vendors. This module controls management's ability to task contract responsibility to certain individuals and offers security through access restrictions to certain reports or contracts.

There are also features in Contract Web that allow for the user to accept contract requests over the Web, although in a limited sense (this is not an e-business application or resource management system capable of handling reverse auctions or tracking supplies). Additionally, Contract Web permits the development of contract templates, such as time-and-material, cost-plus-fixed-fee, firm-fixed-price, or custom-made terms and conditions.

Conclusion: The system would be a smart investment for a small or mid-sized business that has grown too large for internal Microsoft Office contracts management. Its target audience is the private sector, and while theoretically a public sector agency could augment the system for its own tracking and management needs, a significant amount of customization would be required to meet the needs of complex federal contracts or to be compatible with systems already in place.

Selected Review

Written by: *Ted Mahoney*

Software Applications/Systems/Tools Reviewed:
Review of Omnicom's Contracts Applications

Overview: Omniware's Omnicom is an excellent software option. I received a briefing from the company's U.S. representative, who described the six system features as accessible, actionable, adaptive, analytical, mission-critical, and secure.

The information from the Omniware Web site (*www.omniware.com*) indicates Omnicom as a complete contract management software solution, from initial concept to final closeout. The software is a full Web application, as well as a traditional client/server application running on Oracle or SQL Server databases.

Omnicom has an impressive and extensive features list, which includes:

Commercial strategy advisor	Template-based document generation
Supplier positioning	MS Word 98/2000 document
Supply chain stage management	Category-specific contracts
Procurement targeting	Rule-based contract articles
Supplier database	Document change control
Supplier technical approvals	Contract performance monitoring
Supplier performance monitoring	Financial monitoring
Supplier category management	Spend vs. budget control
On-line/Web supplier registration	Bank guarantees
On-line supplier communication	Schedules & milestones
Request for bid documentation	Warranty periods
On-line bidding	Contract closeout
Performance-based bid list selection	Contract document production
Prequalification of bidder	Messages/events database
Bid evaluation	Auditability
Balanced bid value	Traceability
Graphical bid recommendation	Adaptable user security
On-line clarification process	MS Office integration
Automatic Q&A communication	Outlook calendar integration
On-line award/failure notification	E-mail integration
Project timeline tracking	Oracle/SQL server database
Minutes of meetings	Plug-in-free browser environment
Work category management	Workflow-enabled

A Look Inside: These are some of the highlights that I found interesting. The brochure from the site indicates the software, like many others, can automate the documentation creation process and manage the financial, commercial, and administrative aspects for the entire contract life cycle. To maximize efficiency, there are automated workflows, e-mail notifications, and reminders available for integration with your existing work routines. There are also simultaneous multilingual supports on texts, screen labels, and the data/lookup lists. Look out, Berlitz!

Omnicom views the contract as a continual process, not just a document. The system logs all data and document input (plus all changes), making this product compliant with Sarbanes-Oxley Act. Omnicom has a neat "What if?" decision tool, that guides you through a seven-step process on the different aspects of the work to be performed - current and future performance, buyer and seller positioning, benchmarking, improvements, and activity levels. This tool then will make recommendations and arrive at an estimated cost impact on the strategy.

Omnicom is adapted to the company processes. To ensure maximum leverage, all installations are customized to the company and the users. End users can easily perform custom searches and develop graphs and text reports with direct integration into an MS Excel presentation. System administrators are given the ability to completely customize screen layouts, text labels, and certain fields. The integrated report-builder is very similar to Crystal's system.

If you are ready to take your contracts online, Omnicom's e-commerce feature offers a wide range of functionality, including self-maintenance vendor records, on-line documents, competitive bidding with graph and tabular price feedback, and clarifications/ questions and answers. It shows a locked tender/bid-box that can only be opened on a certain date, along with a bid-box log to track who has opened it and what they have reviewed. Maintain up-to-date supplier records in many ways including the self-maintenance, manual input, or ERP interchange. You also can track supplier histories, meeting minutes, and dialogues for future reference. With the on-line solution, you can electronically manage RFQs, RFIs, and even host your own real-time bidding.

For tracking financials, you can pull information from the ERP system for viewing and then perform calculations and apply business logic against them. You also have milestone payment tracking and guarantee against advanced payment (along with liquidated damages and performance bonds).

Conclusion: Omnicom offers flexibility by taking your data and developing an integrated browser design. Omnicom's stated goal is: "Enable enterprises to be agile and adaptive in documenting, tracking, reporting, improving, and sharing knowledge across the company and throughout the world."

SUMMARY & CONCLUSION

So in retrospect, this chapter has focused on the growing complexity of contracts, the need for an enterprise contract management process, and a summary of six of the commercially available contract management software systems/tools/applications to help buyers and sellers improve performance. Realizing the growing global outsourcing trend, the aging of the workforce throughout the U.S. and in many developed countries worldwide, and the increased complexity of contracts - the need for an enterprise contract management process, facilitated by proven effective software systems/tools/applications, is indeed real and significant. My hope is that the Contract Management Process described in this book, combined with the Contract Management Maturity Model (CMMM) discussed in Chapter 13, the Contract Risk and Opportunity Assessment Tool (CMROAT) reviewed in Chapter 14, and the discussion of enterprise contract management systems and tools contained in this chapter will help you and your organization improve your buying and selling business results via better, faster, and more cost effective contract management.

CHAPTER **16**

BUILDING CONTRACTOR TEAMING ARRANGEMENTS

INTRODUCTION

The primary focus of the third step in the Winning Government Contracts Process is building contractor teaming arrangements. Given the growing complexities of products, services, systems, and integrated solutions, in the public sector, most companies are seeking business partners to help them accomplish the work, share the risk, and achieve joint success. As a result, there is a tremendous increase in the formation of a wide-variety of business partnerships commonly called contractor teaming arrangements. It is not uncommon today to find companies working as business partners on one deal and competitors on another deal at the same time. Likewise, we increasingly encounter companies working as a U.S. government prime contractor on one contract, while on another contract serving as a subcontractor under a prime contractor, who is one of their subcontractors on another government contract. If the above stated scenario sounds complicated, then you would be correct. The focus of this chapter is to: (1) review the various business partnerships, or contractor teaming arrangements, which companies are creating to perform U.S. government contracts, (2) understand the key elements which should be included in contractor teaming agreements, and (3) discuss the lessons learned and best practices of forming business partnerships in the U.S. federal government marketplace.

CONTRACTOR TEAMING ARRANGEMENTS

The Federal Acquisition Regulation (FAR) Subpart 9.6 defines a "contractor team arrangement" as an arrangement in which:

1. Two or more companies form a partnership or joint venture to act as a potential prime contractor; or
2. A potential prime contractor agrees with one or more other companies to have them act as its subcontractors under a specified government contract or acquisition program.

The FAR states the government will recognize the "integrity and validity" of contractor team arrangements so long as the relationship is "fully disclosed." Typically, contractor teaming arrangements are formed before a bid or proposal is submitted to the government contracting officer, however, the government often recognizes contractor teaming arrangements entered into after the proposal is submitted to the government.

SIXTEEN

As stated in the FAR definition of contractor team arrangements, business partnerships can take many forms, each with their respective suitability, advantages, and disadvantages. The primary contractor business partnerships include: 1) prime contractor-subcontractor teams, 2) joint ventures, 3) limited liability companies, and 4) private equity ownership agreements.

PRIME CONTRACTOR-SUBCONTRACTOR TEAMING

The most widely used teaming structure, in both the public and private business sectors, is the prime contractor-subcontractor teaming agreement, often referred to as the prime-sub relationship. It is important to note, the rules of contract privity establish a contractual business relationship via two parties. In U.S. federal government contracting, the U.S. government agency serves as the buyer and the prime contractor serves as the seller, thus contract privity exists between the government agency and the prime contractor. Likewise, in a prime-sub relationship, the prime contractor serves as the buyer and the subcontractor serves as the seller, thus contract privity exists between the prime and the sub. Clearly, no contract privity or contractual business relationship exists between a U.S. government agency and a subcontractor. However, the U.S. federal government does exert a lot of power and influence over its selected prime contractors, thus requiring certain rights, consents, reviews, approval of subcontractors, and mandatory flow-down of key contract terms and conditions in all subcontracts.

Prime contractor-subcontractor teaming is most commonly used when each party has a well-defined scope of work, in terms of products and/or services to provide, which can be performed either separately or via an integrated effort with the prime contractor. Except when specifically prohibited by a solicitation, government agencies may properly consider the experience and past performance of subcontractors when evaluating a prime contractor's proposal. (Humphries, 2006)

The prime contractor-subcontractor teaming relationship provides advantages to each of the parties involved. From the government's perspective, it provides a single point of contact, because the prime contractor is held accountable for the subcontractor's performance. From the prime contractor's perspective, it allows them to lead the planning and execution of the work, build strong customer relationships with the government, and flow all revenue recognition through their company. From the subcontractor's perspective, it allows them to do the work they specialize in performing, build a strong relationship with the prime contractor, and create or expand credibility with the government.

The prime contractor-subcontractor team structure also has certain disadvantages to each of the parties. From the government's perspective, it often proves more costly as a result of the tiering of contractors' overhead costs and profits/fees. From a prime contractor's perspective, the selection and management of subcontractors can prove difficult and costly. Despite these potential pitfalls, the prime contractor-subcontractor relationship is the most commonly used teaming arrangement for businesses to work together. Clearly, the prime contractor-subcontractor teaming arrangement should be considered the preferred arrangement unless there are structural issues for the members of the team that prohibit its use. (Garrett, 2007)

JOINT VENTURES

Joint Ventures (JVs), often called consortia, are widely used contractor teaming arrangements. A joint venture is essentially a limited purpose partnership agreement, in which each party (two or more) are jointly and severally liable to both the customer (i.e., the government) and to third parties (i.e., subcontractors). JVs are frequently used in the construction industry and are steadily increasing in use by professional services firms worldwide.

Joint Ventures as a form of contractor teaming arrangement provides advantages to each of the parties involved. From a government perspective, it allows them to secure the resources of two or more firms at the same time to perform the work they require and it may allow them to get the work for a lower price.

From a contractor perspective, as a member of a joint venture team: (1) they can exert more influence and control over contract performance to protect their interest vs. a traditional prime contractor-subcontractor relationship. (2) receive favorable joint venture income tax treatment, and (3) avoid serving as a subcontractor to its competitors.

Joint Ventures as a form of contractor teaming arrangement also has certain disadvantages for each of the parties involved. From a government perspective, a JV may be viewed as lacking a clear or single point of contact, thus creating issues regarding who is really in charge and who has the authority to ensure the work is properly performed. From a Joint Venture team member perspective, each company becomes jointly and severally liable to potentially multiple parties, thus creating higher financial liabilities and risk. Despite these disadvantages, many joint ventures have proven to be wildly successful in both the public and private business sectors.

LIMITED LIABILITY COMPANIES

A Limited Liability Company (LLC) is a form of business arrangement which provides the owners with the limited financial liability of a corporation with the flow-through tax advantages of a partnership. During the past decade, in both the public and private business sectors, there has been a significant growth in the creation and use of LLCs.

The Limited Liability Company form of contractor teaming arrangement offers several advantages. The LLC is an excellent means of structuring a teaming relationship when none of the parties is interested in a subcontractor role. The LLC is considered by both buyers and subcontractors to be a positive teaming arrangement, because the owners of the LLC share the same liability to customers and third parties as do shareholders in a major corporation.

Of course, the use of an LLC does have some disadvantages in its application. For example, the government may become confused as to: who is really in charge when there are multiple owners of the LLC, and how to conduct the evaluation of past performance of individual parties to the LLC after initial formation. Likewise, the LLC structure can lead to division among the owners, which may delay decision-making and create a challenging work environment.

PRIVATE EQUITY OWNERSHIP AGREEMENTS

When a Private Equity (PE) firm decides to purchase a company it typically does so, because the company current owners are looking to sell, and the PE firm believes said company has a lot of potential to grow and achieve highly profitable revenues. A typical PE firm is looking to make a relatively quick turnaround profit usually over a period of 3 to 5 years. The PE firm's involvement with the companies they acquire range quite dramatically depending upon the PE firm's capabilities and the level of support needed by the companies they acquire. Most often, PE firms help their acquired companies to grow via a combination of: improved business practices; key personnel additions and/or changes; and through the acquisition of add-on companies. PE firms typically create a new company board structure, including: members of the PE firm, leaders from the acquired company, and outside experts, selected by the PE firm or jointly selected.

Private equity ownership arrangements do offer certain advantages to all of the parties involved. From the government's perspective, PE ownership is often transparent with the exception that the company typically has access to more resources and expanded capabilities. From the acquired company's view, having a PE ownership agreement can allow a company access to increased capital to fuel product, services, and marketing expansion, plus easy access to additional business expert guidance.

Private equity ownership arrangements do present some distinct disadvantages. For example, depending upon the nature of the works which the other companies perform, who are owned by the same PE firm, an organizational Conflict Of Interest (OCI) may arise, between different companies which are owned by the same PE firm. Another potential disadvantage of PE firms is that sometimes their accessibility to credit or cash may not be available when a company needs the funding for either organic or inorganic growth. A further disadvantage is the potential loss of top talent after the initial sale of the company to the PE firm, which can be very detrimental in the case of professional services firms if the top talent attracts a lot of business. When our economy was booming several years ago, PE firms were rapidly expanding. However, today amidst our global economic crisis, PE firms are often struggling to make their acquisitions profitable for their investors.

CONTRACTOR TEAMING AGREEMENTS: KEY ELEMENTS

The exact focus and intent of a contractor team agreement does vary depending upon the role of the party. In general, contractor teaming agreements should appropriately form an agreement to partner in the event a contract is awarded by a buying organization. Said simply, it is an agreement to agree to potentially work together. Typically, prime contractors or lead parties want as much flexibility in a contractor teaming agreement as possible as to who they select to work with, how much work they are given, and when and where the work is performed. Conversely, subcontractors or minor parties want as much specificity and exclusivity in a contractor teaming agreement as possible to virtually guarantee them as much work as possible and as much control over their work as possible. As a result of these two conflicting priorities, the formation and implementation of contractor teaming agreements has been subject to a great deal of litigation during the past decade.

Table 16–1 provides a brief outline of the 12 key elements which should be contained in most contractor teaming agreements. Following Table 16–1 is a brief discussion of each of these 12 key elements of contractor team assignments.

Table 16-1 Contractor Teaming Agreements — Key Elements	
Purpose	Bid & Proposal (B&P) Costs
Scope of Work	Exclusivity
Confidentiality	Intellectual Property Rights
Flow-down Requirements	Limitation of Liabilities
Ethics	Disputes Resolutions
Payment	Terminations

■ *Purpose*

Every contractor teaming agreement should include a section which describes the overall nature of the products, services, systems, and/or solutions set forth in the agreements. It should at least at a high-level discuss some of the key skills and capabilities each party brings to the subject deal.

■ *Scope of Work*

There are several ways to reflect the scope of work, including: 1) task-oriented statements of what work will be performed, 2) outcome-based or performance-based statements of the end-customer's desired results, or 3) the use of discrete and specific lists of materials, commodities, products, systems, and/or services which will be provided and by whom. The scope of work section is subject to a lot controversy and contention in the formation and execution of contractor team agreements, especially in the description of the relationship between the parties, who does what, and any implied or specific commitments. So, be very careful what wording you agree to between the parties.

■ *Confidentiality*

Today most companies enter into Non-Disclosure Agreements (NDAs) before ever even considering entering into a contractor teaming agreement. Even if you have a signed NDA, it is still important to appropriately include a confidentiality clause in the contractor teaming agreement. Typically, a confidentiality clause will require the parties involved to designate in writing information that is truly proprietary. Usually, confidentiality clauses are mutual, although there may be some unique circumstances which could warrant unilateral determination of confidentiality. The confidentiality clause should contain a period of performance or length of time that the clause will stay in effect and specify whether it will survive the existence of the teaming agreement. In addition, parties to a teaming agreement will usually not be restricted into their use or disclosure of information that a) is located in the public domain, b) is already in their possession, c) is independently developed, and/or d) was properly obtained from another party.

■ *Flow-down Requirements*

Pursuant to the Federal Acquisition Regulation (FAR) Part 44-Subcontracting, U.S. government prime contractors are required to flow-down specified mandatory contract clauses. If the government contract is for the acquisition of designated commercial items, then the number of mandatory flow-down clauses is significantly reduced from 50+ clauses to 11 clauses. In addition, prime contractors may require the flow-down of numerous additional contract terms and conditions to protect their interests and provide performance incentives and/or remedies for non-performance. Thus, it is important to understand all of the appropriate contract and subcontract terms and conditions.

■ *Ethics*

It is critical to ensure contractors select ethical business partners who have developed and implemented effective internal ethics and compliance programs. It is vital to engage in some level of due diligence to review your partner(s) business ethics and internal compliance controls. New U.S. government requirements mandate that all contractors with over $5 million in government contracts have a code of business ethics, provide appropriate ethics training to their employees, and have an appropriate compliance or internal controls program.

■ *Payment*

It is vital that all contractor teaming agreements include appropriate payment terms and conditions for each of the parties involved. It is important to address the various forms of payment which may be used based upon the potential pricing arrangements which may be used. For example, under cost-reimbursement contracts, the contractor teaming agreement should explain how each member of the team will voucher/invoice their allowable and allocable expenses and be paid their fee. Likewise, under a fixed-price type contract, it is critical that the scope of work be appropriately priced and clearly assigned to each of the respective parties. Further, any unusual payment terms and conditions should be specified, i.e., advance payments, milestone-based payments, volume-discounts, discounts for early payment, etc. Also, it is important to establish if subcontractor payments are first contingent upon the prime contractor's receipt of said payment from the government agency, prior to their payment of the subcontractor(s).

■ *Bid & Proposal (B&P) Costs*

Competing for and winning a large complex U.S. government contract can require a significant Bid and Proposal (B&P) investment for all of the parties involved in a contractor teaming agreement. Usually, contractor teaming agreements require each of the parties to provide all of the necessary and appropriate resources to prepare their assigned portion of the bid/proposal and for paying for the respective B&P costs they incur. Likewise, with the growing use of oral presentations by both government agencies and prime contractors, it is important to specify that each party is responsible for preparing, delivering, and paying for their respective portion of any required oral presentations.

■ *Exclusivity*

Typically contractor teaming agreements specify if any exclusivity shall exist in regards to a specific contractor being assured the assignment of certain work. When using a prime-subcontractor teaming agreement, subcontractors generally seek as much clarity regarding the scope of work and exclusivity regarding the assignment of work. Prime contractors generally seek as much flexibility as possible with their subcontractors, and prefer to avoid making any exclusive business arrangements. Clearly the type of contractor teaming agreement selected and the nature of the work significantly affect the willingness of the parties to enter into any exclusivity arrangement.

■ *Intellectual Property Rights*
A contractor teaming agreement should fairly and appropriately protect the intellectual property (IP) rights of each of the parties. Typically, IP clauses limit the data rights to only the pursuit of the target contract, restrict disclosure to those who have a valid "need to know", and prevent broader distribution. In some cases, contractors must be prepared to share their IP with their teaming partners and with U.S. government agencies. However, there are times when a company must fight to protect their IP rights and restrict the use from their business partners. Both government agencies and prime contractors have been known to take advantage of small businesses by inappropriately acquiring data rights and/or violating copyrights, patents, trademarks, etc.

■ *Limitation of Liabilities*
Frequently the parties involved in a contractor teaming agreement will choose to expressly and explicitly state their contractual and financial liability to one another. Typically parties will agree to be jointly and severally liable and any consequential damages are neither contemplatable nor recoverable under the teaming agreement.

■ *Disputes Resolutions*
It is essential that a contactor teaming agreement contain a dispute resolution clause, which addresses the method of dispute resolution, the choice of language, and the choice of law! The most common dispute resolution techniques include negotiations, mediation, facilitation, arbitration, binding or non-binding, and/or litigation. The choice of law relates to which substantive law will govern any dispute. The parties to the contractor teaming agreement will usually select and specify a particular state's law. Clearly, the parties involved in a contractor teaming agreement should do everything ethically possible to mitigate any disputes, and if a dispute arises, seek to promptly and dispassionately resolve their differences without entering into litigation and going to court. We recommend the parties agree to a structured and formal disputes escalation process, which begins at a mid-manager level and rises to appropriate senior executives and/or C-Suite as needed.

■ *Terminations*

It is critical to ensure every contractor teaming agreement include a terminations clause, which permits parties to exit the relationship under certain conditions, including the following:

1. failure to agree,
2. failure to perform,
3. failure to obtain required consents and approvals,
4. financial condition (i.e., bankruptcy),
5. government direction (i.e., suspension, debarment, Anti-Trust, etc.),
6. passage of time (specified period of performance), and
7. mutual agreement of the parties.

CONTRACTOR TEAMING AGREEMENTS: LESSONS LEARNED AND BEST PRACTICES

The following Table 16-2 provides a summary of a few of the many lessons learned and best practices from the various parties involved in contractor teaming agreements.

Table 16-2 Contractor Teaming Agreements	
Lessons Learned	**Best Practices**
1. Be careful what you say, and especially what you verbally promise to another party.	1. Do not make an oral binding commitment to partner or exclusively promise unless you are 100% confident in your commitment, then promptly follow-up in writing.
2. Remember, Non-Disclosure Agreements (NDAs), other confidentiality agreements, and/or Memoranda of Understanding (MOU) are not a formal legal binding teaming agreement, except with regard to the treatment of confidential information.	2. Use NDAs, MOUs, or MOAs as an interim step to a formal binding teaming agreement.
3. Be cautious, if you are a prime contractor, to not make your teaming agreement with your potential subcontractor(s) too specific or definitive.	3. Prime contractors should view and present their teaming agreements as so-called "agreements to agree."
4. Participate in drafting the contractor teaming agreement.	4. Lead the drafting of the contractor teaming agreement to ensure it properly reflects your intent and obligations.
5. Make sure your partners have good business integrity and sound finances.	5. Use NDAs, MOUs, or MOAs as an interim step to a formal binding teaming agreement.
6. Understand that the enforceability of contractor teaming agreements may be difficult.	6. Treat contractor teaming agreements as a business framework.
7. Ensure there is an appropriate exit strategy.	7. Carefully draft a terminations/cancellation clause.

SUMMARY

So, in retrospect, in this chapter we have discussed: the numerous forms of contractor teaming arrangements typically used to win and execute U.S. government contracts, the key elements or clauses which should be included in a contractor teaming agreement, and some contractor teaming agreement lessons learned and best practices. In this world of outsourcing, contractor teaming arrangements and subsequent agreements are critical to business success.

QUESTIONS TO CONSIDER

1. Which of the contractor teaming arrangements discussed has your organization used to win business and execute work?

2. Which of the essential elements to contractor teaming agreements do you consider to be most important?

3. What are your lessons learned and/or best practices of developing and executing contractor teaming agreements?

CHAPTER 17

MANAGING U.S. GOVERNMENT SUBCONTRACTS

INTRODUCTION

Serving as a federal government prime contractor is not easy business, because the U.S. federal government is very demanding. U.S. federal government prime contractors often must select and manage multiple subcontractors and comply with a tremendous number of complex laws, regulations, policies, standards, specifications, and face a growing level of government oversight-audits, reviews, and investigations. This chapter provides a detailed discussion of the critical challenges and proven best practices of U.S. federal government prime contractors in managing their respective supply chains to both comply with all the government's laws, regulations, policies, etc., but also to achieve on-time delivery of quality products and/or services, within budget, which meet or exceed the customer's requirements.

U.S. GOVERNMENT PRIME CONTRACTORS
SUPPLY CHAIN CHALLENGES

Table 17-1. provides a list of ten of the critical challenges which U.S. federal government prime contractors often encounter in building and managing their respective supply chain with their customers and subcontractors. Following Table 17-1. is a brief discussion of each of the stated 10 critical prime contractors supply chain challenges.

Table 17-1 Ten Critical Supply Chain Challenges Facing U.S. Government Prime Contractors
1. Financial pressures, due to global economic downturn, affecting prime contractors and subcontractors
2. Poor demand planning and requirements determination by U.S. federal government agencies
3. Insufficient government contracting and supply chain management team competencies
4. Lack of leverage of suppliers
5. Demanding U.S. government small business subcontracting goals
6. Excessive U.S. government mandatory flow-down of terms and conditions to subcontractors
7. Lack of competition in supplier selection
8. Increased government cost reduction demands
9. Excessive government detailed requirements
10. Increased U.S. government oversight-audits, reviews, and investigations

1. *Financial pressures, due to global economic downturn, affecting prime contractors and subcontractors*

The global economic downturn continues to manifest itself in many ways, and certainly one of them is the risk many companies are facing in terms of some of their suppliers being under significant financial pressures. Many companies in both domestic and international markets are under growing financial pressures, especially smaller companies that are not as well capitalized. A key factor in the current financial struggles of many subcontractors in both the public and private sectors is that their customers often pay even more slowly than usual as prime contractors face their own economic challenges.[2]

Cash flow is the heart of business. Financially strapped prime contractors and subcontractors may be late paying their suppliers as a result of their difficulties in: finding available loans, securing credit, paying higher interest rates, and receiving late payments from some of their customers. A recent survey by CPO Agenda magazine found that more than three quarters of procurement executives said they were facing great pressure to reduce costs – and we're surprised the number isn't even higher. (See Figure 17-1.)[3]

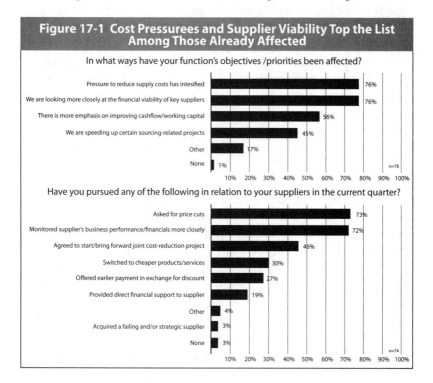

Figure 17-1 Cost Pressurees and Supplier Viability Top the List Among Those Already Affected

In what ways have your function's objectives /priorities been affected?

Pressure to reduce supply costs has intesified	76%
We are looking more closely at the financial viability of key suppliers	76%
There is more emphasis on improving cashflow/working capital	56%
We are speeding up certain sourcing-related projects	45%
Other	17%
None	1% (n=78)

Have you pursued any of the following in relation to your suppliers in the current quarter?

Asked for price cuts	73%
Monitored supplier's business performance/financials more closely	72%
Agreed to start/bring forward joint cost-reduction project	45%
Switched to cheaper products/services	30%
Offered earlier payment in exchange for discount	27%
Provided direct financial support to supplier	19%
Other	4%
Acquired a failing and/or strategic supplier	3%
None	3% (n=74)

2. *Poor demand planning and requirements determination by U.S. federal government agencies*

It may sound amazing to some business professionals, but one of the biggest challenges government prime contractors and sub-contractors encounter is that U.S. federal government agencies do not always know what they want, when they need it, and/or how many they will need! Of course, one of the golden rules to creating a cost-effective and efficient supply chain is to have an accurate demand plan/forecast of the quantity of products and/or services which the customer needs and a timeline as to when they are required. For a variety of reasons, U.S. federal government agencies have historically not done a very good job of accurately aligning their stated needs to their congressionally authorized and appropriated department budgets. As a result, government prime contractors and subcontractors often become frustrated by the in-accuracy of the government's requirements and frequent changes to the quantity, quality, and delivery schedule.

3. *Insufficient government contracting and supply chain management team (SCMT) competencies*

Many U.S. government prime contractors and subcontractors do not have the number of highly-skilled, well-educated, well-trained, and experienced professionals who fully understand the laws, regulations, and best practices of U.S. government contracts and supply chain management. As a result, numerous U.S. government prime contractors and subcontractors struggle to truly optimize their supply chain. Frequent company reorganizations, downsizing, and changing company policies, processes, and practices further complicate companies' ability to enhance both organizational and individual competencies in U.S. government contracting and supply chain management.

4. *Lack of leverage of suppliers*

One of the hallmarks of world class supply chain management companies, such as Wal-Mart, Proctor & Gamble, and IBM, is their ability to effectively leverage suppliers. Leveraging suppliers is a company's ability to negotiate discounts, obtain preferred contract terms and conditions (i.e. payment terms, cycle-time, delivery schedule, extended warranties, etc.), and form mutually success-ful business partnerships.[4] Unfortunately, for a variety of reasons many government prime contractors and subcontractors often struggle to form meaningful supplier relationships, thus prohibiting them from being able to effectively leverage their suppliers.

5. *Demanding U.S. government small business subcontracting goals*
In accordance with the Federal Acquisition Regulation (FAR) Part 19, Small Business Contracting, every U.S. federal government agency is required to establish goals to award a certain percentage of their acquisition budget to U.S. small businesses. In addition, FAR Part 19 mandates that government contracting officers require large businesses awarded specified government contracts valued above $500,000 to create a small business contracting plan to achieve stated goals. Further, FAR Part 19 establishes numerous specific categories of small businesses, including: small disadvantaged businesses, women-owned small businesses, veteran-owned small businesses, HUB-zoned small businesses, and Alaskan and Native American-owned small businesses. Often, U.S. federal government agencies will establish an overall contract goal for prime contractors, for example 20% of the value of the contract is subcontracted to small businesses, frequently with specific subcontracting targets for each specific small business category. Achieving these contract specific small business category targets and overall small business subcontracting goals can prove very challenging in some product and service areas.

6. *Excessive U.S. government mandatory flow-down of contract terms and conditions to subcontractors*
As the old saying goes, "What the big print giveth, the little print taketh away." Clearly, in the world of U.S. government contracts the above statement is true as it pertains to the vast number of complex, detailed, and one-sided mandatory contract clauses, often called terms and conditions (Ts & Cs), which are required by government laws, regulations, and policies. Of course, the U.S. federal government as one of the biggest buyers of products and services in the world has a right to leverage their suppliers and protect its interest. However, the U.S. federal government extended its leverage beyond the rule of contract privity to the prime contractor's subcontractors, via U.S. government mandatory flow-down contract clauses.

Said differently, the U.S. federal government agencies are required via the FAR to ensure the mandatory flow-down of numerous, in most cases 50+, government contract clauses to subcontractors. Further, each government department or agency has developed a list of additional terms and conditions or contract clauses which must be flowed-down to subcontractors, at all levels below the prime contract. For example, a U.S. Department of Defense (DOD) prime contractor, who has received a contract above $500,000, may be required to flow-down over 50 Federal Acquisition Regulation (FAR) contract clauses and another 50+ Department of Defense Federal Acquisition Regulation Supplement (DFARS) contract clauses to their subcontractors, resulting in over 100 detailed, complex, and often expensive to implement subcontract requirements above and beyond what it normally takes to deliver the products and/or services specified.

7. *Lack of competition in supplier selection*
Given the numerous obstacles to successful entry into the U.S. federal government marketplace, including: complexity of requirements, entrenched incumbent competitors, unstable funding, changing requirements, numerous delays, government politics and bureaucracy, and increased government oversight-reviews, audits, and investigations, it is often difficult to maintain real competition in supplier selections. At both the prime contract level and subcontract level(s) it can prove very challenging to maintain two or more viable suppliers especially for some of the highly complex systems and integrated solutions required by the U.S. government agencies.

8. *Increased government cost reduction demands*
As the global economic downturn affects governments and industry worldwide, more U.S. government funding is being directed to support failing industries and financial institutions. Thus, it is widely expected that many U.S. government departments and agencies will receive less funding to support their key contracts and major programs. Clearly, the focus of the Obama administration is on healthcare, house, energy, transportation, and the environment. So, the U.S. federal government departments of Health and Human Services (HHS), Veteran Affairs (VA), Housing and Urban Development (HUD), Transportation, Energy, and the Environmental Protection Agency (EPA) are all expected to receive increased acquisition funding from the U.S. congress with support and approval by President Obama. Likewise, it is widely expected that the Departments of Defense (DOD), Department of Homeland Security (DHS), and the National Aeronautics and Space Administration (NASA) will receive less funding than in previous years. As a result, it is expected that DOD, DHS, and NASA will be highly focused on controlling expenses, especially on the design, production, and operation of major acquisition pro-

grams.[5] Government contractors will increasingly be contractually required to reduce their costs by any and all means possible, within the realm of business ethics.

9. *Excessive government detailed how-to-do-it requirements*

For more than 40 years, U.S. federal government agencies, especially the U.S. Department of Defense (DOD), have developed highly detailed designs, specifications, and standards to ensure they get what they want, how they want it. Unfortunately, this highly detailed and prescriptive government requirements process has often resulted in high costs, over budget, behind schedule, and sometimes poor performing products, services, systems, and integrated solutions. Further, the U.S. government's detailed specification-oriented and statement of work-driven task documents are sometimes inaccurate and/or out-dated. Finally, the U.S. government's traditional detailed "How-to-do-it" requirements process does not allow much flexibility, innovation, or cost-efficiencies to be considered or implemented by industry.

10. *Increased U.S. government oversight-audits, reviews, and investigations*

Today, we live in a world of mistrust or, said simply, a lack of trust in government contracting. As a result of some clear violations of U.S. government laws, regulations, and policies by some government prime contractors and subcontractors, industry is often perceived by the U.S. congress and the public to be crooks. Because of this fundamental lack of trust of industry, U.S. government prime contractors are forced to endure numerous government audits, reviews, and investigations, many with civil and/or criminal penalties associated with non-compliance. Unfortunately, because of the wrong-doings of a relatively small percentage of government prime contractors, the industry as a whole is being forced to endure an unprecedented level of government oversight lead by the Government Accountability Office (GAO), Department Inspector General (IG) offices, Defense Contract Audit Agency (DCAA), Defense Contract Management Agency (DCMA), and many others.

U.S. Government Prime Contractors Supply Chain – Best Practices

Table 17–2 provides a list of ten of the proven effective supply chain best practices as implemented by industry in either the public and/or private sector. Following Table 17–2. is a brief discussion of each of the stated 10 supply chain best practices.

Table 17-2 10 Supply Chain Best Practices for U.S. Government Prime Contractors	
1.	Enhance cash-flow and financial management of suppliers
2.	Understand government needs and contract requirements
3.	Implement a supply chain management professional development program and Center of Excellence
4.	Conduct strategic sourcing and spend analysis
5.	Implement supplier relationship improvement programs
6.	Expand the use of commercial item acquisitions
7.	Enhance market research for supplier sourcing
8.	Implement price-benchmarking clauses
9.	Expand use of performance-based contracts
10.	Benchmark supply chain management processes and performance metrics

1. *Enhance cash-flow and financial management of suppliers*

Many suppliers, in both the public and private sectors, are facing cash-flow issues and growing financial pressures. U.S. government prime contractors must effectively manage their invoice, payment, and cost-flow process with their government agency customers, appropriately requesting: loans, advanced payment, milestone-based payments for results achieved a.k.a. progress-payments, or cost reimbursement for allowable and allocable expenses incurred, depending upon the financial situation and the pricing arrangement agreed to in the contract. Likewise, prime contractors must do all they can afford to do to help their selected subcontractors via contract financing such as collateralized loans, improved payment terms, faster payments, progress payments, and operational assistance when necessary and appropriate. A good supplier is hard to find and if you can help them through a tough financial time, you will most likely have a strong prime-sub business relationship.

2. *Understand customer needs and contract requirements*

In order to become a successful U.S. government prime contractor, it is vital to understand both what are the government customer needs and what are their stated contract requirements. At times the government agencies do not properly develop their contract requirements, thus it is possible for a prime contractor to provide the government the product and services which they contractually required, yet still not meet the government's real needs. The goal of business is for a seller to meet or exceed their customer/buyer's needs, which achieving their company performance goals. Thus, it is essential for a prime contractor to ensure they understand the government's customer's needs and align the needs with the actual contract requirements.

A tool designed to help prime contractors and likewise subcontractors ensure they understand the customers needs and the key contract/subcontract requirements is the customer requirements/Deliverable Matrix (CR/DM). The CR/DM is a simple matrix jointly developed by the buyer and the seller to clearly list all of the critical customer needs and which products, services, or systems will be developed and/or delivered to meet or exceed each contract requirement. Further, top supply chain companies ensure each contract requirement is tracked via a Work Breakdown Structure (WBS), linked to a Responsibility Assignment Matrix (RAM) to assign the work to specific individuals, time-phased via a Master Integrated Schedule (MIS), and has a budget established for each contract deliverable, project, and program.

3. *Implement a supply chain management professional development program and Center of Excellence*
World class companied like IBM, Dell, Toyota, and others have focused on not only creating effective supply chain processes, systems, and performance-metrics, but they have also invested in their most important asset, their people. Specifically, many of the leading global companies like Toyota have made significant investments in the supply chain management education, training, cross-functional work experience for their team members. Further, a few organizations in both the public and private sectors have established a supply chain management Center of Excellence to facilitate processes, tools, training, coaching/mentoring, lessons learned, and best practices via a coordinated and integrated Knowledge Management Center. Plus, many government agencies and companies are using the numerous supply chain management educations and training courses available from colleges and universities worldwide. Today, supply chain management education is offered via classroom-based instruction, computer-based instruction, and interactive online programs like the Supply Chain Management

Master's Certificate Program offered by the University of San Francisco, through the University Alliance online program.

4. *Conduct strategic sourcing and spend analysis*
Leading purchasing organizations worldwide have learned the value and power of conducting spend analysis as a vital element of strategic sourcing. Said simply, a buying/purchasing organization should know how they are spending their money, with whom they are spending the money-byproduct or service, and what is the quality of the products and services they are receiving. Strategic sourcing is a process approach to effectively analyze the supply chain to reduce cycle-time, reduce costs, and improve product and service performance results. Many companies and government agencies have created commodity councils to aggregate their demand planning for specific commercially available raw materials, products, and/or services. Improving demand planning or product/services forecasting is an important first-step for procurement organizations to more effectively leverage their suppliers, through economic-order-quantity buying practices.

5. *Implement supplier relationship improvement programs*
Numerous world class companies like Wal-Mart, IBM, Honda, and others have created, implemented, and maintained highly successful supplier relationship improvement programs. Wal-Mart works with its suppliers to help them improve the quality and marketability of their products. Honda provides all of their suppliers with performance goals/targets and monthly supplier report cards. Further, Honda works with their suppliers to improve their manufacturing processes and find innovated way to reduce cycle-times and drive-out expenses.[6] IBM categories their suppliers based upon performance and had developed a supplier inventive/rewards program. The U.S. Department of Defense (DOD) developed and implemented the DOD Pilot Mentor-Protégé program years ago, which has helped improve the performance of many small businesses working in partnership with a successful major defense prime contractor.

6. *Expand the use of commercial item acquisitions*
The U.S. federal government agencies have tried to increase their use of commercial contracting practices via the implementation of the Federal Acquisition Regulation (FAR) Part 12: Commercial-Item Acquisition. FAR Part 12 provides significant process and

contractual streamlining in comparison to the typical federal contracting process. The use of the Commercial-Item Acquisition process saves significant time and money for the subcontractors, prime contractors, government agencies, and U.S. taxpayers. U.S. government agencies must embrace and require the use of more commercially available products and services, versus creating unique detailed government requirements.

7. *Enhance market research for supplier sourcing*
Many prime contractors and U.S. federal government agencies suffer from the "incumbent contractor syndrome," which can be either positive or negative depending upon the performance of the selected contractor. Continually purchasing products and/or services from a selected contractor over an extended period of time can prove successful if the incumbent contractor is continually improving their people, processes, and performance. However, incumbent contractors have a tendency to become somewhat complacent; thus seeking higher revenues and profits without improving their people, processes, products, and/or pricing. To combat the Incumbent Contractor Syndrome, we recommend the effective use of market research to identify and select the best suppliers.

Market research can be accomplished via numerous methods, including: (1) hiring a professional market research firm (i.e. Dunn & Bradstreet, The Gartner Group, The Hackett Group, or Forrester Research), (2) conducting one-on-one market focus-group meetings with leading suppliers, (3) developing and conducting web-based market surveys, (4) conduct Internet-based searches of available suppliers, (5) contact industry trade associations for lists of available products and/or services providers, (6) review industry/trade magazine and catalogs, and (7) attend industry/trade association conferences and exhibitions.

8. *Implement price-benchmarking clauses*
A benchmarking clause is used in an outsourcing contract as a check against significant price "drift" over time. Such drift is of particular concern in longer term contracts, where major discrepancies can occur between contract prices and market pricing. Most outsourcing projects, especially longer term ones, have complex mechanisms in place for changing contract prices. These mechanisms are the primary drivers of micro-price adjustment and include: year-on-year productivity improvements, inflation adjust-

ments, and adjustments for changes in required service volumes. The underlying commercial basis for including a benchmarking clause is not to treat it as a supplement to these mechanisms, which would cause it to become just another tool to enable an additional micro-price adjustment.[7]

9. *Expand use of performance-based contracts*
Said simply, a Performance-Based Contract (PBC) contains the following essential elements:

- Performance Work Statement (PWS) or Statement of Objectives (SOO)
- Performance standards, measures, and metrics
- Performance incentives (positive and negative)
- Quality Assurance Surveillance Plan (QASP)
- Appropriate pricing arrangement(s)

Without all of the above stated essential elements, a contract lacks the means to truly empowers and motivate a supplier to achieve the art of the possible. Today, too many U.S. government agencies and prime contractors still rely on out-dated, overly legalistic, highly prescriptive, and overly complex contracts containing detailed designs, specifications, and lengthy task-oriented statements of work, which often drive-up costs, extend the acquisition cycle-time, and result in poor performance results. PBCs when effectively structured and intelligently implemented can achieve superior performance results for all of the parties involved.

10. *Benchmark supply chain management processes and key performance indicators*

Establishing and reporting on key performance indicators (KPIs) is critical to the success of any contract. According to the recent 2009 cross-industry benchmarking studies conducted by the Center for Advanced Purchasing Studies (CAPS) research, the most popular commercial procurement KPIs include:

- Purchase spend as a percentage of sales dollars
- Purchasing operating expense as a percentage of sales dollars
- Purchasing operating expense as a percentage of purchase spend
- Purchasing operating expense per purchasing employee
- Purchasing employees as a percentage of company employees
- Purchase spend per purchasing employee
- Managed spend per purchasing employee
- Percentage of purchase spend managed/controlled by purchasing
- Percentage of companies that reported outsourcing some of their procurement activities
- Percentage of managed spend outsourced
- Percentage of purchase spend offshore
- Percentage of purchase spend onshore
- Average annual spend on training per purchasing employees
- Cost avoidance savings as a percentage of total purchase spend
- Cost reduction savings as a percentage of total purchase spend
- Percentage of active suppliers accounting for 80 percent of purchase spend
- Percentage of purchase spend with diversity suppliers
- Percentage of active suppliers who are e-procurement enabled

Most organizations understand the importance and value of conducting benchmarking of their procurement practices and performance metrics or key performance indicators. Today, many senior procurement executives, in both government and industry, are now assessing how their organization adds value to the mission-determining their value proposition. The Hackett Group, a world-class benchmarking firm, has developed a five-stage model for procurement's evolving proposition. See Table 17-3.[8]

SEVENTEEN

Table 17-3				
Supply Management		**Customer Management**		
1 **Supply** **Stage** — **Assurance**	**2** **Price**	**3** **Total Cost of** **Ownership**	**4** **Demand** **Management**	**5** **Value** **Management**
GOAL	Right goods and services at the right time at the right price	Right goods and services AND at the right price	Shift from lowest price to lowest total cost of ownership	Reduce demand activity, complexity, and variability	Increase business value derived from spend rather than just reducing total cost/spend
PROCURE-MENT'S ROLE	Buyer Planner	Negotiator	Supply expert team leader, project manager, supplier manager	Spend/budget consultant ("money manager") and procurement relationship manager	Trusted business advisor and change agent
KEY OUTPUT METRICS	Perfect Order (on-time delivery, defect-free, accurate documentation, etc.)	1. Present Value and/or spend cost savings/ avoidance 2. Performance to market	1. Cost of quality 2. Cost of capital 3. Freight, handling, duties, tariffs, taxes 4. Write-offs and disposal 5. Opportunity cost from lost profits and brand damage	1. Percent of spend/sourcing activity with early demand influence 2. Maverick spend percentage (not channeling demand to best supply) 3. Internal customer satisfaction rating	1. Net Income, Return on Investment, Economic Value Added, Net Present Value, etc. 2. Market cap/ stock price 3. Operation metrics of the spend owners
PRACTICES/ TOOLS	1. Enterprise Resource Planning 2. Supplier scheduling 3. Long term contacts, dual sourcing, etc.	1. Separation of strategic sourcing and tactical buying 2. Basic "n-step" strategic sourcing methodology 3. Price savings tracking 4. Competitive bidding techniques/tools	1. Deep cost modeling and management 2. End-to-end functional teams (suppliers, too) 3. Supplier management, collaboration, and development 4. Working capital management 5. Complexity/ waste reduction (lean, Six Sigma, etc.) 6. Supply chain management (e.g., extended network design, multi-tier sourcing) 7. Design for cost 8. Supply risk mitigation (supplier, capacity, market, network, etc.)	1. Customer Account Management (account managers, co-location, stakeholder surveys, contract centers) 2. Demand visibility (e.g., forecasting project portfolio planning, demand planning) 3. Supply planning and demand supply matching 4. Demand shaping (joint planning/ budgeting, promotions, postponement)	1. Business process sourcing (e.g., make vs. buy, shoring) 2. Design for supply 3. Hoshin Planning and Quality Function Deployment (QFD) 4. Customer's customer focus and customer specific methodologies

SUMMARY

So in retrospect, in this chapter we have provided a detailed discussion of ten critical challenges which U.S. federal government prime contractors typically encounter in managing their respective supply chains in order to both comply with all of the government's laws, regulations, and policies, and to achieve high performance results. Further, we have offered ten supply chain best practices, which have been successfully implemented by numerous world class companies and/or leading government organizations. Too many organizations in both the public and private sectors over promise and under deliver. Remember, the promise of successful outsourcing and contract administration can only be realized through the discipline of effective supply chain management.

QUESTIONS TO CONSIDER

1. How well does your organization manage your subcontractors?

2 Do you know which contract terms and conditions must be flowed-down to your subcontractors?

3. How well does your organization ensure subcontractors provide accurate cost and pricing information?

ENDNOTES

1   Federal Procurement Data System, *FY08 Procurement Statistics,* U.S. Office of Federal Procurement Policy, February 2009.

2   Supply Chain Digest, *If Key Suppliers are Struggling Financially, What Should Procurement Organizations Do?,* scdigest.com, New York NY, January 7, 2009.

3   Supply Chain Digest, *For Procurement Managers, a Bit of Pay Back Time,* scdigest. com, New York NY, January 27, 2009.

4   Garrett, Gregory A., *Contract Negotiations,* CCH, Chicago IL, 2005.

5   Garrett, Gregory A. and Pete McDonald, *Preparing for Change: The Obama Administration Affect on Government Contractors,* Contract Management Magazine, National Contract Management Association, Vienna VA, February, 2009.

6   Garrett, Gregory A., *Commercial Contracting Best Practices,*Contract Management Magazine, National Contract Management Association, Vienna VA, January 2008.

7   Ibid, Note 6.

8   Ibid, Note 6.

APPENDIX

CONTRACT
MANAGEMENT
FORMS

The following templates, checklists, matrixes, and forms are samples of how pertinent information can be formatted and used to help simplify and streamline the contract management process.

Form Number	Title
1	Key Contract Terms and Conditions Checklist
2	Competitive Analysis Matrix
3	Sample Proposal Compliance Matrix
4	Team Member Strengths, Weaknesses, and Interests
5	Things to Know About the Other Party
6	Objectives Identification
7	Objectives Prioritization
8	Create Options for Achieving Negotiation Objectives
9	Objectives and Alternatives– Worst Case, Most Likely, and Best Case
10	Sample Negotiating Planning Summary
11	Negotiation Agenda
12	Offers and Counteroffers Summary
13	Negotiation Results Summary
14	Essential Contract Elements Checklist
15	Preperformance Conference Checklist
16	Invoice Request
17	Invoice and Payment Reconciliation
18	Change Request
19	Contract Change Log
20	Contract Closeout Checklist
21	Postcontract Summary
22	Lessons-Learned Summary
23	Contract Jeopardy/Escalation
24	Customer Relations Checklist
25	Customer Requirements Summary
26	Doability Analysis
27	Subcontractor Evaluation

Form 1 Key Contract Terms and Conditions Checklist

Based on the type of contract to be developed, identify preferred terms and conditions from the following list, and strive to ensure that they are addressed in the contract.

Terms and Conditions

- ❑ Acceptance criteria
- ❑ Change management
- ❑ Delivery
- ❑ Dispute resolution—arbitration
- ❑ Force majeure
- ❑ Glossary of key terms
- ❑ Indemnification
- ❑ Intellectual property rights
- ❑ Invoicing
- ❑ Nondisclosure agreement
- ❑ Packaging and shipment
- ❑ Payments

- ❑ Period of performance
- ❑ Points of contact—authorized representatives
- ❑ Pricing and discounts
- ❑ Product quality
- ❑ Services
- ❑ Software
- ❑ Taxes
- ❑ Termination by mutual agreement
- ❑ Termination for default
- ❑ Testing
- ❑ Training
- ❑ Warranty

Form 2 Competetive Analysis Matrix

Score each competitor on a scale from 1 to 5 (5 = best rating).

Evaluation Factors	Us	Competitors		
		A	B	C
Proven technical solution				
Customer use of equipment (ours vs. competitors')				
Customer preference				
Product price				
Service package				
Timeliness of delivery				
Coproduction within country				
Use of local labor				
Joint venture/political connection				
Training offered				
Financing for customer				
Equity stake financing				
Past performance				
Use of local subcontractors				
Long-term commitment				
Image and reputation industry				
Payment plan for customer				
Total score				

Form 3 Sample Proposal Compliance Matrix

Project Name	Prepared by (Print)	Date Prepared
Customer	Contact	Contact Telephone

Paragraph Number/Title		Category of Reply	Remarks and Reference
3.3	Price comparison		
3.3.1		Complied	Refer to Attachment 3.4.1 for details of discount percent
3.4	Volume sensitivity		
3.4.1		Complied	
3.5	Future price reduction		
3.5.1		Complied	
3.6	Price adjustment		
3.6.1		Complied	
4	Total offer price		
4.1		Complied	
4.2		Information provided	Refer to Attachment 4.2
4.3		Complied	Refer to Chapter 3, "Pricing"
4.4		Complied	Refer to Chapter 3, "Pricing"
4.5		Complied	
4.6		Complied	Repair cost shall not exceed 75% of the unit prices listed in the tender
4.7		Complied	Refer to Chapter 3, "Pricing"
4.8		Complied	
5	Technical proposals		
5.1		Complied	
5.2		Complied	
5.3		Complied	
6	Tender submission		
6.1		Complied	

Form 4 Team Member Strengths, Weaknesses and Interests

Team Member	Team Member
Name	Name
Job Title	Job Title
Phone No.	Phone No.
Fax No.	Fax No.
Strengths 1	Strengths 1
2	2
3	3
Weaknesses 1	Weaknesses 1
2	2
3	3
Interests 1	Interests 1
2	2
3	3

Date Prepared: _____   Lead Negotiator: _____

Form 5 Things to Know About the Other Party

Buyer and Seller

- ❑ What is the organization's overall business strategy?
- ❑ What is its reputation?
- ❑ What is its current company business environment?
- ❑ Who is the lead negotiator?
- ❑ Who are the primary decision makers?
- ❑ What are their key objectives?
- ❑ What are their overall contract objectives?
- ❑ What are their personal objectives?
- ❑ Who or what influences the decision makers?
- ❑ What internal organization barriers do they face?

Seller Only

- ❑ When does the buyer need our products or services?
- ❑ How much money does the buyer have to spend?
- ❑ Where does the buyer want our products and services delivered?
- ❑ What benefits will our products and services provide?
- ❑ What is our company's past experience with this buyer?

Date Prepared: _____   Lead Negotiator: _____

Form 6 Objectives Identification

Seller Objectives	Buyer Objectives
Personal 1	Personal 1
2	2
3	3
4	4
5	5
Professional 1	Professional 1
2	2
3	3
4	4
5	5
6	6
7	7

Date Prepared: _____ Lead Negotiator: _____

Form 7 Objectives Prioritization

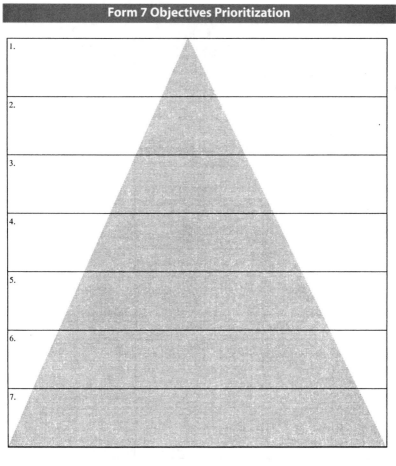

1.

2.

3.

4.

5.

6.

7.

Date Prepared: _____ Lead Negotiator: _____

Form 8 Create Options for Achieving Negotiation Objectives

Seller Objectives	Possible Options	Buyer Objectives

Date Prepared: _____   Lead Negotiator: _____

Form 9 Objectives and Alternatives— Worst Case, Most Likely, and Best Case

Objective:		
Worst Case	Most Likely	Best Case

(Plot your most likely position)

Date Prepared: _____ Lead Negotiator: _____

Form 10 Sample Negotiation Planning Summary

Negotiation Information

Location	Date	Time
1 GCG Corporation, Arlington, VA	1 March 31, 1997	1 9:00 a.m.
2	2	2
3	3	3

Key Objectives (Plot your most likely position)

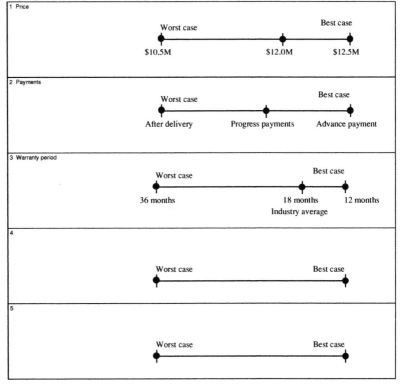

1 Price

Worst case   Best case

$10.5M $12.0M $12.5M

2 Payments

Worst case   Best case

After delivery   Progress payments   Advance payment

3 Warranty period

Worst case   Best case

36 months   18 months   12 months
Industry average

4

Worst case   Best case

5

Worst case   Best case

Form 10—continued

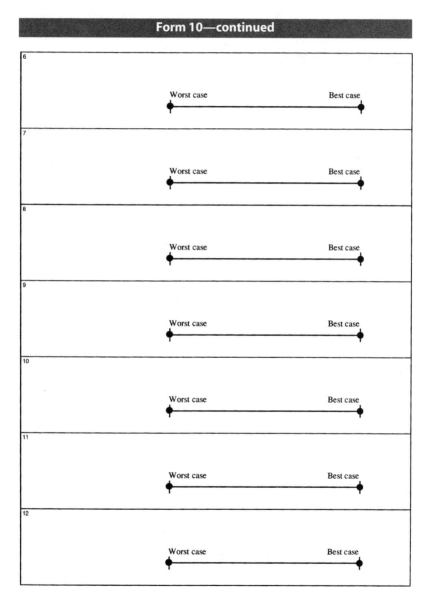

Form 10—continued

Possible Tactics and Countertactics

Objective	Planned Tactics—Buyer	Planned Countertactics—Seller

Contract Price

Range	
Best Case	
Most Likely	
Worst Case	

Date Prepared: _____   Lead Negotiator: _____

Approved by: _____   Date Approved: _____

Form 11 Negotiation Agenda

Contract

Title	Date
Location	Time

Topics or Action   **Time**

❑ Introduce team members   _____

❑ Provide overview and discuss purpose of negotiation   _____

❑ Exchange information on key interests and issues   _____

■ Quantity of products   _____

■ Quality of products and services

■ Past performance

■ Delivery schedule

■ Maintenance

■ Training

❑ Have a break   _____

❑ Review agreement on all key interests and issues   _____

❑ Agree on detailed terms and conditions   _____

❑ Agree on price   _____

❑ Review and summarize meeting   _____

Date Prepared: _____   Lead Negotiator: _____

Form 12 Offers and Counteroffers Summary

Seller	Buyer
Offer	Counteroffer
Offer	Counteroffer
Offer	Counteroffer
Offer	Counteroffer

Date Prepared:_____ Lead Negotiator:_____

Form 13 Negotiation Results Summary

Contract Title	Date of Contract
Parties Involved	Date(s) of Negotiation

Brief Product/Service Description	Location

Agreed-To Price

Key Changes from Approved Proposal

Date Prepared: _____   Lead Negotiator: _____

Form 14 Essential Contract Elements Checklist

Project Name	Prepared by (Print)	Date Prepared
Customer	Contact	Contact Telephone

❑ Deliverables and prices (provide a listing of deliverables and their prices)

❑ Deliverable conformance specifications

❑ Requirements in statement of work (determine SOW requirements not listed as deliverables)

❑ Delivery requirements (list delivery requirements, deliverable packaging and shipping requirements, and service performance instructions)

❑ Deliverable inspection and acceptance

❑ Invoice and payment schedule and provisions (include in contract tracking summary)

❑ Representations and certifications

❑ Other terms and conditions

Form 15 Preperformance Conference Checklist

Project Name	Prepared by (Print)	Date Prepared
Customer	Contact	Contact Telephone

- ❏ Complete requirements analysis (verify and validate the requirements stated in the contract to ensure that the project, when completed according to the requirements statement, will meet the needs of both parties)

- ❏ Summarize contract requirements (complete the contract requirements matrix)

- ❏ Establish the project baseline (ensure that the baseline and specifications are established)

- ❏ Develop in-scope and out-of-scope listings (develop lists of items that buyer and seller consider to be within and outside the scope of the contract; these are useful for establishing and managing expectations and for containing contract cost growth)

- ❏ List the seller's assumptions about the buyer's requirements and understanding of the buyer's expectations

- ❏ Establish preliminary schedule of meetings between the parties

- ❏ Inform your team and other affected parties (brief the team members who will attend the meeting, ensuring that they understand the basic requirements of the contract and the project)

- ❏ Review meeting findings with all affected people in your organization

- ❏ Document who attended, what was discussed, what was agreed to, and what follow-up actions are required (by whom, where, and when)

- ❏ Prepare and send preperformance conference meeting minutes to the other party

Form 15—continued

Deliverables						
Contract Requirements Matrix						
Description	Contract Reference	Delivery Date or Service Dates	WBS Element	Other Reference		

Form 15—continued

Contract Requirements Matrix

Requirements

Description	Contract Reference	Delivery Date or Service Dates	WBS Element	Other Reference

Form 16 Invoice Request

Accounts receivable: Prepare and send an invoice for the following deliverable, and send a copy of the invoice to the requester.

Requester Information

Name (Print)	Signature	Date
Phone	Fax	E-Mail
Project Office	Copies to	

Deliverable Information

Customer	Contract No.	Order No.
Contact	Phone	Fax
Address		
Deliverable		Invoice Amount

Form 17 Invoice and Payment Reconiliation

Project Name			Prepared by (Print)			Date Prepared	
Customer			Contact			Contact Telephone	

Deliverable/ Milestone	Accepted Date	Invoiced Date	Invoice No.	Invoice Amount	Paid Date	Issues/Comments

Form 18 Change Request

Information

Buyer		Change Request No.	Date Requested
Originator	Department/Company	Phone	Fax

Proposed Change

Baseline Description
Change Description
Reason for Change

Affected Documents

WBS No.	SOW Reference	Spec. No.	Drawing No.
WBS No.	SOW Reference	Spec. No.	Drawing No.
WBS No.	SOW Reference	Spec. No.	Drawing No.
Other References			

Seller Authorization

Name (Print)	Signature	Phone	Date

Buyer Disposition

	Approved	Comments (If Appropriate)
	Suspended	
	Disapproved	

Buyer Authorization

Name (Print)	Signature	Phone	Date

Form 19 Contract Change Log

Project Name	Prepared by (Print)	Date Prepared
Customer	Contact	Contact Telephone

Change No.	Description	Date Requested	Date Approved	Effective Date

Form 20 Contract Closeout Checklist

Project Name	Prepared by (Print)	Date Prepared
Customer	Contact	Contact Telephone

Activity				Anticipated Date	Completed Date
	Yes	N/A	No		
1	___	___	___ All products or services required were provided to the buyer.		
2	___	___	___ Documentation adequately shows receipt and formal acceptance of all contract items.		
3	___	___	___ No claims or investigations are pending on this contract.		
4	___	___	___ Any buyer-furnished property or information was returned to the buyer.		
5	___	___	___ All actions related to contract price revisions and changes are concluded.		
6	___	___	___ All outstanding subcontracting issues are settled.		
7	___	___	___ If a partial or complete termination was involved, action is complete.		
8	___	___	___ Any required contract audit is now complete.		
9	___	___	___ The final invoice was submitted and paid.		

Form 21 Postcontract Summary

Summary Information

Buyer	Contract Manager	Phone
Contract Title and No.		Fax

Schedule Performance

Original Planned Start Date	Actual Start Date	Original Planned Finish Date	Actual Finish Date

Cost Performance

Original Contract Price	Final Contract Price	Original Planned Cost	Actual Cost

Technical Performance Summary

Schedule Performance Summary

Buyer Satisfaction

Form 22 Lessons—Learned Summary

Project Name	Prepared by (Print)	Date Prepared
Customer	Contact	Contact Telephone

Executive Summary

Background

Learning Highlights

Recommendation Summary

Technical Performance Summary

Experience

Recommended Process Improvements

Proposed Tools Updates

Form 22—continued

Schedule Performance Summary

Experience
Recommended Process Improvements
Proposed Tools Updates

Contract Management Summary

Experience
Recommended Process Improvements
Proposed Tools Updates

Form 22—continued

Risk Management Summary

Experience

Recommended Process Improvements

Proposed Tools Updates

Financial Management Summary

Experience

Recommended Process Improvements

Proposed Tools Updates

Form 22—continued

Relationship Management Summary

Experience
Recommended Process Improvements
Proposed Tools Updates

Form 23 Contract Jeopardy/Escalation Form

Jeopardy		Escalation		Urgent Escalation	

Date Issue Identified: Control Number:
# of Times Escalated: Date Resolved:

From: Telephone Number: Fax Number:

To: Telephone Number: Fax Number:

Description of Issue:

Background and Discussion of Attempts to Address the Issue:

Impact of Issue on Customer, Scope, Schedule and Financial:

Recommended Action:

Action Plan and Owner:

Resolution:

Escalate to: Date Escalated:

Form 24 Customer Relations Checklist

PROGRAM NAME	PREPARED BY (PRINT)	SIGNATURE	DATE PREPARED

Section #	Topic	Owner	Topic Response	Yes	No	N/A
1.0 Develop Customer Relation Plan:						
	1.1 Select Individuals that will interact with the Customer					
	1.2 Identify the key contacts in the Customer Organization					
	1.3 Identify responsibilities and procedures for customer contact					
	1.4 Determine the frequency of interacting with the Customer					
	1.5 Determine the method of communicating with the Customer					
	1.6 Specify what type of information can and cannot be shared with the Customer					
2.0 The following should be understood by all members of the Team:						
	2.1 Describe the Customer's Needs and Objectives for this program					
	2.2 Identify Customer Expectations					
	2.3 Identify events/actions that may occur that could affect Customer Relations (positively or negatively)					
3.0 The following items should be discussed with the Customer:						
	3.1 Roles and Responsibilities for Lucent and the Customer					
	3.2 Change Control Process					
	3.3 Customer Training					
	3.4 Test & Acceptance Criteria					
	3.5 Frequency of program status					
	3.6 Method of Delivering Status					
	3.7 Type of information and detail to be statused					
	3.8 Transition Plan					

Form 25 Customer Requirements Summary

For Clearly Defined Scope of Work

DOCUMENT PREPARATION INFORMATION

PROGRAM NAME	PREPARED BY (PRINT)	SIGNATURE:	DATE PREPARED

I.	SCOPE OF WORK - What are the program deliverables?
II.	OPERATIONAL NEED - How will the customer use the deliverables?
III.	CURRENT CAPABILITY - What similar systems/products does the customer have in place? Do they have people experienced with them?
IV.	INTERFACES - What other systems/products will the deliverable have to connect with? Are there any other organizations or subcontractors the Program Team will have to work with?
V.	PROGRAM MISSION LIFE - Does the program have to transition to another team (e.g. O&M)
VI.	SCHEDULE - By what dates do the program deliverables have to be completed?
VII.	ID OF USERS - Does the customer have people in place? Will they need training?
VIII.	EVALUATION CRITERIA - How do we evaluate the performance of the deliverables?

Form 26 Doability Analysis

Doable: Yes ☐   No ☐

Summary

Proposal Name and Number:	
Customer:	Country/Region of Operation:
Scope of Deliverables:	Estimated Revenue in US$:
Start Date:	Completion Date:

Prepared by:	Phone #:
Signature:	Comments:

I. Program Description (scope of work):

II. Evaluate Technical Requirements / Availability / Research & Development

III. Evaluate the Feasibility of the Schedule (attach milestone summary schedule)

Form 26—continued

IV. *Evaluate the Reasonableness of the Financial Commitments (attach income statement, balance sheet and cash flow)*

V. *Conduct High Level Risk Assessment. Consider the following risks if appropriate: Pricing, Payment terms, Acceptance, Warranty, Liability, R&D, Implementation, Environmental, etc.*

VI. *Describe significant assumptions implicit in the evaluation of the scope, schedule, and financial commitments*

VII. *Attach the Responsibility Assignment Matrix of Major Deliverables*

Form 27 Subcontractor

DOCUMENT PREPARATION INFORMATION

PROGRAM NAME	PREPARED BY (PRINT)	DATE PREPARED	SIGNATURE

LEVEL	LOW ← → HIGH					NOT REQ	Description
	1	2	3	4	5		
ACCESS TO EQUIPMENT							Owns or can acquire required equipment for job
CONDITION OF EQUIPMENT							Equipment in good repair - maintenance ability
ADEQUATE INSURANCE							Adequate insurance, bonded, etc.
ACCESS TO MANPOWER							Ability to staff and manage required workforce
DEPENDABILITY/REPUTATION							Prior work record of contractor
FLEXIBILITY							Adaptability to work methods
JOB KNOWLEDGE							Knowledge of required work processes
JOB KNOWLEDGE (ability to learn)							Capacity to learn new work processes
PRIOR JOB EXPERIENCE							Prior experience with similar jobs/technology
QUALITY ASSURANCE PROCESS							Documented Q/A process
QUALITY PERFORMANCE							Results of Q/A inspections exist
SAFETY PERFORMANCE							Safety processes/equipment - reports (if available)
LOCAL COUNTRY NATIONAL							Subcontractor based in/has ties to country/region of work site
SUPERVISION EXPERIENCE							Experience as work supervisor
TIMELINESS OF BILLING REPORTS							Process for billing - need for close supervision by PM
WILLINGNESS TO COMPROMISE							Adaptability to work with

Note: Rate the Subcontractor on each of the above characteristics from 1 (least desirable)
to 5 (most desirable). If a particular characteristic does not apply, mark
the 'Not Req.' box (for Not Required) instead. Use the ratings to compare subcontractors.

APPENDIX

UNITED NATIONS CONVENTION ON CONTRACTS FOR THE INTERNATIONAL SALE OF GOODS (1980)

THE STATES PARTIES TO THIS CONVENTION,

BEARING IN MIND the broad objectives in the resolutions adopted by the sixth special session of the General Assembly of the United Nations on the establishment of a New International Economic Order,

CONSIDERING that the development of international trade on the basis of equality and mutual benefit is an important element in promoting friendly relations among States,

BEING OF THE OPINION that the adoption of uniform rules which govern contracts for the international sale of goods and take into account the different social, economic and legal systems would contribute to the removal of legal barriers in international trade and promote the development of international trade,

HAVE DECREED as follows:

PART I: SPHERE OF APPLICATION AND GENERAL PROVISIONS

Chapter I Sphere of Application

Article 1

This Convention applies to contracts of sale of goods between parties whose places of business are in different States:

(a) when the States are Contracting States; or

(b) when the rules of private international law lead to the application of the law of a Contracting State.

The fact that the parties have their places of business in different States is to be disregarded whenever this fact does not appear either from the contract or from any dealings between, or from information disclosed by, the parties at any time before or at the conclusion of the contract.

Neither the nationality of the parties nor the civil or commercial character of the parties or of the contract is to be taken into consideration in determining the application of this Convention.

Article 2

This Convention does not apply to sales:

of goods bought for personal, family or household use, unless the seller, at any time before or at the conclusion of the contract, neither knew nor ought to have known that the goods were bought for any such use;

(b) by auction;

(c) on execution or otherwise by authority of law;

(d) of stocks, shares, investment securities, negotiable instruments or money;

(e) of ships, vessels, hovercraft or aircraft;

(f) of electricity.

Article 3

Contracts for the supply of goods to be manufactured or produced are to be considered sales unless the party who orders the goods undertakes to supply a substantial part of the materials necessary for such manufacture or production.

This Convention does not apply to contracts in which the preponderant part of the obligations of the party who furnishes the goods consists in the supply of labour or other services.

Article 4

This Convention governs only the formation of the contract of sale and the rights and obligations of the seller and the buyer arising from such a contract. In particular, except as otherwise expressly provided in this Convention, it is not concerned with:

(a) the validity of the contract or of any of its provisions or of any usage;

(b) the effect which the contract may have on the property in the goods sold.

Article 5

This Convention does not apply to the liability of the seller for death or personal injury caused by the goods to any person.

Article 6

The parties may exclude the application of this Convention or, subject to article 12, derogate from or vary the effect of any of its provisions.

Chapter II: General Provisions

Article 7

(1) In the interpretation of this Convention, regard is to be had to its international character and to the need to promote uniformity in its application and the observance of good faith in international trade.

(2) Questions concerning matters governed by this Convention which are not expressly settled in it are to be settled in conformity with the general principles on which it is based or, in the absence of such principles, in conformity with the law applicable by virtue of the rules of private international law.

Article 8

(1) For the purposes of this Convention statements made by and other conduct of a party are to be interpreted according to his intent where the other party knew or could not have been unaware what that intent

(2) If the preceding paragraph is not applicable, statements made by and other conduct of a party are to be interpreted according to the understanding that a reasonable person of the same kind as the other party would have had in the same circumstances.

(3) In determining the intent of a party or the understanding a reasonable person would have had, due consideration is to be given to all relevant circumstances of the case including the negotiations, any practices which the parties have established between themselves, usages and any subsequent conduct of the parties.

Article 9

(1) The parties are bound by any usage to which they have agreed and by any practices which they have established between themselves.

(2) The parties are considered, unless otherwise agreed, to have impliedly made applicable to their contract or its formation a usage of which the parties knew or ought to have known and which in international trade is widely known to, and regularly observed by, parties to contracts of the type involved in the particular trade concerned.

Article 10

For the purposes of this Convention:

(a) if a party has more than one place of business, the place of business is that which has the closest relationship to the contract and its performance, having regard to the circumstances known to or contemplated by the parties at any time before or at the conclusion of the contract;

(b) if a party does not have a place of business, reference is to be made to his habitual residence.

Article 11

A contract of sale need not be concluded in or evidenced by writing and is not subject to any other requirement as to form. It may be proved by any means, including witnesses.

Article 12

Any provision of article 11, article 29 or Part II of this Convention that allows a contract of sale or its modification or termination by agreement or any offer, acceptance or other indication of intention to be made in any form other than in writing does not apply where any party has his place of business in a Contracting State which has made a declaration under article 96 of this Convention. The parties may not derogate from or vary the effect or this article.

Article 13

For the purposes of this Convention "writing" includes telegram and telex.

PART II: FORMATION OF THE CONTRACT

Article 14

(1) A proposal for concluding a contract addressed to one or more specific persons constitutes an offer if it is sufficiently definite and indicates the intention of the offeror to be bound in case of acceptance. A proposal is sufficiently definite if it indicates the goods and expressly or implicitly fixes or makes provision for determining the quantity and the price.

(2) A proposal other than one addressed to one or more specific persons is to be considered merely as an invitation to make offers, unless the contrary is clearly indicated by the person making the proposal.

Article 15

(1) An offer becomes effective when it reaches the offeree.

(2) An offer, even if it is irrevocable, may be withdrawn if the withdrawal reaches the offeree before or at the same time as the offer.

Article 16

(1) Until a contract is concluded an offer may be revoked if the revocation reaches the offeree before he has dispatched an acceptance.

(2) However, an offer cannot be revoked:

> (a) if it indicates, whether by stating a fixed time for acceptance or otherwise, that it is irrevocable; or
> (b) if it was reasonable for the offeree to rely on the offer as being irrevocable and the offeree has acted in reliance on the offer.

Article 17

An offer, even if it is irrevocable, is terminated when a rejection reaches the offeror.

Article 18

(1) A statement made by or other conduct of the offeree indicating assent to an offer is an acceptance. Silence or inactivity does not in itself amount to acceptance.

(2) An acceptance of an offer becomes effective at the moment the indication of assent reaches the offeror. An acceptance is not effective if the indication of assent does not reach the offeror within the time he has fixed or, if no time is fixed, within a reasonable time, due account being taken of the circumstances of the transaction, including the rapidity of the means of communication employed by the offeror. An oral offer must be accepted immediately unless the circumstances indicate otherwise.

(3) However, if, by virtue of the offer or as a result of practices which the parties have established between themselves or of usage, the offeree may indicate assent by performing an act, such as one relating to the dispatch of the goods or payment of the price, without notice to the offeror, the acceptance is effective at the moment the act is performed, provided that the act is performed within the period of time laid down in the preceding paragraph.

Article 19

(1) A reply to an offer which purports to be an acceptance but contains additions, limitations or other modifications is a rejection of the offer and constitutes a counter-offer.

(2) However, a reply to an offer which purports to be an acceptance but contains additional or different terms which do not materially alter the terms of the offer constitutes an acceptance, unless the offeror, without undue delay, objects orally to the discrepancy or dispatches a notice to that effect. If he does not so object, the terms of the contract are the terms of the offer with the modifications contained in the acceptance.

(3) Additional or different terms relating, among other things, to the price, payment, quality and quantity of the goods, place

and time of delivery, extent of one party's liability to the other or the settlement of disputes are considered to alter the terms of the offer materially.

Article 20

(1) A period of time for acceptance fixed by the offeror in a telegram or a letter begins to run from the moment the telegram is handed in for dispatch or from the date shown on the letter or, if no such date is shown, from the date shown on the envelope. A period of time for acceptance fixed by the offeror by telephone, telex or other means of instantaneous communication, begins to run from the moment that the offer reaches the offeree.

(2) Official holidays or non-business days occurring during the period for acceptance are included in calculating the period. However, if a notice of acceptance cannot be delivered at the address of the offeror on the last day of the period because that day falls on an official holiday or a non-business day at the place of business of the offeror, the period is extended until the first business day which follows.

Article 21

(1) A late acceptance is nevertheless effective as an acceptance if without delay the offeror orally so informs the offeree or dispatches a notice to that effect.

(2) If a letter or other writing containing a late acceptance shows that it has been sent in such circumstances that if its transmission had been normal it would have reached the offeror in due time, the late acceptance is effective as an acceptance unless, without delay, the offeror orally informs the offeree that he considers his offer as having lapsed or dispatches a notice to that effect.

Article 22

An acceptance may be withdrawn if the withdrawal reaches the offeror before or at the same time as the acceptance would have become effective.

Article 23

A contract is concluded at the moment when an acceptance of an offer becomes effective in accordance with the provisions of this Convention.

Article 24

For the purposes of this Part of the Convention, an offer, declaration of acceptance or any other indication of intention "reaches" the addressee when it is made orally to him or delivered by any other means to him personally, to his place of business or mailing address or, if he does not have a place of business or mailing address, to his habitual residence.

PART III: SALE OF GOODS

Chapter I: General Provisions

Article 25

A breach of contract committed by one of the parties is fundamental if it results in such detriment to the other party as substantially to deprive him of what he is entitled to expect under the contract, unless the party in breach did not foresee and a reasonable person of the same kind in the same circumstances would not have foreseen such a result.

Article 26

A declaration of avoidance of the contract is effective only if made by notice to the other party.

Article 27

Unless otherwise expressly provided in this Part of the Convention, if any notice, request or other communication is given or made by a party in accordance with this Part and by means appropriate in the circumstances, a delay or error in the transmission of the communication or its failure to arrive does not deprive that party of the right to rely on the communication.

Article 28

If, in accordance with the provisions of this Convention, one party is entitled to require performance of any obligation by the other party, a court is not bound to enter a judgement for specific performance unless the court would do so under its own law in respect of similar contracts of sale not governed by this Convention.

Article 29

(1) A contract may be modified or terminated by the mere agreement of the parties.

(2) A contract in writing which contains a provision requiring any modification or termination by agreement to be in writing may not be otherwise modified or terminated by agreement. However, a party may be precluded by his conduct from asserting such a provision to the extent that the other party has relied on that conduct.

Chapter II: Obligations of the Seller

Article 30

The seller must deliver the goods, hand over any documents relating to them and transfer the property in the goods, as required by the contract and this Convention.

Section I. Delivery of the goods and handing over of documents

Article 31

If the seller is not bound to deliver the goods at any other particular place, his obligation to deliver consists:

(a) if the contract of sale involves carriage of the goods–in handing the goods over to the first carrier for transmission to the buyer;

(b) if, in cases not within the preceding subparagraph, the contract relates to specific goods, or unidentified goods to be drawn from a specific stock or to be manufactured or produced, and at the time of the conclusion of the contract the parties knew that the goods were at, or were to be manufactured or produced at, a particular place–in placing the goods at the buyer's disposal at that place;

(c) in other cases–in placing the goods at the buyer's disposal at the place where the seller had his place of business at the time of the conclusion of the contract.

Article 32

(1) If the seller, in accordance with the contract or this Convention, hands the goods over to a carrier and if the goods are not clearly

identified to the contract by markings on the goods, by shipping documents or otherwise, the seller must give the buyer notice of the consignment specifying the goods.

(2) If the seller is bound to arrange for carriage of the goods, he must make such contracts as are necessary for carriage to the place fixed by means of transportation appropriate in the circumstances and according to the usual terms for such transportation.

(3) If the seller is not bound to effect insurance in respect of the carriage of the goods, he must, at the buyer's request, provide him with all available information necessary to enable him to effect such insurance.

Article 33

The seller must deliver the goods:

(a) if a date is fixed by or determinable from the contract, on that date;

(b) if a period of time is fixed by or determinable from the contract, at any time within that period unless circumstances indicate that the buyer is to choose a date; or

(c) in any other case, within a reasonable time after the conclusion of the contract.

Article 34

If the seller is bound to hand over documents relating to the goods, he must hand them over at the time and place and in the form required by the contract. If the seller has handed over documents before that time, he may, up to that time, cure any lack of conformity in the documents, if the exercise of this right does not cause the buyer unreasonable inconvenience or unreasonable expense. However, the buyer retains any right to claim damages as provided for in this Convention.

Section II. Conformity of the goods and third party claims

Article 35

(1) The seller must deliver goods which are of the quantity, quality and description required by the contract and which are contained or packaged in the manner required by the contract.

(2) Except where the parties have agreed otherwise, the goods do not conform with the contract unless they:

(a) are fit for the purposes for which goods of the same description would ordinarily be used;

(b) are fit for any particular purpose expressly or impliedly made known to the seller at the time of the conclusion of the contract, except where the circumstances show that the buyer did not rely, or that it was unreasonable for him to rely, on the seller's skill and judgement;

(c) possess the qualities of goods which the seller has held out to the buyer as a sample or model;

(d) are contained or packaged in the manner usual for such goods or, where there is no such manner, in a manner adequate to preserve and protect the goods.

(3) The seller is not liable under subparagraphs (a) to (d) of the preceding paragraph for any lack of conformity of the goods if at the time of the conclusion of the contract the buyer knew or could not have been unaware of such lack of conformity.

Article 36

(1) The seller is liable in accordance with the contract and this Convention for any lack of conformity which exists at the time when the risk passes to the buyer, even though the lack of conformity becomes apparent only after that time.

(2) The seller is also liable for any lack of conformity which occurs after the time indicated in the preceding paragraph and which is due to a breach of any of his obligations, including a breach of any guarantee that for a period of time the goods will remain fit

for their ordinary purpose or for some particular purpose or will retain specified qualities or characteristics.

Article 37

If the seller has delivered goods before the date for delivery, he may, up to that date, deliver any missing part or make up any deficiency in the quantity of the goods delivered, or deliver goods in replacement of any nonconforming goods delivered or remedy any lack of conformity in the goods delivered, provided that the exercise of this right does not cause the buyer unreasonable inconvenience or unreasonable expense. However, the buyer retains any right to claim damages as provided for in this Convention.

Article 38

(1) The buyer must examine the goods, or cause them to be examined, within as short a period as is practicable in the circumstances.

(2) If the contract involves carriage of the goods, examination may be deferred until after the goods have arrived at their destination.

(3) If the goods are redirected in transit or redispatched by the buyer without a reasonable opportunity for examination by him and at the time of the conclusion of the contract the seller knew or ought to have known of the possibility of such redirection or redispatch, examination may be deferred until after the goods have arrived at the new destination.

Article 39

(1) The buyer loses the right to rely on a lack of conformity of the goods if he does not give notice to the seller specifying the nature of the lack of conformity within a reasonable time after he has discovered it or ought to have discovered it.

(2) In any event, the buyer loses the right to rely on a lack of conformity of the goods if he does not give the seller notice thereof at the latest within a period of two years from the date on which the goods were actually handed over to the buyer, unless this time-limit is inconsistent with a contractual period of guarantee.

Article 40

The seller is not entitled to rely on the provisions of articles 38 and 39 if the lack of conformity relates to facts of which he knew or could not have been unaware and which he did not disclose to the buyer.

Article 41

The seller must deliver goods which are free from any right or claim of a third party, unless the buyer agreed to take the goods subject to that right or claim. However, if such right or claim is based on industrial property or other intellectual property, the seller's obligation is governed by article 42.

Article 42

(1) The seller must deliver goods which are free from any right or claim of a third party based on industrial property or other intellectual property, of which at the time of the conclusion of the contract the seller knew or could not have been unaware, provided that the right or claim is based on industrial property or other intellectual property:

(a) under the law of the State where the goods will be resold or otherwise used, if it was contemplated by the parties at the time of the conclusion of the contract that the goods would be resold or otherwise used in that State; or

(b) in any other case, under the law of the State where the buyer has his place of business.

(2) The obligation of the seller under the preceding paragraph does not extend to cases where:

(a) at the time of the conclusion of the contract the buyer knew or could not have been unaware of the right or claim; or

(b) the right or claim results from the seller's compliance with technical drawings, designs, formulae or other such specifications furnished by the buyer.

Article 43

(1) The buyer loses the right to rely on the provisions of article 41 or article 42 if he does not give notice to the seller specifying the nature of the right or claim of the third party within a reasonable time after he has become aware or ought to have become aware of the right or claim.

(2) The seller is not entitled to rely on the provisions of the preceding paragraph if he knew of the right or claim of the third party and the nature of it.

Article 44

Notwithstanding the provisions of paragraph (1) of article 39 and paragraph (1) of article 43, the buyer may reduce the price in accordance with article 50 or claim damages, except for loss of profit, if he has a reasonable excuse for his failure to give the required notice.

Section III. Remedies for breach of contract by the seller

Article 45

(1) If the seller fails to perform any of his obligations under the contract or this Convention, the buyer may:

(a) exercise the rights provided in articles 46 to 52;

(b) claim damages as provided in articles 74 to 77.

(2) The buyer is not deprived of any right he may have to claim damages by exercising his right to other remedies.

(3) No period of grace may be granted to the seller by a court or arbitral tribunal when the buyer resorts to a remedy for breach of contract.

Article 46

(1) The buyer may require performance by the seller of his obligations unless the buyer has resorted to a remedy which is inconsistent with this requirement.

(2) If the goods do not conform with the contract, the buyer may require delivery of substitute goods only if the lack of conformity constitutes a fundamental breach of contract and a request for substitute goods is made either in conjunction with notice given under article 39 or within a reasonable time thereafter.

(3) If the goods do not conform with the contract, the buyer may require the seller to remedy the lack of conformity by repair, unless this is unreasonable having regard to all the circumstances. A request for repair must be made either in conjunction with notice given under article 39 or within a reasonable time thereafter.

Article 47

(1) The buyer may fix an additional period of time of reasonable length for performance by the seller of his obligations.

(2) Unless the buyer has received notice from the seller that he will not perform within the period so fixed, the buyer may not, during that period, resort to any remedy for breach of contract. However, the buyer is not deprived thereby of any right he may have to claim damages for delay in performance.

Article 48

(1) Subject to article 49, the seller may, even after the date for delivery, remedy at his own expense any failure to perform his obligations, if he can do so without unreasonable delay and without causing the buyer unreasonable inconvenience or uncertainty of reimbursement by the seller of expenses advanced by the buyer. However, the buyer retains any right to claim damages as provided for in this Convention.

(2) If the seller requests the buyer to make known whether he will accept performance and the buyer does not comply with the request within a reasonable time, the seller may perform within the time indicated in his request. The buyer may not, during that period of time, resort to any remedy which is inconsistent with performance by the seller.

(3) A notice by the seller that he will perform within a specified period of time is assumed to include a request, under the preceding paragraph, that the buyer make known his decision.

(4) A request or notice by the seller under paragraph (2) or (3) of this article is not effective unless received by the buyer.

Article 49

(1) The buyer may declare the contract avoided:

(a) if the failure by the seller to perform any of his obligations under the contract or this Convention amounts to a fundamental breach of contract; or

(b) in case of non-delivery, if the seller does not deliver the goods within the additional period of time fixed by the buyer in accordance with paragraph (1) of article 47 or declares that he will not deliver within the period so fixed.

(2) However, in cases where the seller has delivered the goods, the buyer loses the right to declare the contract avoided unless he does so:

(a) in respect of late delivery, within a reasonable time after he has become aware that delivery has been made;

(b) in respect of any breach other than late delivery, within a reasonable time:

(i) after he knew or ought to have known of the breach;

(ii) after the expiration of any additional period of time fixed by the buyer in accordance with paragraph (1) of article 47, or after the seller has declared that he will not perform his obligations within such an additional period; or

(iii) after the expiration of any additional period of time indicated by the seller in accordance with paragraph (2) of article 48, or after the buyer has declared that he will not accept performance.

Article 50

If the goods do not conform with the contract and whether or not the price has already been paid, the buyer may reduce the price in the same proportion as the value that the goods actually delivered had at the time of the delivery bears to the value that conforming goods would have had at that time. However, if the seller remedies any failure to perform his obligations in accordance with article 37 or article 48 or if the buyer refuses to accept performance by the seller in accordance with those articles, the buyer may not reduce the price.

Article 51

(1) If the seller delivers only a part of the goods or if only a part of the goods delivered is in conformity with the contract, articles 46 to 50 apply in respect of the part which is missing or which does not conform.

(2) The buyer may declare the contract avoided in its entirety only if the failure to make delivery completely or in conformity with the contract amounts to a fundamental breach of the contract.

Article 52

(1) If the seller delivers the goods before the date fixed, the buyer may take delivery or refuse to take delivery.

(2) If the seller delivers a quantity of goods greater than that provided for in the contract, the buyer may take delivery or refuse to take delivery of the excess quantity. If the buyer takes delivery of all or part of the excess quantity, he must pay for it at the contract rate.

Chapter III: Obligations of the Buyer

Article 53

The buyer must pay the price for the goods and take delivery of them as required by the contract and this Convention.

Section L Payment of the price

Article 54

The buyer's obligation to pay the price includes taking such steps and complying with such formalities as may be required under the contract or any laws and regulations to enable payment to be made.

Article 55

Where a contract has been validly concluded but does not expressly or implicitly fix or make provision for determining the price, the parties are considered, in the absence of any indication to the contrary, to have impliedly made reference to the price generally charged at the time of the conclusion of the contract for such goods sold under comparable circumstances in the trade concerned.

Article 56

If the price is fixed according to the weight of the goods, in case of doubt it is to be determined by the net weight.

Article 57

(1) If the buyer is not bound to pay the price at any particular place, he must pay it to the seller:

(a) at the seller's place of business; or

(b) if the payment is to be made against the handing over of the goods or of documents, at the place where the handing over takes place.

(2) The seller must bear any increases in the expenses incidental to payment which is caused by a change in his place of business subsequent to the conclusion of the contract.

Article 58

(1) If the buyer is not bound to pay the price at any other specific time, he must pay it when the seller places either the goods or documents controlling their disposition at the buyer's disposal in accordance with the contract and this Convention. The seller may make such payment a condition for handing over the goods or documents.

(2) If the contract involves carriage of the goods, the seller may dispatch the goods on terms whereby the goods, or documents controlling their disposition, will not be handed over to the buyer except against payment of the price.

(3) The buyer is not bound to pay the price until he has had an opportunity to examine the goods, unless the procedures for delivery or payment agreed upon by the parties are inconsistent with his having such an opportunity.

Article 59

The buyer must pay the price on the date fixed by or determinable from the contract and this Convention without the need for any request or compliance with any formality on the part of the seller.

Section II. Taking delivery

Article 60

The buyer's obligation to take delivery consists:

(a) in doing all the acts which could reasonably be expected of him in order to enable the seller to make delivery; and

(b) in taking over the goods.

Section III. Remedies for breach of contract by the buyer

Article 61

(1) If the buyer fails to perform any of his obligations under the contract or this Convention, the seller may:

(a) exercise the rights provided in articles 62 to 65;

(b) claim damages as provided in articles 74 to 77.

(2) The seller is not deprived of any right he may have to claim damages by exercising his right to other remedies.

(3) No period of grace may be granted to the buyer by a court or arbitral tribunal when the seller resorts to a remedy for breach of contract.

Article 62

The seller may require the buyer to pay the price, take delivery or perform his other obligations, unless the seller has resorted to a remedy which is inconsistent with this requirement.

Article 63

(1) The seller may fix an additional period of time of reasonable length for performance by the buyer of his obligations.

(2) Unless the seller has received notice from the buyer that he will not perform within the period so fixed, the seller may not, during that period, resort to any remedy for breach of contract. However, the seller is not deprived thereby of any right he may have to claim damages for delay in performance.

Article 64

(1) The seller may declare the contract avoided:

(a) if the failure by the buyer to perform any of his obligations under the contract or this Convention amounts to a fundamental breach of contract; or

(b) if the buyer does not, within the additional period of time fixed by the seller in accordance with paragraph (1) of article 63, perform his obligation to pay the price or take delivery of the goods, or if he declares that he will not do so within the period so fixed.

(2) However, in cases where the buyer has paid the price, the seller loses the right to declare the contract avoided unless he does so:

(a) in respect of late performance by the buyer, before the seller has become aware that performance has been rendered; or

(b) in respect of any breach other than late performance by the buyer, within a reasonable time:

(i) after the seller knew or ought to have known of the breach; or

(ii) after the expiration of any additional period of time fixed by the seller in accordance with paragraph (1) of article 63, or after the buyer has declared that he will not perform his obligations within such an additional period.

Article 65

(1) If under the contract the buyer is to specify the form, measurement or other features of the goods and he fails to make such

specification either on the date agreed upon or within a reasonable time after receipt of a request from the seller, the seller may, without prejudice to any other rights he may have, make the specification himself in accordance with the requirements of the buyer that may be known to him.

(2) If the seller makes the specification himself, he must inform the buyer of the details thereof and must fix a reasonable time within which the buyer may make a different specification. If, after receipt of such a communication, the buyer fails to do so within the time so fixed, the specification made by the seller is binding.

Chapter IV: Passing of Risk

Article 66

Loss of or damage to the goods after the risk has passed to the buyer does not discharge him from his obligation to pay the price, unless the loss or damage is due to an act or omission of the seller.

Article 67

(1) If the contract of sale involves carriage of the goods and the seller is not bound to hand them over at a particular place, the risk passes to the buyer when the goods are handed over to the first carrier for transmission to the buyer in accordance with the contract of sale. If the seller is bound to hand the goods over to a carrier at a particular place, the risk does not pass to the buyer until the goods are handed over to the carrier at that place. The fact that the seller is authorized to retain documents controlling the disposition of the goods does not affect the passage of the risk.

(2) Nevertheless, the risk does not pass to the buyer until the goods are clearly identified to the contract, whether by markings on the goods, by shipping documents, by notice given to the buyer or otherwise.

Article 68

The risk in respect of goods sold in transit passes to the buyer from the time of the conclusion of the contract. However, if the circumstances so indicate, the risk is assumed by the buyer from the time the goods were handed over to the carrier who issued the documents embodying the contract of carriage. Nevertheless, if at the time of the conclusion of the contract of sale the seller knew or ought to have known that the goods had been lost or damaged and did not disclose this to the buyer, the loss or damage is at the risk of the seller.

Article 69

(1) In cases not within articles 67 and 68, the risk passes to the buyer when he takes over the goods or, if he does not do so in due time, from the time when the goods are placed at his disposal and he commits a breach of contract by failing to take delivery.

(2) However, if the buyer is bound to take over the goods at a place other than a place of business of the seller, the risk passes when delivery is due and the buyer is aware of the fact that the goods are placed at his disposal at that place.

(3) If the contract relates to goods not then identified, the goods are considered not to be placed at the disposal of the buyer until they are clearly identified to the contract.

Article 70

If the seller has committed a fundamental breach of contract, articles 67, 68 and 69 do not impair the remedies available to the buyer on account of the breach.

Chapter V: Provisions Common to the Obligations of the Seller and of the Buyer

Section I. Anticipatory breach and installment contracts

Article 71

(1) A party may suspend the performance of his obligations if, after the conclusion of the contract, it becomes apparent that the other party will not perform a substantial part of his obligations as a result of:

(a) a serious deficiency in his ability to perform or in his creditworthiness; or

(b) his conduct in preparing to perform or in performing the contract.

(2) If the seller has already dispatched the goods before the grounds described in the preceding paragraph become evident, he may prevent the handing over of the goods to the buyer even though the buyer holds a document which entitles him to obtain them. The present paragraph relates only to the rights in the goods as between the buyer and the seller.

(3) A party suspending performance, whether before or after dispatch of the goods, must immediately give notice of the suspension to the other party and must continue with performance if the other party provides adequate assurance of his performance.

Article 72

(1) If prior to the date for performance of the contract it is clear that one of the parties will commit a fundamental breach of contract, the other party may declare the contract avoided.

(2) If time allows, the party intending to declare the contract avoided must give reasonable notice to the other party in order to permit him to provide adequate assurance of his performance.

(3) The requirements of the preceding paragraph do not apply if the other party has declared that he will not perform his obligations.

Article 73

(1) In the case of a contract for delivery of goods by installments, if the failure of one party to perform any of his obligations in respect of any installment constitutes a fundamental breach of contract with respect to that installment, the other party may declare the contract avoided with respect to that installment.

(2) If one party's failure to perform any of his obligations in respect of any installment gives the other party good grounds to conclude that a fundamental breach of contract will occur with respect to future installments, he may declare the contract avoided for the future, provided that he does so within a reasonable time.

(3) A buyer who declares the contract avoided in respect of any delivery may, at the same time, declare it avoided in respect of deliveries already made or of future deliveries if, by reason of their interdependence, those deliveries could not be used for the

purpose contemplated by the parties at the time of the conclusion of the contract.

Section II. Damages

Article 74

Damages for breach of contract by one party consist of a sum equal to the loss, including loss of profit, suffered by the other party as a consequence of the breach. Such damages may not exceed the loss which the party in breach foresaw or ought to have foreseen at the time of the conclusion of the contract, in the light of the facts and matters of which he then knew or ought to have known, as a possible consequence of the breach of contract.

Article 75

If the contract is avoided and if, in a reasonable manner and within a reasonable time after avoidance, the buyer has bought goods in replacement or the seller has resold the goods, the party claiming damages may recover the difference between the contract price and the price in the substitute transaction as well as any further damages recoverable under article 74.

Article 76

(1) If the contract is avoided and there is a current price for the goods, the party claiming damages may, if he has not made a purchase or resale under article 75, recover the difference between the price fixed by the contract and the current price at the time of avoidance as well as any further damages recoverable under article 74. If, however, the party claiming damages has avoided the contract after taking over the goods, the current price at the time of such taking over shall be applied instead of the current price at the time of avoidance.

(2) For the purposes of the preceding paragraph, the current price is the price prevailing at the place where delivery of the goods should have been made or, if there is no current price at that place, the price at such other place as serves as a reasonable substitute, making due allowance for differences in the cost of transporting the goods.

Article 77

A party who relies on a breach of contract must take such measures as are reasonable in the circumstances to mitigate the loss, including loss of profit, resulting from the breach. If he fails to take such measures, the party in breach may claim a reduction in the damages in the amount by which the loss should have been mitigated.

Section III. Interest

Article 78

If a party fails to pay the price or any other sum that is in arrears, the other party is entitled to interest on it, without prejudice to any claim for damages recoverable under article 74.

Section IV. Exemptions

Article 79

(1) A party is not liable for a failure to perform any of his obligations if he proves that the failure was due to an impediment beyond his control and that he could not reasonably be expected to have taken the impediment into account at the time of the conclusion of the contract or to have avoided or overcome it or its consequences.

(2) If the party's failure is due to the failure by a third person whom he has engaged to perform the whole or a part of the contract, that party is exempt from liability only if:

(a) he is exempt under the preceding paragraph; and

(b) the person whom he has so engaged would be so exempt if the provisions of that paragraph were applied to him.

(3) The exemption provided by this article has effect for the period during which the impediment exists.

(4) The party who fails to perform must give notice to the other party of the impediment and its effect on his ability to perform. If the notice is not received by the other party within a reasonable time after the party who fails to perform knew or ought to have known of the impediment, he is liable for damages resulting from such non-receipt.

(5) Nothing in this article prevents either party from exercising any right other than to claim damages under this Convention.

Article 80

A party may not rely on a failure of the other party to perform, to the extent that such failure was caused by the first party's act or omission.

Section V. Effects of avoidance

Article 81

(1) Avoidance of the contract releases both parties from their obligations under it, subject to any damages which may be due. Avoidance does not affect any provision of the contract for the settlement of disputes or any other provision of the contract governing the rights and obligations of the parties consequent upon the avoidance of the contract.

(2) A party who has performed the contract either wholly or in part may claim restitution from the other party of whatever the first party has supplied or paid under the contract. If both parties are bound to make restitution, they must do so concurrently.

Article 82

(1) The buyer loses the right to declare the contract avoided or to require the seller to deliver substitute goods if it is impossible for him to make restitution of the goods substantially in the condition in which he received them.

(2) The preceding paragraph does not apply:

(a) if the impossibility of making restitution of the goods or of making restitution of the goods substantially in the condition in which the buyer received them is not due to his act or omission;

(b) if the goods or part of the goods have perished or deteriorated as a result of the examination provided for in article 38; or

(c) if the goods or part of the goods have been sold in the normal course of business or have been consumed or transformed by the buyer in the course of normal use before he discovered or ought to have discovered the lack of conformity.

Article 83

A buyer who has lost the right to declare the contract avoided or to require the seller to deliver substitute goods in accordance with article 82 retains all other remedies under the contract and this Convention.

Article 84

(1) If the seller is bound to refund the price, he must also pay interest on it, from the date on which the price was paid.

(2) The buyer must account to the seller for all benefits which he has derived from the goods or part of them:

(a) if he must make restitution of the goods or part of them; or

(b) if it is impossible for him to make restitution of all or part of the goods or to make restitution of all or part of the goods substantially in the condition in which he received them, but he has nevertheless declared the contract avoided or required the seller to deliver substitute goods.

Section VI. Preservation of the goods

Article 85

If the buyer is in delay in taking delivery of the goods or, where payment of the price and delivery of the goods are to be made concurrently, if he fails to pay the price, and the seller is either in possession of the goods or otherwise able to control their disposition, the seller must take such steps as are reasonable in the circumstances to preserve them. He is entitled to retain them until he has been reimbursed his reasonable expenses by the buyer.

Article 86

(1) If the buyer has received the goods and intends to exercise any right under the contract or this Convention to reject them, he must take such steps to preserve them as are reasonable in the circumstances. He is entitled to retain them until he has been reimbursed his reasonable expenses by the seller.

(2) If goods dispatched to the buyer have been placed at his disposal at their destination and he exercises the right to reject them, he must take possession of them on behalf of the seller, provided that this can be done without payment of the price and without unreasonable inconvenience or unreasonable expense. This provision does not apply if the seller or a person authorized to take charge of the goods on his behalf is present at the destination. If the buyer takes possession of the goods under this paragraph, his rights and obligations are governed by the preceding paragraph.

Article 87

A party who is bound to take steps to preserve the goods may deposit them in a warehouse of a third person at the expense of the other party provided that the expense incurred is not unreasonable.

Article 88

(1) A party who is bound to preserve the goods in accordance with article 85 or 86 may sell them by any appropriate means if there has been an unreasonable delay by the other party in taking possession of the goods or in taking them back or in paying the price or the cost of preservation, provided that reasonable notice of the intention to sell has been given to the other party.

(2) If the goods are subject to rapid deterioration or their preservation would involve unreasonable expense, a party who is bound to preserve the goods in accordance with article 85 or 86 must take reasonable measures to sell them. To the extent possible he must give notice to the other party of his intention to sell.

(3) A party selling the goods has the right to retain out of the proceeds of sale an amount equal to the reasonable expenses of preserving the goods and of selling them. He must account to the other party for the balance.

PART IV: FINAL PROVISIONS

Article 89

The Secretary-General of the United Nations is hereby designated as the depositary for this Convention.

Article 90

This Convention does not prevail over any international agreement which has already been or may be entered into and which contains provisions concerning the matters governed by this Convention, provided that the parties have their places of business in States parties to such agreement.

Article 91

(1) This Convention is open for signature at the concluding meeting of the United Nations Conference on Contracts for the International Sale of Goods and will remain open for signature by all States at the Headquarters of the United Nations, New York, until 30 September 1981.

(2) This Convention is subject to ratification, acceptance or approval by the signatory States.

(3) This Convention is open for accession by all States which are not signatory States as from the date it is open for signature.

(4) Instruments of ratification, acceptance, approval and accession are to be deposited with the Secretary-General of the United Nations.

Article 92

(1) A Contracting State may declare at the time of signature, ratification, acceptance, approval or accession that it will not be bound by Part II of this Convention or that it will not be bound by Part III of this Convention.

(2) A Contracting State which makes a declaration in accordance with the preceding paragraph in respect of Part II or Part III of this Convention is not to be considered a Contracting State within paragraph (1) of article 1 of this Convention in respect of matters governed by the Part to which the declaration applies.

Article 93

(1) If a Contracting State has two or more territorial units in which, according to its constitution, different systems of law are applicable in relation to the matters dealt with in this Convention, it may, at the time of signature, ratification, acceptance, approval or accession, declare that this Convention is to extend to all its territorial units or only to one or more of them, and may amend its declaration by submitting another declaration at any time.

(2) These declarations are to be notified to the depositary and are to state expressly the territorial units to which the Convention extends.

(3) If, by virtue of a declaration under this article, this Convention extends to one or more but not all of the territorial units of a Contracting State, and if the place of business of a party is located in that State, this place of business, for the purposes of this Convention, is considered not to be in a Contracting State, unless it is in a territorial unit to which the Convention extends.

(4) If a Contracting State makes no declaration under paragraph (1) of this article, the Convention is to extend to all territorial units of that State.

Article 94

(1) Two or more Contracting States which have the same or closely related legal rules on matters governed by this Convention may at any time declare that the Convention is not to apply to contracts of sale or to their formation where the parties have their places of business in those States. Such declarations may be made jointly or by reciprocal unilateral declarations.

(2) A Contracting State which has the same or closely related legal rules on matters governed by this Convention as one or more non-Contracting States may at any time declare that the Convention is not to apply to contracts of sale or to their formation where the parties have their places of business in those States.

(3) If a State which is the object of a declaration under the preceding paragraph subsequently becomes a Contracting State, the declaration made will, as from the date on which the Convention enters

into force in respect of the new Contracting State, have the effect of a declaration made under paragraph (1), provided that the new Contracting State joins in such declaration or makes a reciprocal unilateral declaration.

Article 95

Any State may declare at the time of the deposit of its instrument of ratification, acceptance, approval or accession that it will not be bound by subparagraph (1)(b) of article 1 of this Convention.

Article 96

A Contracting State whose legislation requires contracts of sale to be concluded in or evidenced by writing may at any time make a declaration in accordance with article 12 that any provision of article 11, article 29, or Part II of this Convention, that allows a contract of sale or its modification or termination by agreement or any offer, acceptance, or other indication of intention to be made in any form other than in writing, does not apply where any party has his place of business in that State.

Article 97

(1) Declarations made under this Convention at the time of signature are subject to confirmation upon ratification, acceptance or approval.

(2) Declarations and confirmations of declarations are to be in writing and be formally notified to the depositary.

(3) A declaration takes effect simultaneously with the entry into force of this Convention in respect of the State concerned. However, a declaration of which the depositary receives formal notification after such entry into force takes effect on the first day of the month following the expiration of six months after the date of its receipt by the depositary. Reciprocal unilateral declarations under article 94 take effect on the first day of the month following the expiration of six months after the receipt of the latest declaration by the depositary.

(4) Any State which makes a declaration under this Convention may withdraw it at any time by a formal notification in writing addressed to the depositary. Such withdrawal is to take effect on the

first day of the month following the expiration of six months after the date of the receipt of the notification by the depositary.

(5) A withdrawal of a declaration made under article 94 renders inoperative, as from the date on which the withdrawal takes effect, any reciprocal declaration made by another State under that article.

Article 98

No reservations are permitted except those expressly authorized in this Convention.

Article 99

(1) This Convention enters into force, subject to the provisions of paragraph (6) of this article, on the first day of the month following the expiration of twelve months after the date of deposit of the tenth instrument of ratification, acceptance, approval or accession, including an instrument which contains a declaration made under article 92.

(2) When a State ratifies, accepts, approves or accedes to this Convention after the deposit of the tenth instrument of ratification, acceptance, approval or accession, this Convention, with the exception of the Part excluded, enters into force in respect of that State, subject to the provisions of paragraph (6) of this article, on the first day of the month following the expiration of twelve months after the date of the deposit of its instrument of ratification, acceptance, approval or accession.

(3) A State which ratifies, accepts, approves or accedes to this Convention and is a party to either or both the Convention relating to a Uniform Law on the Formation of Contracts for the International Sale of Goods done at The Hague on 1 July 1964 (1964 Hague Formation Convention) and the Convention relating to a Uniform Law on the International Sale of Goods done at The Hague on 1 July 1964 (1964 Hague Sales Convention) shall at the same time denounce, as the case may be, either or both the 1964 Hague Sales Convention and the 1964 Hague Formation Convention by notifying the Government of the Netherlands to that effect.

(4) A State party to the 1964 Hague Sales Convention which ratifies, accepts, approves or accedes to the present Convention and

declares or has declared under article 52 that it will not be bound by Part II of this Convention shall at the time of ratification, acceptance, approval or accession denounce the 1964 Hague Sales Convention by notifying the Government of the Netherlands to that effect.

(5) A State party to the 1964 Hague Formation Convention which ratifies, accepts, approves or accedes to the present Convention and declares or has declared under article 92 that it will not be bound by Part III of this Convention shall at the time of ratification, acceptance, approval or accession denounce the 1964 Hague Formation Convention by notifying the Government of the Netherlands to that effect.

(6) For the purpose of this article, ratifications, acceptances, approvals and accessions in respect of this Convention by States parties to the 1964 Hague Formation Convention or to the 1964 Hague Sales Convention shall not be effective until such denunciations as may be required on the part of those States in respect of the latter two Conventions have themselves become effective. The depositary of this Convention shall consult with the Government of the Netherlands, as the depositary of the 1964 Conventions, so as to ensure necessary co-ordination in this respect.

Article 100

(1) This Convention applies to the formation of a contract only when the proposal for concluding the contract is made on or after the date when the Convention enters into force in respect of the Contracting States referred to in subparagraph (1)(a) or the Contracting State referred to in subparagraph (1)(b) of article 1.

(2) This Convention applies only to contracts concluded on or after the date when the Convention enters into force in respect of the Contracting States referred to in subparagraph (1)(a) or the Contracting State referred to in subparagraph (1)(b) of article 1.

Article 101

(1) A Contracting State may denounce this Convention, or Part II or Part III of the Convention, by a formal notification in writing addressed to the depositary.

(2) The denunciation takes effect on the first day of the month following the expiration of twelve months after the notification is received by the depositary. Where a longer period for the denunciation to take effect is specified in the notification, the denunciation takes effect upon the expiration of such longer period after the notification is received by the depositary.

DONE at Vienna, this day the eleventh day of April, one thousand nine hundred and eighty, in a single original, of which the Arabic, Chinese, English, French, Russian and Spanish texts are equally authentic.

IN WITNESS WHEREOF the undersigned plenipotentiaries, being duly authorized by their respective Governments, have signed this Convention.

THE UNIFORM COMMERCIAL CODE

Source

Purposes

History

Status

Promulgated by the National Conference of Commissioners on Uniform State Laws and the American Law Institute, with the endorsement of the American Bar Association, under the supervision of the Permanent Editorial Board for the Uniform Commercial Code:

1. To simplify, clarify, and modernize the law governing commercial transactions,

2. To permit the continued expansion of commercial practices through custom, usage, and agreement of the parties, and

3. To make uniform the law among various jurisdictions Original version promulgated in 1951.

- Adopted by Pennsylvania in 1953.
- Revised in 1956, based on comments by New York.
- Second revision in 1958.
- Additional revisions in 1962, 1966, 1972, 1977, and 1987.

Adopted by legislatures of 50 states (Louisiana adopted only Articles 1, 3, 4, 5, 7, and 8), the District of Columbia, Guam, and the Virgin Islands; several states have adopted different versions of the text.

Organization of the Uniform Commercial Code

Article 1.   General Provisions

    Part 1.   Short Title, Construction, Application, and Subject Matter

    Part 2.   General Definitions and Principles of Interpretation

Article 2.   Sales

Part 1.

Part 2.

Part 3.

Part 4.

Part 5.

Part 6.

Part 7.

Article 2A. Leases Part 1. Part 2. Part 3. Part 4.

Part 5.

Short Title, General Construction, and Subject Matter Form, Formation, and Readjustment of Contract General Obligation and Construction of Contract Title, Creditors, and Good Faith Purchasers Performance

Breach, Repudiation, and Excuse

Remedies

General Provisions

Formation and Construction of Lease Contract Effect of Lease Contract

Performance of Lease Contract: Repudiated, Substituted, and Excused

Default

Article 3.

Article 4.

Article 5. Article 6. Article 7.

Commercial Paper

Part 1.	Short Title, Form, and Interpretation
Part 2.	Transfer and Negotiation
Part 3.	Rights of a Holder
Part 4.	Liability of Parties
Part 5.	Presentment, Notice of Dishonor, and Protest
Part 6.	Discharge
Part 7.	Advice of International Sight Draft
Part 8.	Miscellaneous

Bank Deposits and Collections

Part 1.	General Provisions and Definitions
Part 2.	Collection of Items: Depository and Collecting Banks
Part 3.	Collection of Items: Payor Banks
Part 4.	Relationship Between Payor Bank and Its Customer
Part 5.	Collection of Documentary Drafts

Letters of Credit

Bulk Transfers

Warehouse Receipts, Bills of Lading, and Other Documents of Title

Part 1.	General
Part 2.	Warehouse Receipts: Special Provisions
Part 3.	Bills of Lading: Special Provisions
Part 4.	Warehouse Receipts and Bills of Lading: General Obligations
Part 5.	Warehouse Receipts and Bills of Lading: Negotiation and Transfer
Part 6.	Warehouse Receipts and Bills of Lading: Miscellaneous Provisions

Article 8. Article 9.

Article 10. Article 11.

Investment Securities

Effective Date and Repealer

Effective Date and Transition Provisions

Provisions of Note

§ 1-102 (3) Purposes; Rules of Construction; Variation by Agreement

The effect of provisions of this Act may be varied by agreement except as otherwise provided in this Act and except that the obligations of good faith, diligence, reasonableness, and care prescribed by this Act may not be disclaimed by agreement but the parties may, by agreement, determine the standards by which the performance of such obligations is to be measured if such standards are not manifestly unreasonable.

§ 1-103 Supplementary General Principles of Law Applicable

Unless displaced by the particular provisions of this Act, the principles of law and equity, including the law merchant and the law relative to capacity to contract, principal and agent, estoppel, fraud, misrepresentation, duress, coercion, mistake, bankruptcy, or other validating or invalidating cause shall supplement its provisions.

§ 1-106 Remedies to Be Liberally Administered

The remedies provided by this Act shall be liberally administered to the end that the aggrieved party may be put in as good a position as if the other party had fully performed but neither consequential or special nor penal damages may be had except as specifically provided in this Act or by other rule of law.

(2) Any right or obligation declared by this Act is enforceable by action unless the provision declaring it specifies a different and limited effect.

§ 1-107 Waiver or Renunciation of Claim or Right After Breach

Any claim or right arising out of an alleged breach can be discharged in whole or in part without consideration by a written waiver or renunciation signed and delivered by the aggrieved party.

§ 1-108 Severability

If any provision clause of this Act or application thereof to any person or circumstances is held invalid, such invalidity shall not affect other provisions or applications of the Act which can be given effect without the invalid provision or application, and to this end the provisions of this Act are declared to be severable.

§ 1-203 Obligation of Good Faith

Every contract or duty within this Act imposes an obligation of good faith in its performance or enforcement.

§ 1-204 Time; Reasonable Time; "Seasonably"

(1) Whenever this Act requires any action to be taken within a reasonable time, any time that is not manifestly unreasonable may be fixed by agreement.

(2) What is a reasonable time for taking any action depends on the nature, purpose, and circumstances of such action.

(3) An action is taken "seasonably" when it is taken at or within the time agreed or, if no time is agreed to, at or within a reasonable time.

§ 2-101 Short Title

This article shall be known and may be cited as Uniform Commercial Code–Sales.

§ 2-102 Scope; Certain Security and Other Transactions Excluded from This Article

Unless the context otherwise requires, this Article applies to transactions in goods; it does not apply to any transaction which although in the form of an unconditional contract to sell or present sale is intended to operate only as a security transaction nor does this Article impair or repeal any statute regulating sales to consumers, farmers, or other specified classes of buyers.

§ 2-103 Definition and Index of Definitions

(1) In this Article unless the context otherwise requires

(a) "Buyer" means a person who buys or contracts to buy goods.

(b) "Good faith" in the case of a merchant means honesty in fact and the observance or reasonable commercial standards of fair dealing in the trade.

(c) "Receipt" of goods means taking physical possession of them.

§ 2-105 Definitions: Transferability; "Goods"; "Future" Goods; Lot, "Commercial Unit"

"Goods" means all things (including specially manufactured goods) that are movable at the time of identification to the contract for sale other than the money in which the price is to be paid, investment securities (Article 8), and things in action. "Goods" also includes the unborn young of animals and growing crops and other identified things attached to realty as described in the section on goods to be severed from realty (§ 2-107).

(2) Goods must be both existing and identified before any interest in them can pass. Goods which are not both existing and identified are "future" goods. A purported present sale of future goods or of any interest therein operates as a contract to sell.

(3) There may be a sale of a part interest in existing identified goods.

§ 2-106 Definitions: "Contract"; "Agreement"; "Contract for Sale"; "Sale"; "Present Sale"; "Conforming" to Contract; "Termination"; "Cancellation"

In this Article unless the context otherwise requires "contract" and "agreement" are limited to those relating to the present or future sale of goods. "Contract for sale" includes both a present sale of goods and a contract to sell goods at a future time. A "sale" consists in the passing of title from the seller to the buyer for a price (§ 2-401). A "present sale" means a sale which is accomplished by the making of the contract.

Goods or conduct including any part of a performance are "conforming" or conform to the contract when they are in accordance with the obligations under the contract.

"Termination" occurs when either party pursuant to a power created by agreement or law puts an end to the contract otherwise than for its breach. On "termination" all obligations which are still executory on both sides are discharged but any right based on prior breach or performance survives.

"Cancellation" occurs when either party puts an end to the contract for breach by the other and its effect is the same as that of "termination" except that the canceling party also retains any remedy for breach of the whole contract or any unperformed balance.

§ 2-201 Formal Requirements; Statute of Frauds

Except as otherwise provided in this section, a contract for the sale of goods for the price of US$500 or more is not enforceable by way of action or defense unless there is some writing sufficient to indicate that a contract for sale has been made between the parties and signed by the party against whom enforcement is sought or by his authorized agent or broker. A writing is not insufficient because it omits or incorrectly states a term agreed upon, but the contract is not enforceable under this paragraph beyond the quantity of goods shown in such writing.

§ 2-202 Final Written Expression: Parol or Extrinsic Evidence

Terms with respect to which the confirmatory memoranda of the parties agree or that are otherwise set forth in a writing intended by the parties as a final expression of their agreement with respect to such terms as are included therein may not be contradicted by evidence of any prior agreement or of a contemporaneous oral agreement but may be explained or supplemented-

(a) by course of dealing or usage of trade (§ 1-205) or by course of performance (§ 2-208); and

(b) by evidence of consistent additional terms unless the court finds the writing to have been intended also as a complete and exclusive statement of the terms of the agreement.

§ 2-209 Modification, Rescission, and Waiver

(1) An agreement modifying a contract within this Article needs no consideration to be binding.

§ 2-305 Open Price Term

(1) The parties if they so intend can conclude a contract for sale even though the price is not settled. In such a case the price is a reasonable price at the time for delivery if—

(a) nothing is said as to price; or

(b) the price is left to be agreed by the parties and they fail to agree; or

(c) the price is to be fixed in terms of some agreed market or other standard as set or recorded by a third person or agency and it is not so set or recorded.

(2) A price to be fixed by the seller or by the buyer means a price for him or her to fix in good faith.

(3) When a price left to be fixed otherwise than by agreement of the parties fails to be fixed through fault of one party, the other may at his or her option treat the contract as canceled or himself or herself fix a reasonable price.

Where, however, the parties intend not to be bound unless the price be fixed or agreed and it is not fixed or agreed, there is no contract. In such a case, the buyer must return any goods already received or if unable so to do must pay their reasonable value at the time of delivery and the seller must return any portion of the price paid on account.

§ 2-308 Absence of Specified Place for Delivery

Unless otherwise agreed—

(a) the place for delivery of goods is the seller's place of business or if he or she has none, his or her residence; but

(b) in a contract for sale of identified goods which to the knowledge of the parties at the time of contracting are in some other place, that place is the place for their delivery; and

(c) documents of title may be delivered through customary banking channels.

§ 2-312 Warranty of Title and Against Infringement; Buyer's Obligation Against Infringement

(1) Subject to subsection (2), there is in a contract for sale a warranty by the seller that—

(a) the title conveyed shall be good, and its transfer rightful; and

(b) the goods shall be delivered free from any security interest or other lien or encumbrance of which the buyer at the time of contracting has no knowledge.

A warranty under subsection (1) will be excluded or modified only by specific language or by circumstances which give the buyer reason to know that the person selling does not claim title in himself or that he is purporting to sell only such right or title as he or a third person may have.

Unless otherwise agreed a seller who is a merchant regularly dealing in goods of the kind warrants that the goods shall be delivered free of the rightful claim of any third person by way of infringement or the like but a buyer who furnishes specifications to the seller must hold the seller harmless against any such claim which arises out of compliance with the specifications.

§ 2-313 Express Warranties by Affirmation, Promise, Description, Sample

(1) Express warranties by the seller are created as follows:

(a) Any affirmation of fact or promise made by the seller to the buyer which relates to the goods and becomes part of the basis of the bargain creates an express warranty that the goods shall conform to the affirmation or promise.

(b) Any description of the goods which is made part of the basis of the bargain creates an express warranty that the goods shall conform to the description.

(c) Any sample or model which is made part of the basis of the bargain creates an express warranty that the whole of the goods shall conform to the sample or model.

It is not necessary to the creation of an express warranty that the seller use formal words such as "warrant" or "guarantee" or that he have a specific intention to make a warranty, but an affirmation merely of the value of the goods or a statement purporting to be merely the seller's opinion or commendation of the goods does not create a warranty.

§ 2-314 Implied Warranty: Merchantability; Usage of Trade

Unless excluded or modified (§ 2-316), a warranty that the goods shall be merchantable is implied in a contract for their sale if the seller is a merchant with respect to goods of that kind. Under this section the serving for value of food or drink to be consumed either on the premises or elsewhere is a sale.

(2) Goods to be merchantable must be at least such as—

(a) pass without objection in the trade under the contract description; and

(b) in the case of fungible goods, are of fair average quality within the description; and

(c) are fit for the ordinary purposes for which such goods are used; and

(d) run, within the variations permitted by the agreement, of even kind, quality, and quantity within each unit and among all units involved; and

(e) are adequately contained, packaged, and labeled as the agreement may require; and

(f) conform to the promises or affirmations of fact made on the container or label if any.

(3) Unless excluded of modified (§ 2-316), other implied warranties may arise from course of dealing or usage of trade.

§ 2-315 Implied Warranty: Fitness for Particular Purpose

Where the seller at the time of contracting has reason to know any particular purpose for which the goods are required and that the buyer is relying on the seller's skill or judgment to select or furnish suitable goods, there is unless excluded or modified under the next section an implied warranty that the goods shall be fit for such purpose.

§ 2-316 Exclusion of Modification of Warranties

Words or conduct relevant to the creation of an express warranty and words or conduct tending to negate or limit warranty shall be construed wherever reasonable as consistent with each other; but subject to the provisions of this Article on parol or extrinsic evidence (§ 2-202) negation or limitation is inoperative to the extent that such construction is unreasonable.

Subject to subsection (3), to exclude or modify the implied warranty to merchantability or any part of it the language must mention merchantability and in case of a writing must be conspicuous, and to exclude or modify any implied warranty of fitness the exclusion must be a writing and conspicuous. Language to exclude all implied warranties of fitness is sufficient if it states, for example, that "There are no warranties which extend beyond the description on the face hereof."

(3) Notwithstanding subsection (2)–

(a) unless the circumstances indicate otherwise, all implied warranties are excluded by expressions like "as is", "with all faults", or other language which in common understanding calls the buyer's attention to the exclusion of warranties and makes plain that there is no implied warranty; and

(b) when the buyer before entering into the contract has examined the goods or the sample or model as fully as he desired or has refused to examine the goods, there is no implied warranty with regard to defects which an examination ought in the circumstances to have revealed to him; and

(c) an implied warranty can also be excluded or modified by course of dealing or course of performance or usage of trade.

Remedies for breach of warranty can be limited in accordance with the provisions of this Article on liquidation or limitation of damages and on contractual modification of remedy (§ 2-718 and 2-719).

§ 2-317 Cumulation and Conflict of Warranties Express or Implied.

Warranties whether express or implied shall be construed as consistent with each other and as cumulative, but if such construction is unreasonable, the intention of the parties shall determine which warranty is dominant. In ascertaining that intention the following rules apply:

(a) Exact or technical specifications displace an inconsistent sample or model or general language of description.

(b) A sample from an existing bulk displaces inconsistent general language or description.

(c) Express warranties displace inconsistent implied warranties other than an implied warranty of fitness for a particular purpose.

GLOSSARY

GLOSSARY OF KEY CONTRACT MANAGEMENT TERMS

absolute standards

A type of standard used in competitive negotiations to evaluate a proposal. Includes both the maximum acceptable value and the minimum acceptable value for all selected evaluation criteria.

acceptance

(1) The taking and receiving of anything in good part, and as if it were a tacit agreement to a preceding act, which might have been defeated or avoided if such acceptance had not been made. (2) Agreement to the terms offered in a contract. An acceptance must be communicated, and (in common law) it must be the mirror image of the offer.

act of God

An inevitable, accidental, or extraordinary event that cannot be foreseen and guarded against, such as lightning, tornadoes, or earthquakes.

actual authority

The power that the principal intentionally confers on the agent or allows the agent to believe he or she possesses.

actual damages

See *compensatory damages.*

affidavit

A written and signed statement sworn to under oath.

agency

A relationship that exists when there is a delegation of authority to perform all acts connected within a particular trade, business, or company. It gives authority to the agent to act in all matters relating to the business of the principal.

agent

An employee (usually a contract manager) empowered to bind his or her organization legally in contract negotiations.

allowable cost

A cost that is reasonable, allocable, and within accepted standards, or otherwise conforms to generally accepted accounting principles, specific limitations or exclusions, or agreed-on terms between contractual parties.

apparent authority
The power that the principal permits the perceived agent to exercise, although not actually granted.

as is
A contract phrase referring to the condition of property to be sold or leased; generally pertains to a disclaimer of liability; property sold in as-is condition is generally not guaranteed.

assign
To convey or transfer to another, as to assign property, rights, or interests to another.

assignment
The transfer of property by an assignor to an assignee.

best value
The best trade-off between competing factors for a particular purchase requirement. The key to successful best-value contracting is consideration of life-cycle costs, including the use of quantitative as well as qualitative techniques to measure price and technical performance trade-offs between various proposals. The best-value concept applies to acquisitions in which price or price-related factors are *not* the primary determinant of who receives the contract award.

bid
An offer in response to an invitation for bids (IFB).

bilateral contract
A contract formed if an offer states that acceptance requires only for the accepting party to promise to perform. In contrast, a *unilateral contract* is formed if an offer requires actual performance for acceptance.

bond
A written instrument executed by a seller and a second party (the surety or sureties) to ensure fulfillment of the principal's obligations to a third party (the obligee or buyer), identified in the bond. If the principal's obligations are not met, the bond

ensures payment, to the extent stipulated, of any loss sustained by the obligee.

breach of contract

(1) The failure, without legal excuse, to perform any promise that forms the whole or part of a contract. (2) The ending of a contract that occurs when one or both of the parties fail to keep their promises; this could lead to arbitration or litigation.

buyer

The party contracting for goods and/or services with one or more sellers.

cancellation

The withdrawal of the requirement to purchase goods and/or services by the buyer.

change in scope

An amendment to approved program requirements or specifications after negotiation of a basic contract. It may result in an increase or decrease.

change order/purchase order amendment

A written order directing the seller to make changes according to the provisions of the contract documents.

claim

A demand by one party to contract for something from another party, usually but not necessarily for more money or more time. Claims are usually based on an argument that the party making the demand is entitled to an adjustment by virtue of the contract terms or some violation of those terms by the other party. The word does not imply any disagreement between the parties, although claims often lead to disagreements. This book uses the term *dispute* to refer to disagreements that have become intractable.

clause

A statement of one of the rights and/or obligations of the parties to a contract. A contract consists of a series of clauses.

compensable delay

A delay for which the buyer is contractually responsible that excuses the seller's failure to perform and is compensable.

compensatory damages

Damages that will compensate the injured party for the loss sustained and nothing more. They are awarded by the court as the measure of actual loss, and not as punishment for outrageous conduct or to deter future transgressions. Compensatory damages are often referred to as "actual damages." See also *incidental* and *punitive damages.*

competitive negotiation

A method of contracting involving a request for proposals that states the buyer's requirements and criteria for evaluation; submission of timely proposals by a maximum number of offerors; discussions with those offerors found to be within the competitive range; and award of a contract to the one offeror whose offer, price, and other consideration factors are most advantageous to the buyer.

condition precedent

A condition that activates a term in a contract.

condition subsequent

A condition that suspends a term in a contract.

consideration

(1) The thing of value (amount of money or acts to be done or not done) that must change hands between the parties to a contract. (2) The inducement to a contract – the cause, motive, price, or impelling influence that induces a contracting party to enter into a contract.

constructive change

An oral or written act or omission by an authorized or unauthorized agent that is of such a nature that it is construed to have the same effect as a written change order.

contingency

The quality of being contingent or casual; an event that may but does not have to occur; a possibility.

contingent contract

A contract that provides for the possibility of its termination when a specified occurrence takes place or does not take place.

contra proferentem

A legal phrase used in connection with the construction of written documents to the effect that an ambiguous provision is construed most strongly against the person who selected the language.

contract

(1) A relationship between two parties, such as a buyer and seller, that is defined by an agreement about their respective rights and responsibilities. (2) A document that describes such an agreement.

contract administration

The process of ensuring compliance with contractual terms and conditions during contract performance up to contract closeout or termination.

contract closeout

The process of verifying that all administrative matters are concluded on a contract that is otherwise physically complete – in other words, the seller has delivered the required supplies or performed the required services, and the buyer has inspected and accepted the supplies or services.

contract interpretation

The entire process of determining what the parties agreed to in their bargain. The basic objective of contract interpretation is to determine the intent of the parties. Rules calling for interpretation of the documents against the drafter, and imposing a duty to seek clarification on the drafter, allocate risks of contractual ambiguities by resolving disputes in favor of the party least responsible for the ambiguity.

contract management

The art and science of managing a contractual agreement(s) throughout the contracting process.

contract type

A specific pricing arrangement used for the performance of work under the contract.

contractor

The seller or provider of goods and/or services.

controversy

A litigated question. A civil action or suit may not be instigated unless it is based on a "justiciable" dispute. This term is important in that judicial power of the courts extends only to cases and "controversies."

cost

The amount of money expended in acquiring a product or obtaining a service, or the total of acquisition costs plus all expenses related to operating and maintaining an item once acquired.

cost-plus-award fee (CPAF) contract

A type of cost-reimbursement contract with special incentive fee provisions used to motivate excellent contract performance in such areas as quality, timeliness, ingenuity, and cost-effectiveness.

cost-plus-fixed fee (CPFF) contract

A type of cost-reimbursement contract that provides for the payment of a fixed fee to the contractor. It does not vary with actual costs, but may be adjusted if there are any changes in the work or services to be performed under the contract.

cost-plus-incentive fee (CPIF) contract

A type of cost-reimbursement contract with provision for a fee that is adjusted by a formula in accordance with the relationship between total allowable costs and target costs.

cost-plus-a-percentage-of-cost (CPPC) contract

A type of cost-reimbursement contract that provides for a reimbursement of the allowable cost of services performed plus an agreed-on percentage of the estimated cost as profit.

cost-reimbursement (CR) contract
> A type of contract that usually includes an estimate of project cost, a provision for reimbursing the seller's expenses, and a provision for paying a fee as profit. CR contracts are often used when there is high uncertainty about costs. They normally also include a limitation on the buyer's cost liability.

cost-sharing contract
> A cost-reimbursement contract in which the seller receives no fee and is reimbursed only for an agreed-on portion of its allowable costs.

cost contract
> The simplest type of cost-reimbursement contract. Governments commonly use this type when contracting with universities and nonprofit organizations for research projects. The contract provides for reimbursing contractually allowable costs, with no allowance given for profit.

counteroffer
> An offer made in response to an original offer that changes the terms of the original.

default termination
> The termination of a contract, under the standard default clause, because of a buyer's or seller's failure to perform any of the terms of the contract.

defect
> The absence of something necessary for completeness or perfection. A deficiency in something essential to the proper use of a thing. Some structural weakness in a part or component that is responsible for damage.

defect, latent
> A defect that existed at the time of acceptance but would not have been discovered by a reasonable inspection.

defect, patent
> A defect that can be discovered without undue effort. If the defect was actually known to the buyer at the time of acceptance, it is patent, even though it otherwise might not have been discoverable by a reasonable inspection.

definite-quantity contract

A contractual instrument that provides for a definite quantity of supplies or services to be delivered at some later, unspecified date.

delay, excusable

A contractual provision designed to protect the seller from sanctions for late performance. To the extent that it has been excusably delayed, the seller is protected from default termination or liquidated damages. Examples of excusable delay are acts of God, acts of the government, fire, flood, quarantines, strikes, epidemics, unusually severe weather, and embargoes. See also *forbearance* and *force majeure clause.*

design specification

(1) A document (including drawings) setting forth the required characteristics of a particular component, part, subsystem, system, or construction item. (2) A purchase description that establishes precise measurements, tolerances, materials, in-process and finished product tests, quality control, inspection requirements, and other specific details of the deliverable.

direct cost

The costs specifically identifiable with a contract requirement, including but not restricted to costs of material and/or labor directly incorporated into an end item.

direct labor

All work that is obviously related and specifically and conveniently traceable to specific products.

direct material

Items, including raw material, purchased parts, and subcontracted items, directly incorporated into an end item, which are identifiable to a contract requirement.

dispute

A disagreement not settled by mutual consent that could be decided by litigation or arbitration. Also see *claim.*

e-business
> Technology-enabled business that focuses on seamless integration between each business, the company, and its supply partners.

e-commerce
> A subset of e-business, Internet-based electronic transactions.

electronic data interchange (EDI)
> Private networks used for simple data transactions, which are typically batch- processed.

elements of a contract
> The items that must be present in a contract if the contract is to be binding, including an offer, acceptance (agreement), consideration, execution by competent parties, and legality of purpose.

enterprise resource planning (ERP)
> An electronic framework for integrating all organizational functions, evolved from Manufacturing Resource Planning (MRP).

entire contract
> A contract that is considered entire on both sides and cannot be made severable.

e-procurement
> Technology-enabled buying and selling of goods and services.

estimate at completion (EAC)
> The actual direct costs, plus indirect costs allocable to the contract, plus the estimate of costs (direct or indirect) for authorized work remaining.

estoppel
> A rule of law that bars, prevents, and precludes a party from alleging or denying certain facts because of a previous allegation or denial or because of its previous conduct or admission.

ethics
> Of or relating to moral action, conduct, motive, or character (such as ethical emotion). Also, treating of moral feelings, duties, or conduct; containing precepts of morality; moral.

Professionally right or befitting; conforming to professional standards of conduct.

e-tool

An electronic device, program, system, or software application used to facilitate business.

exculpatory clause

The contract language designed to shift responsibility to the other party. A "no damages for delay" clause would be an example of one used by buyers.

excusable delay

See *delay, excusable.*

executed contract

A contract that is formed and performed at the same time. If performed in part, it is partially executed and partially executory.

executed contract (document)

A written document, signed by both parties and mailed or otherwise furnished to each party, that expresses the requirements, terms, and conditions to be met by both parties in the performance of the contract.

executory contract

A contract that has not yet been fully performed.

express

Something put in writing, for example, "express authority."

fair and reasonable

A subjective evaluation of what each party deems as equitable consideration in areas such as terms and conditions, cost or price, assured quality, timeliness of contract performance, and/or any other areas subject to negotiation.

Federal Acquisition Regulation (FAR)

The government-wide procurement regulation mandated by Congress and issued by the Department of Defense, the General Services Administration, and the National Aeronautics and Space Administration. Effective April 1, 1984, the FAR supersedes both the Defense Acquisition Regulation (DAR) and the Federal Procurement Regulation (FPR). All federal agencies are authorized to issue regulations implementing the FAR.

fee

An agreed-to amount of reimbursement beyond the initial estimate of costs. The term "fee" is used when discussing cost-reimbursement contracts, whereas the term "profit" is used in relation to fixed-price contracts.

firm-fixed-price (FFP) contract

The simplest and most common business pricing arrangement. The seller agrees to supply a quantity of goods or to provide a service for a specified price.

fixed cost

A cost that, for a given period of time and range of activity, does not change in total and thus becomes progressively smaller on a per-unit basis as volume increases.

fixed price

A form of pricing that includes a ceiling beyond which the buyer bears no responsibility for payment.

fixed-price incentive (FPI) contract

A type of contract that provides for adjusting profit and establishing the final contract price using a formula based on the relationship of total final negotiated cost to total target cost. The final price is subject to a price ceiling, negotiated at the outset.

fixed-price redeterminable (FPR) contract

A type of fixed-price contract that contains provisions for subsequently negotiated adjustment, in whole or in part, of the initially negotiated base price.

fixed-price with economic price adjustment

A fixed-price contract that permits an element of cost to fluctuate to reflect current market prices.

forbearance

An intentional failure of a party to enforce a contract requirement, usually done for an act of immediate or future consideration from the other party. Sometimes forbearance is referred to as a nonwaiver or as a onetime waiver, but not as a relinquishment of rights.

force majeure clause

Major or irresistible force. Such a contract clause protects the parties in the event that a part of the contract cannot be performed due to causes outside the control of the parties and could not be avoided by exercise of due care. Excusable conditions for nonperformance, such as strikes and acts of God (e.g., typhoons) are contained in this clause.

fraud

An intentional perversion of truth to induce another in reliance upon it to part with something of value belonging to him or her or to surrender a legal right. A false representation of a matter of fact, whether by words or conduct, by false or misleading allegations, or by concealment of that which should have been disclosed, that deceives and is intended to deceive another so that he or she shall act upon it to his or her legal injury. Anything calculated to deceive.

free on board (FOB)

A term used in conjunction with a physical point to determine (a) the responsibility and basis for payment of freight charges and (b) unless otherwise agreed, the point at which title for goods passes to the buyer or consignee. *FOB origin* – The seller places the goods on the conveyance by which they are to be transported. Cost of shipping and risk of loss are borne by the buyer. *FOB destination* – The seller delivers the goods on the seller's conveyance at destination. Cost of shipping and risk of loss are borne by the seller.

functional specification

A purchase description that describes the deliverable in terms of performance characteristics and intended use, including those characteristics that at minimum are necessary to satisfy the intended use.

general and administrative (G&A)

(1) The indirect expenses related to the overall business. Expenses for a company's general and executive offices, executive

compensation, staff services, and other miscellaneous support purposes. (2) Any indirect management, financial, or other expense that (a) is not assignable to a program's direct overhead charges for engineering, manufacturing, material, and so on, but (b) is routinely incurred by or allotted to a business unit, and (c) is for the general management and administration of the business as a whole.

horizontal exchange
A marketplace that deals with goods and services that are not specific to one industry.

imply
To indirectly convey meaning or intent; to leave the determination of meaning up to the receiver of the communication based on circumstances, general language used, or conduct of those involved.

incidental damages
Any commercially reasonable charges, expenses, or commissions incurred in stopping delivery; in the transportation, care and custody of goods after the buyer's breach; or in connection with the return or resale of the goods or otherwise resulting from the breach.

indefinite-delivery/indefinite-quantity (IDIQ) contract
A type of contract in which the exact date of delivery or the exact quantity, or a combination of both, is not specified at the time the contract is executed; provisions are placed in the contract to later stipulate these elements of the contract.

indemnification clause
A contract clause by which one party engages to secure another against an anticipated loss resulting from an act or forbearance on the part of one of the parties or of some third person.

indemnify
To make good; to compensate; to reimburse a person in case of an anticipated loss.

indirect cost
Any cost not directly identifiable with a specific cost objective but subject to two or more cost objectives.

indirect labor

All work that is not specifically associated with or cannot be practically traced to specific units of output.

Internet

The World Wide Web.

intranet

An organization specific internal secure network.

joint contract

A contract in which the parties bind themselves both individually and as a unit.

liquidated damages

A contract provision providing for the assessment of damages on the seller for its failure to comply with certain performance or delivery requirements of the contract; used when the time of delivery or performance is of such importance that the buyer may reasonably expect to suffer damages if the delivery or performance is delinquent.

mailbox rule

The idea that the acceptance of an offer is effective when deposited in the mail if the envelope is properly addressed.

market research

The process used to collect and analyze information about an entire market to help determine the most suitable approach to acquiring, distributing, and supporting supplies and services.

memorandum of agreement (MOA)/ memorandum of understanding (MOU)

The documentation of a mutually agreed-to statement of facts, intentions, procedures, and parameters for future actions and matters of coordination. A "memorandum of understanding" may express mutual understanding of an issue without implying commitments by parties to the understanding.

method of procurement

The process used for soliciting offers, evaluating offers, and awarding a contract.

monopoly
>A market structure in which the entire market for a good or service is supplied by a single seller or firm.

monopsony
>A market structure in which a single buyer purchases a good or service.

negotiation
>A process between buyers and sellers seeking to reach mutual agreement on a matter of common concern through fact-finding, bargaining, and persuasion.

net marketplace
>Two-sided exchange where buyers and sellers negotiate prices, usually with a bid-and-ask system, and where prices move both up and down.

novation agreement
>A legal instrument executed by (a) the contractor (transferor), (b) the successor in interest (transferee), and (c) the buyer by which, among other things, the transferor guarantees performance of the contract, the transferee assumes all obligations under the contract, and the buyer recognizes the transfer of the contract and related assets.

offer
>(1) The manifestation of willingness to enter into a bargain, so made as to justify another person in understanding that his or her assent to that bargain is invited and will conclude it. (2) An unequivocal and intentionally communicated statement of proposed terms made to another party. An offer is presumed revocable unless it specifically states that it is irrevocable. An offer once made will be open for a reasonable period of time and is binding on the offeror unless revoked by the offeror before the other party's acceptance.

oligopoly
>A market dominated by a few sellers.

option
>A unilateral right in a contract by which, for a specified time, the buyer may elect to purchase additional quantities of the

supplies or services called for in the contract, or may elect to extend the period of performance of the contract.

order of precedence

A solicitation provision that establishes priorities so that contradictions within the solicitation can be resolved.

outsourcing

A contractual process of obtaining another party to provide goods and/or services that were previously done internal to an organization.

overhead

An accounting cost category that typically includes general indirect expenses that are necessary to operate a business but are not directly assignable to a specific good or service produced. Examples include building rent, utilities, salaries of corporate officers, janitorial services, office supplies, and furniture.

overtime

The time worked by a seller's employee in excess of the employee's normal workweek.

parol evidence

Oral or verbal evidence; in contract law, the evidence drawn from sources exterior to the written instrument.

parol evidence rule

A rule that seeks to preserve the integrity of written agreements by refusing to permit contracting parties to attempt to alter a written contract with evidence of any contradictory prior or contemporaneous oral agreement (*parol* to the contract).

payment bond

A bond that secures the appropriate payment of subcontracts for their completed and acceptable goods and/or services.

performance bond

A bond that secures the performance and fulfillment of all the undertakings, covenants, terms, conditions, and agreements contained in the contract.

performance specification

A purchase description that describes the deliverable in terms of desired operational characteristics. Performance specifications tend to be more restrictive than functional specifications, in that they limit alternatives that the buyer will consider and define separate performance standards for each such alternative.

pricing arrangement

An agreed-to basis between contractual parties for the payment of amounts for specified performance; usually expressed in terms of a specific cost-reimbursement or fixed-price arrangement.

prime/prime contractor

The principal seller performing under the contract.

private exchange

A marketplace hosted by a single company inside a company's firewall and used for procurement from among a group of preauthorized sellers.

privity of contract

The legal relationship that exists between the parties to a contract that allows either party to (a) enforce contractual rights against the other party and (b) seek remedy directly from the other party.

procurement

The complete action or process of acquiring or obtaining goods or services using any of several authorized means.

procurement planning

The process of identifying which business needs can be best met by procuring products or services outside the organization.

profit

The net proceeds from selling a product or service when costs are subtracted from revenues. May be positive (profit) or negative (loss).

program management

Planning and execution of multiple projects that are related to one another.

progress payments

An interim payment for delivered work in accordance with contract terms; generally tied to meeting specified performance milestones.

project management

Planning and ensuring the quality, on-time delivery, and cost of a specific set of related activities with a definite beginning and end.

proposal

Normally, a written offer by a seller describing its offering terms. Proposals may be issued in response to a specific request or may be made unilaterally when a seller feels there may be an interest in its offer (which is also known as an unsolicited proposal).

proposal evaluation

An assessment of both the proposal and the offeror's ability (as conveyed by the proposal) to successfully accomplish the prospective contract. An agency shall evaluate competitive proposals solely on the factors specified in the solicitation.

punitive damages

Those damages awarded to the plaintiff over and above what will barely compensate for his or her loss. Unlike compensatory damages, punitive damages are based on actively different public policy consideration, that of punishing the defendant or of setting an example for similar wrongdoers.

purchasing

The outright acquisition of items, mostly off-the-shelf or catalog, manufactured outside the buyer's premises.

quality assurance

The planned and systematic actions necessary to provide adequate confidence that the performed service or supplied goods will serve satisfactorily for the intended and specified purpose.

quotation

A statement of price, either written or oral, which may include, among other things, a description of the product or service; the terms of sale, delivery, or period of performance; and payment. Such statements are usually issued by sellers at the request of potential buyers.

reasonable cost

A cost is reasonable if, in its nature and amount, it does not exceed that which would be incurred by a prudent person in the conduct of competitive business.

request for proposals (RFP)

A formal invitation that contains a scope of work and seeks a formal response (proposal), describing both methodology and compensation, to form the basis of a contract.

request for quotations (RFQ)

A formal invitation to submit a price for goods and/or services as specified.

sealed-bid procedure

A method of procurement involving the unrestricted solicitation of bids, an opening, and award of a contract to the lowest responsible bidder.

severable contract

A contract divisible into separate parts. A default of one section does not invalidate the whole contract.

several

A circumstance when more than two parties are involved with the contract.

single source

One source among others in a competitive marketplace that, for justifiable reason, is found to be most worthy to receive a contract award.

solicitation

A process through which a buyer requests, bids, quotes, tenders, or proposes orally, in writing, or electronically. Solicitations can take the following forms: request for proposals (RFP), request for quotations (RFQ), request for tenders, invitation to bid (ITB), invitation for bids, and invitation for negotiation.

solicitation planning

The preparation of the documents needed to support a solicitation.

source selection

The process by which the buyer evaluates offers, selects a seller, negotiates terms and conditions, and awards the contract.

Source Selection Advisory Council

A group of people who are appointed by the Source Selection Authority (SSA). The Council is responsible for reviewing and approving the source selection plan (SSP) and the solicitation of competitive awards for major and certain less-than-major procurements. The Council also determines what proposals are in the competitive range and provides recommendations to the SSA for final selection.

source selection plan (SSP)

The document that describes the selection criteria, the process, and the organization to be used in evaluating proposals for competitively awarded contracts.

specification

A description of the technical requirements for a material, product, or service that includes the criteria for determining that the requirements have been met. There are generally three types of specifications used in contracting: performance, functional, and design.

standard

A document that establishes engineering and technical limitations and applications of items, materials, processes, methods, designs, and engineering practices. It includes any related criteria deemed essential to achieve the highest practical degree of uniformity in materials or products, or interchangeability of parts used in those products.

statement of work (SOW)

That portion of a contract describing the actual work to be done by means of specifications or other minimum requirements, quantities, performance date, and a statement of the requisite quality.

statute of limitations

The legislative enactment prescribing the periods within which legal actions may be brought upon certain claims or within which certain rights may be enforced.

stop work order

A request for interim stoppage of work due to nonconformance, funding, or technical considerations.

subcontract

A contract between a buyer and a seller in which a significant part of the supplies or services being obtained is for eventual use in a prime contract.

subcontractor

A seller who enters into a contract with a prime contractor or a subcontractor of the prime contractor.

supplementary agreement

A contract modification that is accomplished by the mutual action of parties.

technical factor

A factor other than price used in evaluating offers for award. Examples include technical excellence, management capability, personnel qualifications, prior experience, past performance, and schedule compliance.

technical leveling

The process of helping a seller bring its proposal up to the level of other proposals through successive rounds of discussion, such as by pointing out weaknesses resulting from the seller's lack of diligence, competence, or inventiveness in preparing the proposal.

technical transfusion

The disclosure of technical information pertaining to a proposal that re-suits in improvement of a competing proposal. This practice is not allowed in federal government contracting.

term

A part of a contract that addresses a specific subject.

termination

An action taken pursuant to a contract clause in which the buyer unilaterally ends all or part of the work.

terms and conditions (Ts and Cs)

All clauses in a contract, including time of delivery, packing and shipping, applicable standard clauses, and special provisions.

unallowable cost

Any cost that, under the provisions of any pertinent law, regulation, or contract, cannot be included in prices, cost-reimbursements, or settlements under a government contract to which it is allocable.

uncompensated overtime

The work that exempt employees perform above and beyond 40 hours per week. Also known as competitive time, deflated hourly rates, direct allocation of salary costs, discounted hourly rates, extended work week, full-time accounting, and green time.

Uniform Commercial Code (UCC)

A U.S. model law developed to standardize commercial contracting law among the states. It has been adopted by 49 states (and in significant portions by Louisiana). The UCC comprises articles that deal with specific commercial subject matters, including sales and letters of credit.

unilateral

See *bilateral contract.*

variance

The difference between projected and actual performance, especially relating to costs.

vertical exchange

A marketplace that is specific to a single industry.

waiver

The voluntary and unilateral relinquishment a person of a right that he or she has. See also *forbearance.*

warranty

A promise or affirmation given by a seller to a buyer regarding the nature, usefulness, or condition of the goods or services furnished under a contract. Generally, a warranty's purpose is to delineate the rights and obligations for defective goods and services and to foster quality performance.

warranty, express

A written statement arising out of a sale to the consumer of a consumer good, pursuant to which the manufacturer, distributor, or retailer undertakes to preserve or maintain the utility or performance of the consumer good or provide compensation if there is a failure in utility or performance. It is not necessary to the creation of an express warranty that formal words such as "warrant" or "guarantee" be used, or that a specific intention to make a warranty be present.

warranty, implied

A promise arising by operation of law that something that is sold shall be fit for the purpose for which the seller has reason to know that it is required. Types of implied warranties include implied warranty of merchantability, of title, and of wholesomeness.

warranty of fitness

A warranty by the seller that goods sold are suitable for the special purpose of the buyer.

warranty of merchantability

A warranty that goods are fit for the ordinary purposes for which such goods are used and conform to the promises or affirmations of fact made on the container or label.

warranty of title

An express or implied (arising by operation of law) promise that the seller owns the item offered for sale and, therefore, is able to transfer a good title and that the goods, as delivered, are free from any security interest of which the buyer at the time of contracting has no knowledge.

web portals
A public exchange in which a company or group of companies list products or services for sale or provide other transmission of business information.

BIBLIOGRAPHY

Ahern, Dennis M., Aaron Clouse and Richard Turner, *CMMI Distilled: A Practical Introduction to Integrated Process Management*, Addison-Wesley Longman Publishing Co., Boston MA, 2001.

The American Law Institute and National Conference of Commissioners on Uniform State Laws, *Uniform Commercial Code: 1987 Official Text with Comments, 10th ed.*, West Publishing Co., St. Paul MN, 1990.

Badgerow, Dana B., Gregory A. Garrett, Dominic F. DiClementi and Barbara M. Weaver, *Managing Contracts for Peak Performance*, National Contract Management Association, Vienna VA, 1990.

Barlow, C. Wayne and Glenn P. Eisen, *Purchasing Negotiations*, CBI Publishing Co., Boston MA, 1983.

Bazerman, Max and Margaret A. Neale, *Negotiating Rationally*, The Free Press, New York NY, 1992.

Binnendijk, Hans, ed., *National Negotiating Styles*, Foreign Service Institute, U.S. Department of State, Washington DC, 1987.

Black, Henry C., Joseph R. Nolan, Jacqueline M. Nolan-Haley, M.J. Connolly, Stephan C. Hicks and Martina N. Alibrandi, *Black's Law Dictionary, 6th ed.*, West Publishing Co., St. Paul MN, 1990.

Bockrath, Joseph T., *Contracts, Specifications, and Law for Engineers, 4th ed.*, McGraw-Hill Inc., New York NY, 1986.

Bova, Regina M., *The Desktop Guide to Basic Contracting Terms, 4th ed.*, National Contract Management Association, Vienna VA, 1994.

Bunnik, Edward C. and Gregory A. Garrett, *Creating a World-Class PM Organization: A Success Story*, PM Network Magazine, Project Management Institute, September 2000.

Burt, David N., Donald W. Dobler and Stephen L. Starling, *World Class Supply Management*, McGraw-Hill/Irwin, New York NY, 2003.

Callaway, Edward A., *Software Applications/Systems/Tools Reviewed: Accudraft's DocsEngine Portal: Writing the Contract Correctly and Quickly Through Automation,* Contract Management Magazine, National Contract Management Association, Vienna VA, 2004.

Cavinato, Joseph L. and Ralph G. Kauffman, *The Purchasing Handbook: A Guide for the Purchasing and Supply Professional,* 6th ed., McGraw-Hill, New York NY, 1999.

Clarkson, Kenneth W., Roger L. Miller, Stephen A. Chaplin and Bonnie Blaire, *West's Business Law: Alternate UCC Comprehensive Edition,* West Publishing Co., St. Paul MN, 1981.

Cohen, Herb, *You Can Negotiate Anything,* L. Stuart, Secaucus NJ, 1980.

Corbin, Arthur L., *Corbin on Contracts,* West Publishing Co., St. Paul MN, 1993.

Covey, Stephen R., *The Seven Habits of Highly Effective People,* Simon and Schuster, Inc., New York NY, 1989.

Crawford, J. Kent, *Project Management Maturity Model: Providing a Proven Path to Project Management Excellence,* Marcel Dekker AG, 2002.

Curtis, Bill, William E. Hefley and Sally A. Miller, *The People Capability Maturity Model: Guidelines for Improving the Workforce,* Addison Wesley Longman, Reading MA, 2002.

Dayal, Kunjan, *Software Applications/Systems/Tools Reviewed: Contracting With the Hummingbird: Fast, Powerful, Versatile,* Contract Management Magazine, National Contract Management Association, Vienna VA, 2004.

Dickover, Ryan D., *Software Applications/Systems/Tools Reviewed: Reviewing Cobble Stone Systems: Contract Web,* Contract Management Magazine, National Contract Management Association, Vienna VA, 2004.

Dobler, Donald W., David N. Burt and Lamar Lee, Jr., *Purchasing and Materials Management: Text and Cases, 5th ed.*, McGraw-Hill, New York NY, 1990.

Engelbeck, Marshall R., *Acquisition Management Handbook*, Management Concepts, Vienna VA, 2002.

Fisher, Roger, *Getting Ready to Negotiate: The Getting to Yes Workbook*, Penguin Books, New York NY, 1995.

Fisher, Roger and Scott Brown, *Getting Together*, Penguin Books, New York NY, 1989.

Fisher, Roger and William Ury, *Getting to Yes: Negotiating Agreement Without Giving In, 2d ed.*, Penguin Books, New York NY, 1991.

Fisher, Roger, Elizabeth Kopelman and Andrea K. Schneider, *Beyond Machiavelli: Tools for Coping with Conflict*, Harvard University Press, Cambridge MA, 1994.

Frame, J. Davidson, *Managing Projects in Organizations: How to Make the Best Use of Time, Techniques, and People*, Jossey-Bass Publishers, San Francisco CA, 1995.

Garrett, Gregory A. and Dr. Rene Rendon, *Contract Management Organizational Assessment Tools*, National Contract Management Association, Vienna VA, 2005.

Garrett, Gregory A., *Commercial Contracting Best Practices*, Contract Management Magazine, National Contract Management Association, Vienna VA, February 2008.

Garrett, Gregory A., *Contract Negotiations: Skills, Tools and Best Practices*, CCH, Chicago IL, 2005.

Garrett, Gregory A. and Pete McDonald, *Preparing for Change: The Obama Administration Affect on Government Contractors*, Contract Management Magazine, National Contract Management Association, Vienna VA, February 2009.

Garrett, Gregory A., *World Class Contracting, 4th ed.*, CCH, Chicago IL, 2007.

Gates, Bill, *Business @ The Speed of Thought: Using a Digital Nervous System*, Warner Books USA, New York NY, 1999.

Government Accountability Office, *Defense Acquisitions, DOD Has Paid Billions in Award and Incentive Fees Regardless of Acquisition Outcomes*, Report GAO-06-66.

Harris, Phillip R. and Robert T. Moran, *Managing Cultural Differences*, Gulf Publishing Co., Houston TX, 1996.

Hendon, Donald W. and Rebecca A. Hendon, *World-Class Negotiating: Dealmaking in the Global Marketplace*, John Wiley & Sons, New York NY, 1990.

Humphries, Robert and Andrew D. Irwin, *Teaming Agreements, 3rd ed.*, Briefing Papers, Thomson West, New York NY, September 2006.

Jugdev, Kam and J. Thomas, *Project Management Maturity Models: The Silver Bullets of Competitive Advantage*, Project Management Institute, University of Calgary, Calgary Canada, 2002.

Karrass, Chester L., *Give and Take: The Complete Guide to Negotiating Strategies and Tactics*, Harper Collins, New York NY, 1993.

Karrass, Gary, *Negotiate to Close: How to Make More Successful Deals*, Simon and Schuster, New York NY, 1985.

Kerzner, Harold, *Kerzner's Project Management Maturity Model*, John Wiley & Sons, Hoboken NJ, 2001.

Kirk, Dorthy, *Managing Expectations*, PM Network Magazine, Project Management Institute, Upper Darby PA, August 2000.

Koren, Leonard and Peter Goodman, *The Haggler's Handbook: One Hour to Negotiating Power*, W.W. Norton & Co., New York NY, 1992.

Kwak, Young Hoon and William Ibbs, *The Berkley Project Management Process Maturity (PM2) Model, Measuring the Value of Project Management*, 2000.

Leenders, Michael R., Harold E. Fearon and Wilbur B. England, *Purchasing and Materials Management, 9th ed.*, Richard D. Irwin, Inc., Homewood IL, 1989.

Liebesny, Herbert J., *Foreign Legal Systems: A Comparative Analysis, 4th ed.*, The George Washington University, Washington DC, 1981.

Loudin, Kathlyn H., *Software Applications/Systems, Tools Reviewed: diCarta: A Proven Contract Management Solution*, Contract Management Magazine, National Contract Management Association, Vienna VA, 2004.

Mahoney, Ted, *Software Applications/Systems/Tools Reviewed: Review of Omnicom's Contracts Applications*, Contract Management Magazine, National Contract Management Association, Vienna VA, 2004.

Monroe, Kent B., *Pricing: Making Profitable Decisions, 2d ed.*, McGraw-Hill Publishing Co., New York NY, 1990.

Morice, Joseph, *Software Applications/Systems/Tools Reviewed: Upside Software: Making Your Job Easier*, Contract Management Magazine, National Contract Management Association, Vienna VA, 2004.

Nash, Ralph C., Jr. and John Cibinic, *Formation of Government Contracts, 3rd ed.*, CCH, Chicago IL, 1998.

Nash, Ralph C., Jr. and John Cibinic, *Administration of Government Contracts, 3rd ed.*, CCH, Chicago IL, 1995.

Nash, Ralph C., Jr., Karen R. O'Brien and Steven L. Schooner, *The Government Contracts Reference Book: A Comprehensive Guide to the Language of Procurement, 2d ed.*, CCH, Chicago IL, 1998.

Nierenberg, Gerard, *The Art of Negotiating*, Penguin Books, New York NY, 1989.

O'Connell, Brian, *B2B.com: Cashing-in on the Business-to-Business e-Commerce Bonanza*, Adams Media Corp., Holbrook MA, 2000.

O'Connor, Robert, *Contract Management: An Enterprise Process Perspective*, Contract Management Magazine, National Contract Management Association, Vienna VA, November 2004.

Ohmae, Kenichi, *The Borderless World: Power and Strategy in the Interlinked Economy*, Harper Collins, New York NY, 1991.

Project Management Institute Standards Committee, *A Guide to the Project Management Body of Knowledge*, Project Management Institute, Upper Darby PA, 1996.

Raedels, Alan R., *The Supply Management Process: Managing Key Supply Processes*, Institute for Supply Management, Tempe AZ, 2000.

SCDigest editorial staff, *For Procurement Managers, a Bit of Pay Back Time*, Supply Chain Digest, New York NY, January 7, 2009.

SCDigest editorial staff, *If Key Suppliers Are Struggling Financially, What Should Procurement Organizations Do?*, Supply Chain Digest, New York NY, January 7, 2009.

Stein, Janice G., *Getting to the Table: The Processes of International Prenegotiation*, Johns Hopkins University Press, Baltimore MD, 1989.

Ury, William, *Getting Past No: Negotiating Your Way from Confrontation to Cooperation*, Bantam Books, New York NY, 1993.

U.S. Office of Federal Procurement Policy, Federal Data System, *FY08 Procurement Statistics*, February 2009.

Zartman, I. William, *The Fifty Percent Solution*, Yale University Press, New Haven CT, 1987.

Zartman, I. William, *The Negotiation Process*, Sage Publications, Beverly Hills CA, 1978.

INDEX